CALLED TO DEFEND

An imprint of 1517 the Legacy Project

Called to Defend: An Apologetics Handbook

Published by:
NRP Books
PO Box 54032
Irvine, CA 92619-4032

Cover design by Scribe Inc. (scribenet.com)

Printed in the United States of America

Publisher's Cataloging-In-Publication Data
(Prepared by The Donohue Group, Inc.)

Names: Locklair, Valerie.
Title: Called to defend : an apologetics handbook / by Valerie Locklair.
Description: Irvine, CA : NRP Books, an imprint of 1517 the Legacy Project, [2017] | Includes bibliographical references and index. | Summary: "This book provides a helpful introduction to apologetics for middle school students, using a variety of disciplines with which they are already familiar. Students will learn to defend their faith in an age appropriate way."—Provided by publisher.
Identifiers: ISBN 9781945978647 (hardcover) | ISBN 9781945978654 (softcover) | ISBN 9781945978661 (ebook)
Subjects: LCSH: Apologetics—Juvenile literature. | Apologetics—Handbooks, manuals, etc. | Preteens—Religious life—Juvenile literature. | CYAC: Apologetics. | Religion.
Classification: LCC BT1103 .L63 2017 (print) | LCC BT1103 (ebook) | DDC 239—dc23

NRP Books, an imprint of 1517. The Legacy Project, is committed to packaging and promoting the finest content for fueling a new Lutheran Reformation. We promote the defense of the Christian faith, confessional Lutheran theology, vocation and civil courage.

For my brother,
Daniel,
a knight of the cross and a true friend.
Thank you for your continued encouragement,
friendship, and prayers.
Philemon 1:4-7.

Contents

Foreword

Called to Defend takes on a challenge of seemingly daunting proportions: not only does the author call the reader to take seriously St. Peter's largely ignored admonition to be "ready always to give a defense" (1 Pet. 3:15), but she sounds a clarion call that this biblically commanded apologetical task be aggressively and creatively introduced to that slice of contemporary culture seemingly the least inclined to be receptive to its aims—namely, the middle school student.

But enter the fray Valerie Locklair does and does so undeterred by the legion of war stories of the youth group leader (no doubt a catechized, confirmed regular church attendee, with even a "mission trip" on his or her resume), who went off to college and came home ten weeks into an Intro to Philosophy class as a convinced atheist. To be sure, the statistics of those who dump the Christian religion after going to college are telling and provide clear and convincing evidence of the cost that has been paid by the church for ignoring St. Peter's admonition. Like Luther's unbelieving man stumbling down the street and bouncing from one extreme and bankrupt philosophy to another, the church's response to the objections raised by unbelievers has been either to wall off contact with the secular world and to consider objections to the faith to be the result of the sinful rebellion to be expected of the non-elect (witness "fundamentalism" and aspects of Calvinist orthodoxy) or to absorb the secular world and become indistinguishable from it and to consider the "settled truths" of postmodernism and Darwinian naturalism as hopelessly irrefutable (witness "liberalism" of the theological brand as well as the implicit belief of most of mainline denominational Christianity). The consequence is that we have sent out a generation of young Christians from our churches utterly without any armor whatsoever and in a day when such armor has never been more necessary.

While a renaissance of interest in apologetics has been occurring in some unlikely quarters like orthodox Lutheranism and Anglicanism, American evangelicalism has never lost its interest in equipping the church to defend the faith once delivered. What has not dawned on even the evangelical church is the need to introduce apologetics at an age thought impervious to serious theological and apologetical content. In fact, and as Ms. Locklair powerfully demonstrates, classical education recognized (as the sainted Dorothy Sayers notes in her marvelous essay on "Regaining the Lost Tools of Learning") that the polemical nature of the middle school years is actually a natural ally to the teaching of the apologetical task. Some of us have long argued that classical education and its trivium suggest that catechism and confirmation (roughly akin to the grammar and dialectic phases) should occur before the middle school years and that apologetics (paralleling the rhetoric phase) should start in middle school in order to take advantage of the natural polemical and confrontational aspect of that period of social, physical, and intellectual development. Valerie Locklair provides both the philosophy and practicum for just that approach.

Ms. Locklair attacks the idea that apologetics is "above" the capabilities of middle schoolers and in fact turns that argument on its head by arguing that it is fatal to fail to teach apologetics to middle schoolers—namely, that Christianity has (as Sayers notes) compelled the mind of man (including middle schoolers) "not because it is the most cheering view of the world or of man's existence, but because it is truest to the facts." Rather than let those critical middle school years be dissipated in futile efforts to make the middle school church experience a theological version of *Ferris Bueller's Day Off*, she invites (even demands) that we equip the next generation of Fidei Defensores with the apologetical tools they most assuredly need now as secularism pushes down to more and more vulnerable ages. We ignore her call at our peril, for if the next generation is not presented the "many infallible proofs" asserted by St. Luke (Acts 1:3), we can be sure they will either leave the faith once delivered or end up holding to a Christianity unrecognizable by the Apostolic band.

It was our pleasure at the International Academy of Apologetics in Strasbourg, France, to have Ms. Locklair defend the thesis that later became the basis for this important volume. There she combined theological and apologetical acumen with zeal for those who "are the least among us" and presented a compelling case that to be ready always to defend the faith was not directed to a particular age or station in life. In the process, she has a critical message that needs to be heard by the Church Militant of all ages.

On the Feast of the Holy Innocents
December 28, 2017
Santa Barbara, California
Craig A. Parton,
trial lawyer and United States Director
of the International Academy of Apologetics
(www.apologeticsacademy.eu)

PART ONE

THE THEORETICAL FOUNDATIONS

CHAPTER 1

Introduction

We live on a battlefield. Whether we are blissfully, naively blasé or vividly aware of the combat going on around us, we were born into a world at war. There is no demilitarized zone and no neutral ground. Every day we send our children out into a minefield, and most of them are totally unprepared for what they find.

You see, it doesn't look like a battlefield. On the contrary, it looks like paradise. There is no forbidden fruit, no "right" or "wrong," and all ideas are equally beautiful, alluring, and welcome. No thought is turned away, no matter how eccentric, shocking, or controversial—except perhaps those that are labeled as narrow-minded and phobic—while emotions, dreams, and euphoric highs paint the world in candy-coated ecstasy. There are no demons here, no dragons to slay, no evil to shun. Welcome to postmodernism. Check your outdated definitions at the door and we'll get along just fine.

Our culture has become the ultimate altar. Youth serums, surgeries, meditation, and holistic health all clamor that if we try *this*, buy *this*, or do *this*, we will never age. We've each become Peter Pan chasing Neverland. Our greatest fear is seeing a wrinkle in the mirror or finding a silver strand on our hairbrush, and in our quest for immortality, we've completely ignored the new-and-improved twenty-first-century face of child sacrifice.

Oh, it isn't called that, of course. It has prettier names, names like education, sensitivity training, acceptance, reform, and—"Yes, yes, yes," you interrupt, "I've heard all this before—that's why I picked up this handbook." If you have any interest in this at all, it is safe to assume that you are concerned about the current state of affairs in our society and the impact it is having on our children. While you may be slightly unnerved by my bold "child sacrifice" statement, you aren't particularly surprised or unduly shocked; but you may be wondering, Why *this* handbook? Why do we need apologetics instruction to begin with? Why for this age range? Why interdisciplinary? And so on.

I was educated at home mainly by my mother, who raised and taught five children, and my father, who was (and still is) a distinguished professor at a Lutheran university. While I did attend Sunday school and catechism class like most of my Lutheran peers, the majority of my religious education was accomplished at home. I vividly remember bringing home anecdotes from Sunday school that my parents and I fact-checked on various occasions. Two examples in particular stick out in my mind. The first was quite shocking to me—the second less so but equally troublesome.

Around fourth or fifth grade, I was in a certain Sunday school class where we were discussing the Christmas account. The instructor had just finished reading the annunciation of the virgin birth. She paused and then said, "I'm not sure if Mary was a virgin when Jesus was born."

The second incident happened a few years later. My family had moved and changed churches, and I was enrolled in catechism class. It was a small class of three or four students, and the majority of class periods were spent trying to keep one or two disruptive individuals from swaying the whole class into utter anarchy. I can imagine how frustrating that must have been for the pastor at that time. What I can't imagine is why he gave the response he did to a simple question.

It was a typical weekday evening, and the class was a bit calmer than usual. One of the routine troublemakers was a trifle subdued. In a rare spirit of attentiveness, he appeared to be listening as the pastor discussed sharing faith with friends and peers at school. The young man, "James," paused and seemed to be considering something.

"Um." He coughed uncomfortably and shook his long hair out of his eyes, attempting to cover the sincerity of his question by assuming a carefree attitude. "Yeah, but what if you're, like, talking to a terrorist and he has a bomb strapped on you and he asks you if you're a Christian and if you say yes he's going to kill you?"

The room was momentarily silent. This was after 9/11 and years before the publicized ISIS beheadings, but it still raised uncomfortable questions in the minds of the tweens gathered in that study room. I looked at the pastor, expecting one of the beautiful Scripture passages about the certainty of salvation for all who trust in Jesus and have the strength to speak His name in all circumstances.

The pastor looked at the young man coldly. "When you're deployed to the Middle East and actually facing that situation, let me know and we'll talk. Until then I doubt you have to worry about it."

I stared at him in shock. James mumbled something incoherent and began doodling on his folder while I wondered if feeling sick to my stomach was enough of an excuse to leave class early. Had our declaration of the gospel just been downgraded from a lifelong joy to a situational ethic to be taken out when it's convenient and to be hidden when it may save our lives? Is our faith in Christ alone until we're confronted with earthly danger, and then we're allowed to take a page from our sinful nature's self-help book and deny our Savior to extend our mortal lives?

Both of these accounts come from within Christendom and within Lutheranism. If we think that we will be saved because of the initials on our church's signboard, we are deceiving ourselves. I say this not to point out the speck in my brother's eye but to highlight the plank within our own lives. We're not preparing children for the real world, the real questions they will face, and the real heartaches they will experience.

Because we live in a postmodern world, we need an apologetic that is able to interact with culture and at the same time not be overcome by it. We need to be sufficiently in the world if we are to, by grace, carry out our commission to be salt and light, but we must also realize that there is a grave difference between sodium chloride and sodium hypochlorite. We do no one any favors—and indeed we perform a great disservice to our neighbors—if we treat truth as a slipshod handle for something that makes you happy, brings you fulfillment, or "works" for you. How, then, do we approach this in a culture where truth is seen as entirely subjective?

I once had a heartbreaking conversation with a friend concerning truth. We were discussing faith, and he requested hard evidence for why I believed what I believed. In the midst of the conversation, he shook his head and said, "What you're saying is probably true—but I can't accept it." Truth—objective truth for truth's sake—for this young man was not enough. While he said that he was seeking hard evidence, what he was really seeking was a tender, personal, and intimate reassurance that there was something unchanging, something absolute in a world where he had been told his entire life that truth, far from being the revealed word of God, was an experience that you had to create for yourself. He ended the conversation by rejecting any further comments from me. I can't help but feel that I have seen how the rich young man looked as he walked away from his Lord.

A day doesn't go by that I don't mourn for that young man. For the first time in my life, I saw a personal glimpse of how the Spirit groaned as Jesus sighed, "O Jerusalem, Jerusalem . . . How often would I have gathered your children together as a hen gathers her brood under her wings, and you were not willing!"[1] I recount this story not to highlight my piety—indeed, were it not for the grace of God and the knowledge that He brings good out of all things, I would be scourging myself day and night for what I consider a deep and painful failure—but as a warning. We dare not forget that we are dealing with eternal souls who will spend forever glorified with Christ or screaming in hell. We dare not focus on ourselves, our worthiness, or our false humility in our interactions with the world around us. We are not discussing opponents to beat, debates to win, or intellectuals to snub. We are talking about individuals created in the image of God and loved with an everlasting love by the Creator of all men.

In a time when there is no right or wrong, we must be sure that our apologetic is touching the heart as well as the mind. When Jesus Christ became man, He became fully human; because of this, Christianity has an incredibly holistic approach to offer to a world that sees the universal issue not as "How can I be saved?" but "How can I be happy?"[2] The postmodernist has done away with the old paradigm that held that "if you have the right teaching, you will experience God" in favor of the newer, hipper, more inclusive paradigm of "if you experience God, you will have the right teaching."[3] Our world today is increasingly concerned with experience, emotion, and the unholy trinity of "Me, Myself, and I." How can Christians adequately defend the faith to a generation that refuses to believe that there is a need for a war at all?

St. Paul tells us that we are to be all things to all people (1 Cor. 9:19–23). The other side of the coin is that Jesus Himself says that believers are not of the world, as He Himself is not (John 17:16). The narrow Lutheran middle ground must follow the footpath of Scripture and no other guiding line. Emotions, experiences, and desires must never be allowed to become the magisterial reasons by which we live, confess, or defend our faith. At the same time, we must avoid the presuppositional logic so rampant in certain Christian denominations today—the lunch buffet, "here, try Christianity, you'll like it and it's right because we say it's right" approach. If we offer as our defense the ideas that Christianity will make you happier, healthier, and more fulfilled, we've done nothing but offer something that yoga, spiritism, and the local gym all claim to provide.

The point of all apologetics is to get the "attacker" (the one questioning) to the cross of Christ as quickly as possible. Our goal doesn't change with the passing of time or the changing of fads, and we must be careful lest we change our tactics so much that we become indistinguishable from the babblings of the Gentiles and those who cry "Peace! Peace!" when there is no peace. However, we must learn to speak gently to the tender-minded and meet them where they stand. We must learn to share our story—as C. S. Lewis phrased it, the "true myth"[4]—in order to introduce our friend, neighbor, or coworker to the God who became flesh and is well acquainted with our sorrows, emotions, and deepest desires. We must train ourselves to be ready to give a defense to the heart as well as to the mind.

A sound, doctrinally adequate apologetic for the tender-minded is something that is surprisingly difficult to come by. Many take the "tell your story" paradigm too far and turn the apologetic into a personal testimony. The problem with that, of course, is that unless you have been crucified and raised from the dead, your word could, in theory, be just as useful (or useless) as anyone else's opinion. Maybe Christianity just "worked" for you the way meditation, full-contact sparring, or burning incense works for your neighbor down the street. We must be on guard to teach our children that those who come to them with questions may be moved by different approaches. As my earlier story of the young man illustrated, some who claim that they need hard evidence are actually looking for the reassurance that *truth* is a living, breathing, personal concept that can meet their deepest unspoken needs.

This was one of the driving forces that moved me to write this handbook: there is a distinct lack of apologetics training that appropriately differentiates between tough-minded and tender-minded approaches. As noted Christian professor and writer Gene Edward Veith Jr. says, the time has come to focus on a postmodern (*not* a postmodern*ist*) approach to apologetics.[5] Neither our proclamation nor our defense of the gospel should ever bow to cultural bias. However, would you defend yourself against a samurai sword in the same manner you would defend yourself against a bullet, assuming that you were not simply going to run away and hide? Different offensive techniques on the part of the unbeliever necessitate different defensive techniques on the part of the church.

It is also important for students to realize that personality can correlate to or suggest the need for a certain apologetic approach. A rudimentary understanding of *introverts* and *extroverts* is helpful when one is interacting with and answering the questions of diverse and distinct individuals. It is difficult to "help and support" our neighbor and to "explain everything in the kindest way" if we do not understand his needs.[6] The questions of an extrovert will appear different from the questions of an introvert, even if the heart of the matter is the same in both cases. We tend too often to think of apologetics as being used in conversation with blustering, loud critics who complain about everything from the weather, to the stock market, to religion with hardly a pause for air in between. We rarely think of the timid, quiet receptionist who sees a beautiful painting of the Madonna and Child by Ilian Rachov and wants to know more. We are quick to label individuals as "quiet" or "loud" (which, incidentally, are *not* synonymous with "introverted" and "extroverted," but more on that later) without a second thought and with very little idea of how to interact with either one other than by ignoring them both equally.

This brings us to the last question to be addressed in this introduction—namely, why interdisciplinary? Much of what our children face in the realm of academia today is compartmentalized, prepackaged, and simplified. Some of this is necessary—indeed, if there were no distinction among subjects, then students of any age would quickly become frustrated, burned out, and technically illiterate in any meaningful subject. We must be cautious to feed young minds bite-sized pieces of information that can be easily digested. However, we must also guard against making the information so easy to swallow that it hardly merits a second glance or a thoughtful investigation. The middle school years dovetail well with the drawing of connections among subjects, ideas, and beliefs. Should not the logic stage support this foray into interdisciplinary thought?

Steffen M. Iverson, a faculty member of the University of Southern Denmark's Philosophy, Education, and the Study of Religions Department, put it this way when discussing the need for an interdisciplinary approach (to mathematics in particular):

> In the educational system knowledge is still in a very large scale separated into distinct blocks by different subjects. This separation of knowledge has shown itself to be very efficient in producing and teaching new knowledge, but does not necessarily provide the students with the skills necessary to navigate through the constantly increasing amount of accessible information. Interdisciplinary activities between different subjects can help to develop a broader context of meaning or understanding for the student, and in this way contribute to the ongoing scholarly development and provide the student with the tools necessary to deal with complex problem solving in the future.[7]

If we fail to appropriately emphasize the relationships among subject A, subject B, and the world around us as a whole, we are hindering the expansion of a child's mind toward a deeper understanding of critical thinking. If students using this handbook have already been exposed to the basic principles of the faith and the quadrivium, the next logical step is to make sure they find the once-lost tools of learning. This stage should provide a test arena for the child to grow in grace, knowledge, and discernment.

Discernment is an oft-overlooked yet vitally important virtue in childhood, adolescence, and adulthood. The ability to distinguish between concepts and ideas is in many ways as important as being able to find the ways in which they complement one another. In the postmodern society we find ourselves traversing, discernment is all but eliminated. When it is allowed at all, it is muddled with subjective sentiments that vaguely appeal to "doing the right thing," "finding one's bliss," or "doing no harm." If there is no absolute truth, there is no need to discern between it and its illusionary antithesis.[8] There is my truth, your truth, and Uncle Harry's truth, with their definitions being roughly equivalent to whatever happens to make an individual happy at any given moment in time.

Are we not doing the same thing—albeit unconsciously—if we stringently classify knowledge within the tight bounds of subject areas? Are we not unintentionally creating "scientific truth," "English truth," "historical truth," and so on? What little objectivity secular (and sometimes, dare I say it, even private) education allows is neatly tucked away into its own 84 × 28 × 23 box and buried in a subject yard where it could not possibly contaminate another discipline. Artists scoff at the frigidity of science, mathematicians ridicule poetry, and little Johnny is taught that math is "something you do in the morning" between 9:45 and 10:30 a.m.[9]

Ironically, this is the same approach to which many church bodies succumb far too quickly and willingly. Religious truth is limited to an hour and a half most Sunday mornings (except when our favorite sports team is playing) and has very little to do with the other 166 and a half hours in the week. Religious studies, when offered at all, are often confined to their own class periods, and students can open and close the Bible, an evolutionary textbook, and fiction about transgenderism and homosexuality in the course of one twenty-four-hour period. (Think of *George*, a 2015 novel about a boy who identifies as a girl, aimed at an audience ages 8–12.) Science textbooks must scramble to cover psychology's push for increasing gender-fluidity education for younger and younger students, and sadly, this may be one of the strongest examples of interdisciplinary thought in action in our schools today.

What can be done? We can withdraw into our monasteries of piety and refuse to be in the world at all. We can teach our children nothing of other religions, forbid them to question their own faith, and build charming picket fences around the law as the Pharisees did. Far above the cities, we will keep ourselves pure of the smog, and we will effectively poison our souls with the intoxication of self-focused idolatry. If the tragedy of a dying world, oblivious to the flames of hell itself that are engulfing it, does not move us to pray earnestly for any means of witness and conversation possible, we must examine our hearts and pray that God Almighty would save us from ourselves. If we do not allow our children to question their faith, what will they do when they meet the honest skeptic who has *no* idea why anyone would believe in a God who allowed the death of an infant sister?

Conversely, we can become so passionate about saving the lost, winning souls for Jesus, and building our New Jerusalem on this earth that we can distort our message. No longer does Satan have to bodily slither from the leafy crevices of a perfect world to plant doubt. We are too busy hemming and hawing and justifying our position with "Did God *really* say?" that Screwtape and Wormwood must be having a leisurely lunch while we effectively trample the pearl of the gospel in the pigpen. We can hedge our defenses to the questions "Why would anyone believe in a God of love who condemns people to hell?" and "Isn't the Bible a book of fables written by a group of monks in the twelfth century?" with half-truths. We can teach our children to forsake the "evils of logic" and focus on the "reality of love" in order to have another hand to hold while singing "Kumbaya." We know Jesus is alive because we feel it in our hearts, and once everyone else feels it too, everything will be all right. There's no need for apologetics, logic, or true objectivity at all. We can be like Princess Unikitty in *The LEGO Movie*, building our own Cloud Cuckoo Land with "no rules! No government, no babysitters, no bedtime, no frowny faces, no bushy mustaches, and no negativity of any kind! . . . And there's also no consistency! Any idea is a good idea, except for the not-happy ones."[10] Spoiler alert: it didn't work out too well for Cloud Cuckoo Land.

Or we can once again tread the narrow, unpopular, predominantly Lutheran middle. We can stand unapologetically on the word of God and pray for the grace and strength to defend it. We can, by the work of the Holy Spirit, teach our children to speak the truth in love.

How Should This Handbook Be Used?

This handbook is intended to be a field guide as you begin your apologetics training, and it is intended to be read by both a middle school–aged student and his or her parent, instructor, or guardian.

You will notice throughout this book that I touch on several different subject areas. You are encouraged to draw connections between these areas and your general schooling. Home educators are especially encouraged to use this handbook in conjunction with their own curriculum, but anyone and everyone is encouraged to draw connections between apologetics and other subject areas.

In many ways, this handbook is a skeleton. It is designed to support and expand upon the historic quadrivium and, if the child using this book is home-educated, to dovetail with the curricula that child is already using. It's designed to be "plugged in" wherever it fits. For example, the mathematics section should be read in light of whatever mathematics curriculum you are currently using. I would suggest integrating sections when and where they make sense, although this handbook can also be used from start to finish on its own as a separate "subject."[11]

This book is necessarily, well, "reading heavy." There will be a lot of material for the student to read and understand, and sometimes (or, as I suggest, *always*) this will require outside reading or studying a section more slowly. If you come across something that you deem is too advanced for a middle schooler, I would encourage you not to automatically dismiss it. Learning (of any sort) never happens within a comfort zone. It's an uncomfortable fact that learning requires you to stretch and grow, and your child's reaching *upwards* toward knowledge that may be beyond his level is to be preferred to speaking *down* to him.

If, on the other hand, you find a section that is simply too challenging or too involved for your child, skip it. There's no rule that says you have to use every unit the way it is presented here. If you take nothing else away from this handbook, take this: encourage your child to ask questions about his faith, and when he does, *listen*. If you don't know the answer, help him find it. There is a world that is waiting to bombard him with sugar-coated answers to all of life's questions. Help him distinguish between Turkish delight and the Fruit of the True Vine.

Notes

1 Matthew 23:37. Unless otherwise noted, Scripture references are taken from the ESV (English Standard Version) Bible.

2 Gene Edward Veith Jr., *Postmodern Times* (Wheaton: Crossway, 1994), 216.

3 Ibid., 211.

4 C. S Lewis, "Letter to Arthur Greeves, Oct 18th, 1931," in *The Collected Letters of C. S. Lewis, Volume I: Family Letters 1905–1931*, ed. Walter Hooper (New York: HarperCollins, 2004), 976–77.

5 See Veith, *Postmodern Times.*

6 Martin Luther, *Luther's Small Catechism with Explanation* (St. Louis: Concordia, 1986), 10, 11 (explanations to 5th and 8th commandments).

7 Bharath Sriraman, Viktor Freiman, and Nicole Lirette-Pitre, eds., *Interdisciplinarity, Creativity, and Learning: Mathematics with Literature, Paradoxes, History, Technology, and Modeling* (Charlotte: Information Age Publishing, 2009), 148.

8 See Craig Parton, *Religion on Trial* (Eugene: Wipf & Stock, 2008), 5.

9 Heidi Hayes Jacobs, *Interdisciplinary Curriculum: Design and Implementation* (Alexandria: Association for Supervision and Curriculum Development, 1989), accessed February 18, 2016, http://www.ascd.org/publications/books/61189156/chapters/The-Growing-Need-for-Interdisciplinary-Curriculum-Content.aspx.

10 *The LEGO Movie*, directed by Phil Lord and Christopher Miller (2014; Burbank, CA: Warner Bros, 2014), DVD.

11 See the following section on "Criteria, Principles, and Overview" for more information.

CHAPTER 2

Criteria, Principles, and Overview

This handbook should not be limited to those pursuing home education for their children. The concept of this course would work equally well in a Sunday school, Vacation Bible School, or even private school environment. Any child would be able to learn from this course, and adults wishing to use it in other venues should note that the principles put forth here and in other places in the course itself translate very well to a myriad of environments. The primary reason that homeschoolers are singled out by name is due to the fact that confessional, Lutheran home educators sometimes feel themselves at a loss in a sea of predominantly reformed curriculum. It is important for everyone concerned, however, to realize that we do not exist in a vacuum and that apologetics instruction should be a primary responsibility for all Christian parents, whether they homeschool or not.

Homeschool Criteria

> The freedom to tailor an academic program to your child's particular interests and needs is one of home education's greatest advantages . . . when you teach your child at home, *you* make the final decision on which books you'll use and how much time you'll spend on schoolwork.
>
> —Susan Wise Bauer and Jessie Wise, *The Well-Trained Mind*[1]

Everyone has heard of the stereotypical *homeschoolers*. They do school in their pajamas! They're four grades ahead of everyone else! They don't have any friends! And so on and so forth, ad nauseam. Some individuals erroneously equate homeschooling with the act of wearing jean skirts and participating in international spelling bees. Contrary to popular belief, educating a child at home does carry with it some commonly agreed-upon criteria for success. I will examine some of these criteria and describe how this handbook fulfills the required conditions.

Principles of Homeschooling Curricula

The typical concern among parents considering homeschooling often centers on whether or not they have the required skill set to *teach*. Many people mistakenly equate a teaching license or an education degree with the ability to impart knowledge and facilitate the pursuit of wisdom. It is not assumed that the homeschooling parent has an extensive background in education or an expert grasp on every subject that will be encountered throughout the child's studies. It is, however, assumed that homeschooling is something that the parents, for one reason or another, are passionate about. It would surely take something extreme to have the family sacrifice time, income, and energy for the sake of educating a child at home. Some scoff that it would take nothing short of an act of God for them to consent to spending the entire school day with their children. Many homeschoolers would smilingly agree that it is indeed an act of God—a blessed gift of grace in the form of *vocation*, or the calling He bestows on each and every one of us to be "masks of God" to carry out His will on this earth.[2]

Individuals and families choose to homeschool for a variety of reasons. It is a gross generalization to say that all homeschoolers are Christians. There are many resources available for Islamic, Buddhist, and atheistic home educators.[3] The criteria for a successful homeschool curriculum will vary between differing religious and secular sources—for the sake of this handbook, it is assumed that the criteria we are interested in fulfilling are those of a Christian home-education program.

The academic benefits of homeschooling are undeniable—many students who are educated at home score higher on standardized tests than students enrolled in public schools.[4] However, Veith points out that "morality and character" appear to take precedence over academic achievement for the homeschooling family.[5]

In other words, many home educators are looking for an environment for their children that deals with the transcendent as well as the immanent. The question is not only will my child learn the skills needed to be a member of our society, but also will he learn what is true, good, and beautiful?[6] For the Christian parent in a postmodern society, this is an admittedly tall order. Now more than ever, our children need the foundation of a strong faith and a strong apologetic. Absolute truth is an extremely unpopular concept in our world today. One has only to flip through a Disney Channel or Nickelodeon lineup to see examples of postmodern thought aimed at even the youngest of viewers. Your child needs to learn not only *what*—or rather, *who*—is true, good, and beautiful, but also how to defend it; for who is good but God alone, who is true but truth Himself, and who is more beautiful than the flawless lover of our souls?

Another benefit of homeschooling is that a curriculum can be molded to fit the child instead of the other way around. Homeschoolers are used to either creating their own curricula or "piecemeal-ing" one together from existing sources.[7] Dr. Ruth Beechick advises that "if you find yourself struggling to mold your child to a book [or series of books], try reversing priorities. It's the child you are teaching, not the book. Bend the book, or find another; make the studies fit the child."[8] When the parent is also the teacher, he or she will already be in tune with the child's mind-set, strengths, and weaknesses. If this handbook is too advanced for your ten-year-old, you can choose sections of it to use, you can choose to not use it at all, or you can set it aside for when your child is older. Remember that learning is meant to be challenging but not overwhelmingly so, especially at this point in your child's life. Use discretion and don't be afraid to edit in order to fit your child's needs.

Personal Requirements: A Classical Dialogue

Aside from state requirements, there are many requirements within homeschooling circles that can be used to weigh the appropriateness of any one curriculum. Although all-in-one curricula exist that contain the core areas that should be addressed at each grade level, many homeschooling instructors opt to pick and choose curricula on a per-subject basis instead. One of the strengths of educating a child at home is the freedom the instructor has to select teaching material that adequately meets the child's needs and the instructor's criteria. However, lest we fall into sloshy subjectivity and find ourselves turning into postulating postmodernists, I will lay out ways of evaluating a home education curriculum and how this handbook in particular drew from and fulfills these criteria.

Within the past several years, classical education has seen a resurgence in the conservative education community's consciousness. Home educators and Christian school teachers are developing an increasing interest in the tenets of classicalism—namely, that such an approach to education "cultivates wisdom and virtue by nourishing the soul on truth, goodness, and beauty."[9] Apologetics, it can be argued, places the same emphasis on the "three transcendentals" and fits well within the framework of classical education. The three units of this book are based loosely on these three themes, with truth corresponding to understanding, goodness to judgment, and beauty to reasoning, paralleling the three acts of mind.

This handbook's interdisciplinary section was inspired by the quadrivium, the four ancient liberal arts currently experiencing a renaissance among the classical community. The historical quadrivium consisted of arithmetic, geometry, astronomy, and music—I will explain later in this section why this handbook deviates from the traditional four subjects. First, we need to examine something called the trivium and its impact on your child's current stage of development.

The Trivium

Many home and private school instructors are rediscovering the classical proponents of a liberal arts education, and with this rediscovery comes an increased awareness of and appreciation for "the trivium." The trivium comprises grammar, rhetoric, and logic. Susan Wise Bauer, coauthor of one of the most well-known resources for those interested in a classical approach to home education, summarizes the trivium as the "three-part process of training the mind,"[10] and Gene Edward Veith Jr. notes that it is primarily linguistic in nature.[11]

After noting that the trivium occurs prior to the quadrivium—the four subject areas of arithmetic, geometry, music, and astronomy—Dorothy Sayers highlights the fact that unlike its successor, the trivium is not concerned with *subjects.*

> Now the first thing we notice is that two at any rate of these "subjects" are not what we should call "subjects" at all: they are only methods of dealing with subjects. Grammar, indeed, is a "subject" in the sense that it does mean definitely learning a language—at that period it meant learning Latin. But language itself is simply the medium in which thought is expressed. The whole of the Trivium was, in fact, intended to teach the pupil the proper use of the tools of learning, before he began to apply them to "subjects" at all.[12]

The first stage of this three-part process occurs around elementary school, in grades one through three or four.[13] The grammar stage focuses on understanding the basic facts of any discipline.[14] Observation and memory are emphasized in subjects from arithmetic (think of multiplication and division tables) to history (memorization of names and dates) and literature (short poem memorization).[15] The grammar stage comprises "the years in which the building blocks for all other learning are laid," and so the learning of facts is emphasized in order to build the meaning and integration of those facts into a solid web of learning at later stages.[16]

The stage to which this handbook most closely correlates is the aptly named "logic stage." Depending on which curricula you sample, you will receive differing answers about when the logic stage begins. For the purposes of this book, the assumption is made that the logic stage and the middle school years are, if not virtually indistinguishable, at least simultaneously simpatico. Although parents of toddlers and very young children may disagree, the logic stage has been associated with a child's increased interest in questioning the facts instead of simply being content to memorize them, with "why?" being a frequently used query. Abstract thought begins to occur in the mind of the middle school child, and with it comes the ability to apply a developing sense of logic to academic subjects.[17]

"Somewhere around fourth grade," Susan Wise Bauer and Jessie Wise tell us, "the growing mind begins to switch gears . . . The mind begins to generalize, to question, to analyze—to develop the capacity for abstract thought."[18] Critical thinking skills are emerging, and the middle school child is beginning to interact with information in a new way. Instead of seeing black-and-white facts ("*i* before *e* except after *c*"), the child is beginning to notice exceptions to rules ("What about weird? Weigh? Neigh? Sleigh?") and to question *why* things are the way they are. Anyone who was been on the receiving end of a query such as "Yes, but *why* does three plus three equal six?" will tell you that "passively accepting information" is no longer the middle schooler's modus operandi.[19]

Dorothy Sayers summarized the "pert age" as being "characterized by contradicting, answering back, liking to 'catch people out' (especially one's elders); and by the propounding of conundrums. Its nuisance-value is extremely high."[20] The questioning, searching, and finding of relationships between subjects and ideas that occurs at this stage makes it an ideal time to introduce the young mind to apologetics.

Why is it, then, that so often education at this level—religious and secular—gets the story wrong? Secular education falls off the wagon by encouraging children to question anything and everything (one thinks of gender reassignment surgeries performed on prepubescent children), effectively destroying any foundation for facts whatsoever. Touting "critical thinking skills" without adhering to the facts of reality is akin to teaching piano skills without a keyboard.[21] However, at this stage in life, the child has progressed beyond simply recognizing the ivories as a component of a musical instrument and is now able to interact with them, sense patterns in the combination of keys pressed, and understand the relationships between the patterns and increasingly abstract concepts (e.g., minor keys being used to denote sadness, thoughtfulness, and so on).

The same is true of religious studies. The child who is receiving a religious education in general (and a Lutheran one, specifically) should have a basic understanding of the core doctrines of the faith by the middle school age. This handbook is less concerned with whether a child can define the term "doctrine" and more interested in whether she can draw connections between teachings and begin to elucidate them in her daily interactions with her peers. The child's mind and heart have been prepared for this, hopefully, by sound teaching in the grammar school years.[22]

"But wait!" you say. Surely this is all much too complex for the mind of a ten- or eleven-year-old to grasp? I am of the opinion that if grown-ups left off with much of the detailing, charting, and prioritizing of what is and is not too complex for the child's mind, our children would learn more and our grown-ups would be much improved for being taken down a peg. While I am not advocating that we begin instructing our toddlers in advanced neuroscience, I am saying that the compartmentalization of knowledge is an open flame that should be handled with fear and trembling.

While it would be overly simplistic to say that this is *the* critical time in a child's development, it should be noted that the logic stage has a unique bearing on a child's developing worldview. A student in the logic stage is learning not only *that* Martin Luther nailed his Ninety-Five Theses to a door in Germany in 1517, but *why* he did it, the result of that, and *why* it matters five hundred years later. This insight into the middle school years seems to be lacking in today's education circles. A quick look at middle school and high school curricula in both public and private sectors reveals a distinct lack of logic instruction outside of a mathematics course or (for high school students) the occasional honors-level computing class. "Logic" is considered an advanced subject to be pushed off until the student is more mature instead of a framework to aid the child in academic and personal growth. At a time when a child's mind is prepared for the challenges of logic, we are not providing him with adequate instruction.

The same rings true for Christian apologetics instruction. When it is offered at all, it is offered at the high school and college levels. We are not encouraging middle schoolers to question, investigate, and interact with their faith on a level appropriate to their developing minds and worldviews. We are sending them off to high school and assuming that any gaps in their learning will be filled at least by the time they graduate college. We are sending them out into a world at war without adequate armor, expecting that armor will come when they are prepared to understand it instead of when they actually need it.

The Quadrivium

Because this handbook is intended to be interdisciplinary and yet maintain a primary focus on apologetics, an attempt has been made to incorporate elements of the quadrivium (or an updated version, the quadrivium with a twist, if you will). I have noted that the historic foursome consists of arithmetic, geometry, music, and astronomy. This book takes a slightly different approach to these subject areas. I discuss this in some detail in the "Note to Instructors" that precedes each subject, but I will give a general overview here of the rationale behind it.

The mathematics section came to be almost by accident. I knew that I wanted to incorporate analytical thinking and contrast that with synthetic statements, but I wasn't sure how. I happened to be watching TV one day when I saw Dr. Jason Lisle presenting on Mandelbrot sets and numbers. That was the link I had been searching for, and it paralleled beautifully with my epiphany (which some would affectionately term a "blinding flash of the obvious") that Einstein's Gulf would be the unifying thread throughout all four subject areas (more on that later). I decided to sidestep the question of "is this arithmetic or is this geometry?" by terming the section simply "Mathematics," thereby hopefully incensing fewer mathematicians than I may have otherwise.

With mathematics out of the way, I originally planned to incorporate astronomy as the second major subject area. After running into writer's block more times than I care to recall, I had another blinding flash of the obvious: namely, this wasn't working. On top of that, astronomy has been dealt with so well in numerous other publications by people with PhDs who actually have an inkling of what they're doing when they observe the night sky. It happened that at the time I was banging my head against the wall and trying to write something halfway coherent, I had a conversation with my father, Dr. Gary Locklair, chair of the computer science department at Concordia University Wisconsin, on the subject of computer science as a liberal art. Cue the light bulb moment. Being an information technology major as an undergraduate, I suddenly realized how Einstein's Gulf is present in computer science as well—and how the problem-solving paradigm could be applied to apologetics. Enter the computer science section.

That left me with two remaining sections to go if I was to have anything resembling a quadrivium. I had already decided that I was going to have a section on history, mainly due to my realization that Lessing's Ditch is Einstein's Gulf in theological garb. This section flowed the most easily, for whatever reason, even though I was painfully aware that I had now abandoned all hope of following the historic quadrivium in any meaningful way.

The final section had been termed something like "Creative Arts" in this work's initial outline, which was my way of saying I had no idea what on earth I was going to write about, but it was going to be something relating to music, art, writing, or some kind of visual art. I settled on creative writing for the extremely subjective reason that I've always loved to write. After a halfhearted attempt at forcing the section to be about art and some nebulous concept of color theory, I finally let myself write what I actually wanted to . . . and promptly ran smack into a quote in a writing manual that was Einstein's Gulf all over again, this time with ink-stained thumbs and the sharp eyes of the most diligent writer.

My fate was sealed. The quadrivium had been replaced with a misfit band of rogue subjects. True writers (like Eloise Jarvis McGraw) say that the mark of a story worth telling is its inability to be pigeonholed and forced into being something that it isn't. I hope this is true, and it is also my hope that this transgression will be overlooked and that the subjects I chose will serve to bring apologetics to life for the student.

Havighurst's Developmental Tasks

I have spoken with individuals who, after hearing that I wanted to encourage apologetics instruction for middle schoolers, began reciting a laundry list of why this was a very bad idea. One of the most common objections I hear is that middle school students simply do not have the capacity to grasp anything more complex than Captain Underpants or the latest Pokémon video game. With all due respect to the good captain, Jigglypuff, and other critics, this simply is not the case. In order to support this assertion, I want to briefly show how instructing fourth through eighth graders in the defense of the faith makes sound, psychosomatic sense.

Noted professor of education and human development and educational theory pioneer Robert J. Havighurst developed six stages of learning and growth that begin at birth and continue until death. He termed these stages "the developmental tasks of life," explaining that "a developmental task is a task which arises at or about a certain period in the life of the individual, successful achievement of which leads to his happiness and to success with later tasks, while failure to leads to unhappiness in the individual, disapproval by the society, and difficulty with later tasks."[23] While Havighurst wrote from a distinctly secular perspective with more than a tincture of humanism (e.g., his belief that "religion [is] almost completely the product of learning at the hands of society"[24]), these developmental tasks provide a useful framework for explaining why the middle school years are the ideal time to introduce a child to apologetics.

Havighurst was influenced by the idea of "sensitive periods for learning," which are limited periods of time when a child is ready to accept and process certain stimuli in order to learn a task that she may not be able to adequately grasp after this defined period. For example, Havighurst references the supposed critical period for learning to talk—between the ages of two and three—and notes that if the child does not learn to talk during this period, he is likely to be "emotionally disturbed" and "maladjusted."[25] It is worth noting that this appears in contrast to the documented existence of the human brain's neuroplasticity, the startling discovery that "our brains rewire to create new connections, set out on new paths, and assume new roles," and the fact that this continual learning occurs not only in childhood but also throughout adulthood.[26] However, Havighurst realized that these sensitive periods for learning serve as ideal learning opportunities. Once the child is physically, mentally, and emotionally equipped to achieve a task, the "teachable moment" has arrived wherein the task can be learned well enough to provide a foundation for future development.

The two stages of particular interest to us overlap with the middle school–aged child (roughly ages ten to fourteen): the *middle childhood* (ages six to twelve) and the *adolescence* (ages thirteen to eighteen) stages, each with their unique, required developmental tasks. Middle childhood has nine tasks to be accomplished, adolescence has eight, and both stages parallel beautifully with the logic stage and provide additional support for an apologetics handbook aimed at the middle school child. Although all of these tasks have something to offer in terms of supporting this book, for the sake of space I will focus on only the most relevant from each stage.

Middle Childhood Tasks

> Middle childhood—or the period from about six to twelve years of age—is characterized by three great outward pushes. There is the thrust of the child out of the home and into the peer group, the physical thrust into the world of games and work requiring neuromuscular skills, and the mental thrust into the world of adult concepts, logic, symbolism, and communication.[27]

Havighurst defines nine tasks that should occur in middle childhood, around the ages of six to twelve. All nine are listed below:

1. Learning physical skills necessary for ordinary games
2. Building a wholesome attitude toward oneself as a growing organism
3. Learning to get along with age-mates
4. Learning an appropriate masculine or feminine social role
5. Developing fundamental skills in reading, writing, and calculating
6. Developing concepts necessary for everyday living
7. Developing conscience, morality, and a scale of values
8. Achieving personal independence
9. Developing attitudes toward social groups and institutions[28]

It does not take an overly active imagination to see how each of these nine tasks could correlate to an apologetics handbook, but I will especially focus on tasks two, six, and seven.[29]

Building a Wholesome Attitude toward Oneself

Developing a healthy awareness of oneself is perhaps one of the most stressed aspects of a young child's emotional and physical maturation in today's world. Positive body image is touted to younger and younger audiences, and discipline is urged only if it does not negatively impact the sensitive self-concept of the young. While these attitudes are not necessarily in and of themselves wrong, we are finding increasing numbers of educators and behavioral specialists who do not have wholesome attitudes toward themselves and who are thus unable to pass along appropriate self-awareness to their pupils. I needn't give you the chilling exposé of behavioral psychologists supporting pedophilia, sexual aberrance in preteenagers, and all manner of education that no more suits a child of five or six than does a golden ring in a pig's snout. We're inundated with these articles every time we browse an online news publication or (horror of horrors) read "Dear Abby" on Yahoo's home page.

Havighurst stresses almost exclusively the physical dimension of this developmental task, noting that "success in this task leads to a well-balanced personality."[30] The difficulty is that he considers the culture as a leading arbitrator of what is the correct view of "physical normality," which, unsurprisingly, Havighurst links closely with attitudes toward sexual activity.[31] He glosses over the fact that everyone seems to have a different idea of how to discover one's true self, and developing a wholesome attitude toward oneself as a growing organism appears to suggest that one first has some general concept of what or who one is. The solution for Havighurst was the teaching of "health habits" through television, movies, and athletics that portray "glamorous figures" to "impress [the habits] favorably upon children."[32] Some parents may find it disturbing that their child should look to actors of *Magic Mike* fame or *Sports Illustrated* models as examples of "wholesome, realistic attitude[s]"[33] concerning one's physical and psychological development.

Some may say that apologetics is too advanced a subject for a middle school–aged child. The reality is that your child is going to learn apologetics whether he receives formal training in it or not—the only question is what object of faith he will see as worth defending and how solid his defense will be. Michael Berg, a Lutheran professor and apologetics scholar, puts it simply: "I would [argue] that all Christians do apologetics, and the only question is whether we do it well or poorly."[34] A Christian middle school child will be facing new pressures, and homeschooling or enrolling him in private school will not protect him from the influences he will face. He will quickly learn how to give a defense for his actions and beliefs, whether that defense is founded on his feelings, the latest Disney Channel star, or the person of Christ. "Know Thyself" is a pithy, gilded statement that has ignited debate, discussion, and introspection for hundreds of years. At a time when this philosophy is introduced to the young mind in earnest, it would be well if we also added the statement "Know Thy Savior" to his defensive repertoire.

Developing Concepts Necessary for Everyday Living

"A concept," Havighurst explains, "is an idea which stands for a large number of particular sense perceptions, or which stands for a number of ideas of lesser degrees of abstraction."[35] The child at this age needs to develop a storehouse of concepts that can be used for higher-level thinking and the ability to interact with the world and with other concepts of greater or lesser complexity. This ability to discover and use concepts in everyday life—sometimes referred to as "higher-order" or "critical" thinking and "problem solving"—is the hallmark by which many define the logic stage.[36]

Havighurst notes that a child's concepts, provided they are "true to reality," primarily emerge from his "concrete experiences" within the home, peer group, and school.[37] A child's concept of a dog, for example, may stem from his experience with the family pet. Concepts, it would seem, should be grounded in reality if they are to be of use to the child at this stage and throughout his development. Life would be very difficult indeed if one were unable to differentiate between an artichoke and an automobile.

Havighurst affirms this when he notes that "the greatest peril in the school learning of concepts is that they may lack sufficient concrete basis in experience to make them trustworthy."[38] He gives the example of an American child learning about (and forming "erroneous concepts of") life in Holland who is unable to form concepts about "diet, disease, and agriculture" that could be learned in his own environment. Those domestic concepts could then be compared and contrasted to the foreign environment of life in another country, and he thus concludes that "it may be urged that the school curriculum be as full of concrete experience as possible in the early years, so as to help the child build concepts on a realistic basis."[39]

As Christians, we have a (quite literally) perfect example of this. Jesus Christ became fully man (concrete) while retaining His godhood (analogous to a concept). It is erroneous to think that anyone, child or adult, can know God without knowing Jesus Christ.[40] A child's developing concept of the world, or what we would term his worldview, must be grounded in reality for the sake of not only his mind and body but also his soul. Without the concrete basis to guide him, it is uncertain which sources are trustworthy and which are misinformed or malicious. Orthodox Lutheran apologetics is centered on Christ as the word made flesh, the concept made concrete, and as the only source of ultimate truth. St. John writes:

> And the Word became flesh and dwelt among us, and we have seen his glory, glory as of the only Son from the Father, full of grace and truth. (John bore witness about him, and cried out, "This was he of whom I said, 'He who comes after me ranks before me, because he was before me.'") For from his fullness we have all received, grace upon grace. For the law was given through Moses; grace and truth came through Jesus Christ. No one has ever seen God; the only God, who is at the Father's side, he has made him known.[41]

While the young child needs everyday experiences to develop the concepts necessary for everyday life, she also needs the factual revelation of truth for her eternal salvation. Where is the truth to be found? How can we recognize it? Can we be sure we have the truth and not a cleverly constructed fable? Apologetics provides the map to the answer that the child of ten is not only equipped to handle but needs to experience in order to grow in grace and knowledge.[42]

Developing Conscience, Morality, and a Scale of Values

Havighurst, like famed psychologist Jean Piaget before him, believes that middle childhood is the critical stage for learning what he loosely terms the "morality of cooperation," or "inner moral control, respect for moral rules, and the beginning of a rational scale of values," which allows one to function in a modern society.[43] He also insists that morality and conscience are almost entirely social constructs and equates the mores of a culture with individual moral conscience.[44] It follows that distinguishing between what is good and what is bad is largely (if not entirely) dependent on the situation.

This poses apologetic concerns on several levels (e.g., if morality is determined by society, what happens when societies are in conflict? Who is right?). We must remember that the child at the logic stage is asking "Why?" and not simply about academic areas. At some level, she is beginning to question why she is the way that she is and whether or not there is meaning to life. Coming-of-age stories sense this longing to know who one is and what one's purpose is—children being chosen for an important destiny is a recurring theme in literature aimed at tweens and teenagers. Frequently these destinies involve hard decisions, which, often as not, are influenced by postmodernism and situation ethics.

Case in point: in Shannon Hale's bestselling novel *Princess Academy: Palace of Stone*, the heroine, Miri, begins her scholarly training at the prestigious Queen's Castle with an introduction to the subject of ethics. The headmaster highlights an exquisite painting on the wall of the classroom. It is one of only a few surviving works by a master painter, and it is, in his words, simply "perfection." Master Filippus turns and poses a question to the class:

> Imagine the Queen's Castle catches fire. Besides yourself, there is only one other person in the building—a confessed murderer of a child, chained in the dungeon. If you save the murderer, he will not harm you but will live the remainder of his life in another prison, and the painting will burn. If you save the painting, the man will burn. Which would you choose—the murderer or the painting?[45]

The classroom erupts with different opinions—the man should be saved, some claim, since he still has the ability to do good, whereas the painting is not a living thing. But the painting, others argue, is irreplaceable. At the end of the story, Miri achieves a sort of enlightenment: "*Which would you save, the murderer or the painting?* [Miri] knew her answer now: both. She would find a way."[46]

Your child will be exposed to many different moral and ethical theories long before high school. *Palace of Stone* gives us only one example.[47] This *inclusive or* (not good *or* evil, but *both*) example of postmodern truth appears throughout our culture today. If we leave it to society to mold our children's ethics, we are taking a dangerous gamble of possibly eternal consequence. As I discussed in the previous section on developing concepts, how can we be sure that our concept of morality is based on reality—something that is not only true but also good and beautiful? What about those times when we cannot save both the murderer and the painting? How do we decide? How do we decide to attempt to save *both* and what makes this decision *right?* How do we as Christians defend our adherence to absolute truth and transcendental moral law to a world intoxicated by postmodern situation ethics? When the ideas of the world come calling, we must teach our children to distinguish between truth and error and to provide a solid defense for the one true faith.

Adolescence Tasks

> The period from twelve to eighteen is primarily one of physical and emotional maturing . . . Adolescents who are growing up to adulthood . . . have the basic psychosocial task which [developmental psychologist Erik] Erikson calls *achievement of identity.* They must become persons in their own right—persons who are in charge of their lives, who know *who* they are.[48]

Although Havighurst's developmental tasks of adolescence indicate that adolescence continues from age twelve to eighteen, there are still many of the eight tasks that can be of use to the child between the ages of ten and fourteen. Havighurst terms some tasks as "recurrent"—that is, they never truly end but occur over a long period of time, sometimes throughout one's lifetime.[49]

1. Achieving new and more mature relations with age-mates of both sexes
2. Achieving a masculine or feminine social role
3. Accepting one's physique and using the body effectively
4. Achieving emotional independence of parents and other adults
5. Preparing for marriage and family life

6. Preparing for an economic career
7. Acquiring a set of values and an ethical system as a guide to behavior—developing an ideology
8. Desiring and achieving socially responsible behavior

As with the middle childhood tasks, it is possible to correlate the relationship between this handbook and any one of the tasks listed above. For the sake of space and due to the fact that I am focusing on children up to the age of fourteen, I will only examine two tasks in this section: numbers seven and eight.

Acquiring a Set of Values and an Ethical System as a Guide to Behavior: Developing an Ideology

Havighurst quotes Erikson to support his claim that one's ideology is the central element of the main goal of adolescence: achieving identity. Erikson defines an ideology as "a coherent body of shared images, ideas, and ideals which (whether based on a formulated dogma, an implicit *Weltanschauung* [worldview], or highly structured world image, a political creed or a way of life) provides for the participants a coherent if systematically simplified over-all orientation in space and time, in means and end."[50] The young adolescent is becoming interested in questions of morality, ethics, and religions. Havighurst identifies two educational implications of this:

> (a) To help students acquire a worthwhile combination of expressive and instrumental values that will maintain the positive qualities of a highly productive economy and add the aesthetic and ethical values which bring more beauty and love into the lives of the people;
> (b) To help students learn how to apply these values in their personal and civic lives.[51]

This sounds very much like discerning between tough-minded ("maintain the positive qualities of [the] economy") and tender-minded ("add the aesthetic and ethical values"). One's worldview, while very often containing elements of both mentalities, will generally lean toward being tough-minded or tender-minded. This is a useful distinction when learning about one's own worldview as well as the worldview of others. Christianity is unique among the world's religions in that it provides ultimate meaning centered on a historical fact—namely, the resurrection of Jesus Christ. How do we help students apply these values? As Lutherans we understand the distinction between the civic (kingdom of the left hand) and the sacred (kingdom of the right hand). We also understand that our faith will extend to every area of our lives. Christianity offers the personal reassurance to the tender heart and the factual truth to the toughened mind, capable of adding aesthetic beauty and providing solid answers to everyone around us.

How do young minds acquire a set of values, and how can these values be defended? If the world's ideologies are incompatible (as I will discuss in this handbook), which, if any of them, is true? "How can a young man keep his way pure?"[52] The child's developing mind will open him up to new facets of his worldview and those of his peers. To many people, the Bible is only one possible way of developing a set of morals (and, in our world today, one that is often criticized and reviled). Why should the Bible be of any more consequence than the Koran or one's personal feelings about ethics? Our young people are increasingly asking philosophical and religious questions of ultimate meaning. To quote Dr. John Warwick Montgomery, "When the Greeks of our day come seeking Jesus (John 12:20, 21), let us make certain they find Him,"[53] and let us make certain that we are equipping our young people with the desire and ability to make this great introduction.

Desiring and Achieving Socially Responsible Behavior

Havighurst describes the goal of this task as being able "to develop a social ideology; to participate as a responsible adult in the life of the community, region, and nation; to take account of the values of society in one's personal behavior."[54] The pull of the world is strong, especially on a young mind newly adrift in a sea of abstract thought, conceptual analysis, and heightened awareness. The intense desire to belong haunts the young adolescent in much the same way the fear of the dark haunts the young child—both seem to suggest that one will be safe from the unknown if one can remain in the light of community. Havighurst sees loyalty to one's community as a basis for socially responsible behavior, noting that "the adolescent must develop an ideology that is in harmony with the values and the facts of his society."[55]

This is a very appealing suggestion to many individuals, adolescents and adults alike. An adherence to old-fashioned ideals can lead to loneliness and rejection by one's peers. The desire to belong can lead to the spurning of unpopular ideas and the embracing of new morals. A young adolescent from a conservative household is facing new and oftentimes unexpected pressures—and not just in the oft-discussed realms of alcohol consumption and sexual behavior. Belief in absolute truth is unfashionable among many young people. A desire to belong can cause the adolescent to turn his back on a faith that society deems unacceptable.

This is something that many people talk about but few actually address in any meaningful manner. Trendier church services, a more social gospel, and hip-swaying contemporary worship songs appeal to the superficial signs of a deeper problem. Somewhere along our postmodern line, we lost the idea that truth is enough, and we lost it because we shunned the name of truth. I grew up in a community of conservative, evangelical friends and peers. I can count on one hand those who still claim the name of Christ and adhere to the Bible as the only source of truth. What happened?

For many of my former friends, the call of the world was too strong. Those who desired marriage found that it was difficult to find companionship with any sort of biblical foundation. The *cornerstone* was the first to go in order to make way for a newer, airier, more sensual building. Those who desired meaningful employment found that it was a faux pas to mention Jesus in the workplace. Cue the purging of the mind of all religion.

Like Peter, we're extraordinarily quick to say, "Though they all fall away because of You [Jesus], I will never fall away!"[56] And like Peter, all of us fail. In our search for socially responsible behavior, we have all missed the mark. In our interactions with society, we dare not approach it with a "holier-than-thou" attitude. However, "whereof one can speak, thereof one must not be silent."[57] We have a faith solidly founded on fact, an apologetic extended to us and mandated by the Holy Spirit.[58]

What is "socially responsible behavior"? Christ gives us the answer: "And Jesus came and said to them, 'All authority in heaven and on earth has been given to me. Go therefore and make disciples of all nations, baptizing them in the name of the Father and of the Son and of the Holy Spirit, teaching them to observe all that I have commanded you.'"[59] And if the Spirit has moved through us to proclaim the word of God and the hearers have questions, what then? Enter apologetics: "always [be] prepared to make a defense to anyone who asks you for a reason for the hope that is in you; yet do it with gentleness and respect."[60] May our desire be the same as that of our Lord: that all men be saved and come to the knowledge of the truth.[61] We, who by the grace of God know this truth, should teach our young people to wield apologetics effectively—and unapologetically—in its defense.

Notes

1 Susan Wise Bauer and Jessie Wise, *The Well-Trained Mind: A Guide to Classical Education at Home*, 3rd ed. (New York: W. W. Norton & Company, 2009.), xxv, xxvi.

2 Gene Edward Veith Jr., *The Spirituality of the Cross: The Way of the First Evangelicals*, rev. ed. (St. Louis: Concordia, 2010), 71.

3 A quick Internet search reveals countless such organizations, and some religious affiliations have resources by country, such as *The Resources of Islamic Homeschool in the UK*, http://www.rahmahmuslimhomeschool.co.uk.

4 Gene Edward Veith Jr., *Classical Education: The Movement Sweeping America*, 3rd ed. (Washington, DC: Capital Research Center, 2015), 86.

5 Ibid.

6 Adapted from the ancient philosophical idea of the transcendentals. See Wouter Goris and Jan Aertsen, "Medieval Theories of Transcendentals," *The Stanford Encyclopedia of Philosophy*, Summer 2013 Edition, ed. Edward N. Zalta, accessed July 29, 2017, http://plato.stanford.edu/archives/sum2013/entries/transcendentals-medieval/.

7 "Choosing Christian Curriculum," *Exploring Homeschooling*, accessed July 14, 2017, http://www.exploringhomeschooling.com/ChoosingChristianCurriculum.aspx.

8 Ruth Beechick, *You Can Teach Your Child Successfully* (Fenton, MI: Mott Media, 1999), vii.

9 Veith, *Classical Education*, 13.

10 Bauer and Wise, *The Well-Trained Mind*, 13.

11 Veith, *Classical Education*, 17.

12 Dorothy Sayers, "The Lost Tools of Learning," *GBT*, accessed February 18, 2016, http://www.gbt.org/text/sayers.html.

13 Different home- and classical-schooling resources hold varying ideas about when each process occurs. Some think that certain stages begin earlier and carry on later—for example, author Laura M. Berquist thinks that the logic stage begins around grade seven, Susan Wise Bauer and Jessie Wise think this occurs at grade five, and this handbook proposes that it begins in grade four.

14 Veith, *Classical Education*, 17.

15 Laura Berquist, *Designing Your Own Classical Curriculum* (Warsaw, ND: Ignatius Press, 1995), 18.

16 Bauer and Wise, *The Well-Trained Mind*, 13.

17 Ibid., 14.

18 Ibid., 229.

19 Ibid., 231.

20 Sayers, "The Lost Tools of Learning."

21 Bauer and Wise, *The Well-Trained Mind*, 231.

22 If a middle schooler's parent is using this handbook expecting a child to learn both the core concepts of the faith and its defense, he would be well advised to look elsewhere. While every attempt has been made to outline the "mere Christianity" we are defending, it would be useful if a child already had an elementary background in the core teachings of the Christian faith (as detailed firstly in Holy Scripture and secondarily in Luther's Small and Large Catechisms and *The Book of Concord*).

23 Robert Havighurst, *Developmental Tasks and Education*, 4th printing (New York: David McKay, 1976), 2.

24 Ibid.

25 Ibid., 2, 12.

26 Mario Beauregard and Denyse O'Leary, *The Spiritual Brain* (New York: HarperOne, 2007), 103, 104ff.

27 Havighurst, *Developmental Tasks and Education*, 19.
28 Ibid., 19–35.
29 Task 5, "Developing fundamental skills in reading, writing, and calculating," fits very well with the interdisciplinary approach used in this handbook. However, due to the fairly self-explanatory title, we will not unpack it in detail but simply say that this book has attempted to fulfill this task's goal as well.
30 Havighurst, *Developmental Tasks and Education*, 21.
31 Ibid.
32 Ibid.
33 Ibid., 20.
34 Michael Berg, "An Apology for Apologetics," *Kingdom Workers*, accessed July 29, 2017, http://kingdomworkers.com/articleapologetics1.php.
35 Havighurst, *Developmental Tasks and Education*, 27.
36 Bauer and Wise, *The Well-Trained Mind*, 230.
37 Havighurst, *Developmental Tasks and Education*, 27.
38 Ibid., 28.
39 Ibid.
40 John 14:6.
41 John 1:14–18.
42 See 2 Peter 3:18.
43 Havighurst, *Developmental Tasks and Education*, 29.
44 Ibid., 30.
45 Shannon Hale, *Princess Academy: Palace of Stone* (New York: Bloomsbury, 2012), 43.
46 Ibid., 307.
47 *Palace of Stone* is an excellent book for a discerning young reader. Along with its prequel, *Princess Academy*, it brings up many interesting philosophies and discussion points. I highly recommend that you consider reading it with your child.
48 Havighurst, *Developmental Tasks and Education*, 44.
49 Ibid., 40.
50 Quoted in ibid., 69.
51 Ibid., 73.
52 Psalm 119:9.

53 John Warwick Montgomery, *Faith Founded on Fact: Essays in Evidential Apologetics* (Edmonton: Canadian Institute for Law, Theology, and Public Policy, 2001), 42.

54 Havighurst, *Developmental Tasks and Education*, 75.

55 Ibid., 76.

56 Matthew 26:33.

57 John Warwick Montgomery, *Tractatus Logico-Theologicus* (Eugene: Wipf & Stock, 2013), 205.

58 1 Peter 3:15.

59 Matthew 28:18–20.

60 1 Peter 3:15.

61 1 Timothy 2:4.

PART TWO

THE HANDBOOK

A Note to Instructors Regarding Assignments

Assignment suggestions will appear after relevant sections in the handbook. Some assignments will be project or essay based, and others will be more like discussion questions. In addition to the suggested assignments, ask your child if there is a particular section that she is having trouble understanding and tailor your assignments to aid her comprehension. If there is a section your child especially enjoys, let her investigate it further.

I have not developed exams in conjunction with this handbook simply because it is aimed at home-based educators (and other educators in similarly small environments) who will have more one-on-one contact with their students. You as the instructor will be able to tell if your child has a grasp of the subject matter or not without the use of testing. If you choose to issue exams, they may be developed following the assignment suggestions.

Some of the suggested readings may contain material that is too advanced for your child, either in terms of comprehension or subject propriety. You are encouraged to browse the assigned readings before handing them off to your child. If a specific reading deals with concepts beyond your child's age, I encourage you to read sections aloud to your child instead of abandoning the assignment altogether. Mold the assignments to fit your child, keeping in mind that putting one's armor on is rarely a comfortable experience. The trick lies in girding oneself appropriately for war while at the same time not being crushed by the weight of the armor. There is no need for your child to be unduly disturbed by age-inappropriate material—just remember that the dragons will attack whether your child is ready or not. The first time your child experiences mental stress should not be in the heat of battle but in the (still uncomfortable) confines of the training hall. May God bless your efforts at discernment as you strive to be good stewards of His precious lambs.

Unit One

Focus on Understanding ("Truth")

And [Jesus] called the people to Him and said, "Hear and understand."

—Matthew 15:10

"Do you believe in God?" The young man looked up at his instructor. His face was open and honest and his eyes were slightly widened.

"Yes, of course," his teacher answered, looking a bit uncomfortable.

"Oh." The boy thought for a moment. Then he shrugged and said, "For me, I think I believe more in the ancient Greek gods. You know, Zeus, Poseidon, Hades." His face lit up. "Hades! I love how you contact him!"

All right, students, this is your first test. Take a guess at which time period, from the beginning until the present day, this conversation occurred. Got it? Write it down.

What if I told you that this conversation occurred in modern-day America, in a small town in the Midwest? Would you be surprised? I certainly was when I heard it. Or when I had a fifth grader gush to me about how much she enjoyed studying ancient Egypt because of all the gods. "I just love their religion," she exclaimed and proceeded to recite a list of her favorite Egyptian deities and their powers. While you may not have witnessed a conversation as extreme as I did, maybe you've heard similar comments from the media, friends, or relatives. Before we can dive into *defending* our faith, we need to examine why this is necessary—don't all religions basically say the same thing? How do you know that what you're defending is the truth? Is truth even *knowable?*

At the beginning of this unit, I want you as a student to begin a portfolio that you will add to as you move through this handbook. It can be a spiral-bound notebook, a three-ring binder, or a document on your computer. Throughout this book, I will ask you to add things to your portfolio. Although I will give end-of-unit assessment suggestions for your instructors, I am more interested in providing you with ongoing resources than I am in having you pass a standardized exam.

Here is your first assignment.

Assignments and Discussion Questions

1. Select a medium (physical notebook, word processor document on a computer, or your own creation) you wish to use for your portfolio.
2. Write your name, your grade or age, your instructor's or mentor's name, your school name (if applicable), the subject, and the date on the first page. Follow your instructor's guidelines for the formatting. Here is one suggestion:
   Valerie Locklair
   4th Grade
   Mrs. Jessica Fletcher
   Phoenix Institute
   Apologetics
   October 2, 2015
3. On the next page, write down a question or two that you have about your faith or how to discuss it with others. For example, maybe you've never understood *how* we got the Bible or *who* decided which books to include, or maybe you wonder if there's really any

evidence for the life of Jesus. Don't be bashful! Think of the questions that make you uncomfortable, and write them down. "How do we know the Bible is true?" is a legitimate question, and there is nothing shameful about having questions about your faith.

4. Find a blank page near the end of your portfolio (leave enough space if you're using a physical notebook—allow yourself about five pages) and write "Book Suggestions" at the top. Throughout this handbook, you will discover resources that you will want to read. You will want to keep track of both the book suggestions and those books that you have read. Maybe you would like to color-code them or draw a checkbox next to them so you can keep track of which books you have read. Be creative!
5. What religious ideas do you hear frequently among your friends? Were you ever surprised to find out that someone didn't believe the same things that you do?

Our focus for unit one will be on defining our terms and understanding what our goal is. We'll explore what apologetics is and why we need it and investigate the basics of Christianity and the importance of truth. As you read the following sections, you may want to take notes in your notebook, especially if there's something that you don't quite understand and may need to investigate further later on. For now, let's get started by figuring out what exactly apologetics is.

CHAPTER 1
Becoming CPR Certified

> Beloved, although I was very eager to write to you about our common salvation, I found it necessary to write appealing to you to contend for the faith that was once for all delivered to the saints.
>
> —Jude 1:3

Why do you believe what you believe?

Have you ever been asked this question? Maybe a friend or relative has questioned why you believe some "book" that is full of so-called outdated rules. Maybe someone has asked you how you know what you believe is true. How do you know you're not wrong? Isn't it prideful to think that *you're* right and everyone else is wrong? Maybe you've heard someone ask questions like this and you've secretly breathed a sigh of relief that *you* don't have to answer. Maybe you've asked these questions yourself—or you would, if you weren't embarrassed or worried about what people would think. Maybe you're afraid that you don't know the answer.

This handbook is for you. Throughout the next three units, you'll learn about something called *apologetics*—and not just any apologetics but Christ-centered, orthodox Lutheran apologetics.

Simply stated, *apologetics* means "a defense." It comes from the Greek word *apologia*, which St. Peter uses in 1 Peter 3:15: "But in your hearts honor Christ the Lord as holy, always being prepared to make a *defense* to anyone who asks you for a reason for the hope that is in you; yet do it with gentleness and respect [emphasis mine]." Apologetics is *defensive*, not offensive. Just like a good martial artist, one does not swing apologetics around wildly, anxiously looking for a fight. The strong martial artist is prepared to physically defend herself if she is attacked. The strong apologist[1] is prepared to verbally give a defense if she is confronted with questions.

Apologetics is not a fancy term for getting into arguments or debates. This is not to say that apologists can't debate others, but apologetics itself is not debating. Let's be perfectly clear: Apologetics is *not* preaching, personal testimony, philosophy, or "logic-ing someone to a conclusion" (while I appreciated the originality of the new verb creation, I sadly couldn't agree with the individual who said this to me). "Arguing" (which is perhaps the verb that the individual was looking for) is actually a technical term that may *aid* apologetics but can never be synonymous with it (which I will discuss later). Neither is apologetics evangelism because proclaiming the gospel—"Christ died for sinners and [you qualify]"[2]—can occur whether anyone directly questions you or not. Apologetics should always be done in response to a question posed by someone else—say, a friend, relative, or classmate.

Recap: *Apologetics* means "a defense." It comes from the Greek word *apologia*, which is a technical, legal term that literally means "from [apo] intelligent reasoning [logos]."[3] Interestingly, *logos* is also the word used in John 1:1.

Clarification

Apologetics is made up of three parts: **clarification**, **positive evidences**, and **refutation**.[4] Think of these components as "Apologetics CPR." Clarification is what I'm doing right now—I'm addressing some common misconceptions about apologetics and stating what it actually *is*. A large part of clarifying something is being able to define it. That's why it's important for you to study new vocabulary terms as you come across them. As you will see throughout this handbook, *understanding*—both your own position and the positions of those around you—is key to doing apologetics. There are types of apologetics other than Christian apologetics—*everyone* does apologetics. Though not every person or religion will have a formal, organized "apologetic," we all defend why we believe something, whether we realize that is what we are doing or not.

Recap: Clarification: "The act of using definitions and coherent language to clear up misunderstandings about a belief or set of beliefs." This is also a huge part of communication. In order to truly have a relationship with someone, both parties need to communicate and practice good listening skills. We will revisit this later in unit two. A clarifying statement is one that states what one actually believes. The three creeds (Apostles', Nicene, and Athanasian) are prime examples of clarifying statements.

Review Questions

Practice stating precisely *what* you believe the core of Christianity is. Try not to give any "justification" for it at all, and be as precise as possible. For instance, "I believe in Jesus" can be taken as too vague. What *specifically* do you believe about Jesus? That He was a historical figure? That He had some good pointers on how to live a good life? That He is the Son of God? If you haven't already, choose one of the three Christian creeds to memorize.

Positive Evidences

Positive evidences can be divided into two broad categories: evidences for those *inside of* Christendom who wonder why we need to do apologetics at all and evidences for Christianity to those *outside of* the faith. The latter—which will be expanded upon later in this book—can come in many different types: scientific (such as evidences for or against a finely tuned, specially created universe), historical (such as arguments for the truthfulness of the Bible), artistic (such as pointing out the aesthetic beauty of a worldview or story), and more. For now, let's address a **positive evidence** for why Christians in general—and Lutherans in particular—should bother with apologetics in the first place.

Simultaneously Lutheran and Apologist

Perhaps you've heard it said that Lutherans really shouldn't be concerned with apologetics. It is, the claim goes, a waste of time and an obnoxious form of the magisterial use of reason (thinking that man can, in essence, set himself up as the sole definer of truth and worker of his own salvation)[5], and this position parallels the idea that Christians should learn to accept matters of faith based on, well, faith. I won't take the time to fully address this issue, but I would like to respond to it briefly, since this handbook is built on the assumption that Lutherans should be not only *doing* apologetics but also *teaching* it to their children—in the church and at home. It should be noted that my concern is not *whether* some Lutherans follow liberal thinking and consider apologetics to be an affront to true faith (they do) but whether they *ought* to feel this way and if there is any Lutheran basis for believing it. Is it the case that we should not "attempt to 'establish evidentially' the Bible's claim to be the Word of God" or endeavor to "'demonstrate' the veracity of the gospel to the non-Christian"?[6] As Dr. Montgomery notes in his essay "Lutheran Theology and the Defense of Biblical Faith," we ought to be asking, "Should orthodox Lutheranism share the antiapologetical bed with contemporary theology, or have we inadvertently picked up the wrong room key altogether?"[7]

Now, if one is interested in discovering what Luther and the Reformers taught concerning apologetics, I recommend Dr. Montgomery's essay "Christian Apologetics in the Light of the Lutheran Confessions" for a thorough examination.[8] (If you're wondering, the fact is that the Confessions are strongly proapologetic.) I'll cut right to the point: the Bible not only allows for the saints to perform apologetical tasks—it mandates that they do so. This deceptively simple fact is often overlooked in our Lutheran churches, which is ironic since most (all?) confessional Lutherans pride themselves on having a strong *Sola Scriptura* foundation.[9]

Consider a few brief examples. Elijah on Mount Carmel demonstrated visible evidence to the pagan priests of Baal (and to all of Israel) that the LORD, He is God (1 Kings 18). Paul, speaking to the philosophers on the Areopagus, gave perhaps the most recognizable apologetic in church history (Acts 17). My favorite example is Jesus offering tactile confirmation of His resurrection by urging Thomas to touch His hands and His side (John 20:27). Examples like this abound throughout Scripture, but for those who require pithy biblical certainty, take a look at 1 Peter 3:15. Notice, please, that statement isn't a suggestion. It's a mandate. Apologetics is not "dogmatics, preaching, philosophy," or optional.[10] If one is to accept the

Bible as the inspired, inerrant word of God—a stance upon which the mainstream, confessional Lutheran church bodies of the WELS (Wisconsin Evangelical Lutheran Synod), ELS (Evangelical Lutheran Synod), and LCMS (Lutheran Church–Missouri Synod) agree—one must come face-to-face with the fact that, concerning apologetics, God "is there, and He is not silent."[11]

In addition, our faith is not founded on faith. Faith in faith is a meaningless statement—it is, logically speaking, nonsense.[12] Faith is a relational term that must have an object. I can have faith in many things, but whenever an individual strays into the "faith based on faith" paradigm, it inevitably turns into "faith in myself." Think about it: Is our faith validated by how firmly we believe it? Is our spirituality dependent on how ardently we adhere to it? Does a boulder turn into a lollipop if we fervently believe it is candy? Lutherans should be wary of anything that smacks of "faith because of faith," or the idea that the veracity of our faith is somehow proven by our sincerity. How are we saved? By grace *through* faith, Ephesians 2 tells us, not by means of our own ideas about our beliefs. Faith is a relational term that always implies an object—something in which we *have* faith. As Lutherans, our object is *solus Christus*—Christ alone. The more we resist the objective nature of faith, the more we unwittingly exchange the *true object* for the house built on sand. We replace the certainty of Christ crucified and raised on the third day for our own emotional ecstasies concerning Him. If we know He lives because of our spiritual feelings, we would do well to remember that houses of sand—devoid of the chief cornerstone—are attractive nesting spots for roving demons (see Luke 11:24ff.).

But surely, some Lutherans protest, "the Bible says it, I believe it, and that settles it."[13] Well, yes—but this statement completely misses the issue. The same could be said (and *is* said) by Muslims: "The Koran says it, I believe it, and that settles it." This is an impregnable argument because it *assumes the very thing that remains to be demonstrated*—in other words, the veracity of the Bible over and against competing authority claims.[14] Instead of setting up our confession to be dismissed as simply another unprovable claim, what if we took the approach of pointing to the person of Jesus Christ as a historical, verifiable figure who just happened to overcome death itself, and then investigate what He has to say about religion?

I could say more on this topic, and for further reading concerning Lutherans and the defense of the faith, see this unit's suggested reading list. For now, let's review the definition of "positive evidences" and move on to defining "refutation," the third facet of our apologetical task.

Recap: Positive Evidences: "The reasons and facts offered by a belief or set of beliefs as to why one should accept it in preference to other religions." There can be at least two types of positive evidences: those intended to provide positive reasons to people *inside* the worldview as to how and why apologetics fits into it (e.g., my discussion of how apologetics is distinctly Lutheran) and those intended to provide reasons for belief to people *outside* of the worldview. There are at least two types of positive evidences for those *outside* of a worldview, which are designed to meet people where they are and provide the resources that individuals need at any given moment. I will discuss something called *tough-minded* and *tender-minded* apologetics in unit two. For now, just be aware that there are different categories of evidences.

Review Questions

Think about the clarification that you worked on earlier. Do you have positive evidences to support it? What are some positive evidences that you have heard people give? What does it mean that "faith always has an object"?

Refutation

The "refutation" aspect of apologetics may contribute to why some people shy away from giving a solid defense. To refute something means to disprove or point out the errors in it. You see, other worldviews will have positive evidences that will be used to support them. Blindly ignoring these evidences is not a good idea (we'll find out more about why this is later on). We need to be able to reasonably and lovingly point out the holes in other worldviews. Others may try to refute your *worldview*, and at some point as you make your defense, you will have to refute other worldviews.

This means, however, that you need to *understand* opposing *positive evidences*. In order to do this, you may need to ask for *clarification* if you don't understand someone's position. It is important to ensure that you are actually addressing the issue and not inadvertently criticizing the wrong thing! In other words, don't assume someone's position. We'll see in later units why this is so important.

Refutation is important, but it is also important to remember that just because you can disprove someone else, it doesn't prove that you are right. You must both show the inadequacy of a competing worldview and be able to offer a reasonable case as to why another viewpoint is superior. Refutations should also be given in a loving way. Shouting, "You're wrong and you're also stupid!" is not only hurtful to others, it is harmful to your own cause. I will discuss in this handbook fair, respectful ways to point out flaws in other worldviews.

Recap: Refutation: "The act of pointing out flaws and fallacies in belief systems." To refute something well, you must thoroughly understand the other point of view and take opposing evidences seriously. Refutation addresses someone's position; it does not wage personal attacks against others.

Review Questions

What refutations have you heard concerning a worldview? Has anyone ever tried to refute what you believe? What were their objections to your beliefs?

Before I define our terms any further, I need to set the stage a little bit. Let's consider the following questions: Why is a defense necessary? What kind of attack are we under? And why does it matter?

Why Is There a War?

> Religions are worldviews. They claim to address the primary questions of our existence—where we came from, where we are going, and why we are going where we are going. Everyone is religious because everybody has a worldview, even if that worldview is that we come from a totally purposeless beginning and are returning to dust and that this life is largely what novelist William Faulkner called "sound and fury, signifying nothing."
>
> —Craig Parton, *Religion on Trial*[15]

Maybe you've heard that all religions basically teach the same thing. A recent Internet "meme" I saw compared the "primary teachings" of nine religions and came to the conclusion that they all said basically the same thing: we should be kind to each other. "Tolerance" and "Coexist" bumper stickers flood our highways and city streets. We don't want to imply that someone's belief is less true than our own. What works for you may not work for me, and if I'm happy, that's all that matters. Can't we all just get along?

After all, don't all religions teach basically the same thing? Both Muslims and Christians pray to "God," and Buddhists meditate, which is almost the same thing. A Mormon uncle, a Muslim neighbor, and a Christian friend all claim to follow the Ten Commandments.[16] What about nonreligious people? Where do they fit into all this?

To begin my survey of this issue, I am going to accept a basic definition of religion, simplified by Craig Parton, a noted lawyer, scholar, and apologist: "Religions are worldviews."[17] Even people who claim to be nonreligious do, in fact, believe in *something* that explains how and why they view the world in the way that they do. Phillip E. Johnson, a retired law professor at UC Berkeley, explains what a worldview is and why it's so important in this way:

> It would be an understatement to say that worldview is an important topic. I would rather say that understanding how worldviews are formed, and how they guide or confine thought, is the essential step toward understanding everything else. Understanding worldview is a bit like trying to see the lens of one's own eye. We do not ordinarily see our own worldview, but we see everything else by looking through it. Put simply, our worldview is the window by which we view the world, and decide, often subconsciously, what is real and important, or unreal and unimportant.[18]

You see, very rarely will you hear your friend say in normal, day-to-day conversation, "I'm a thoroughly postmodern agnostic and that's why I believe in relative truths." Many times the individuals you interact with may not even know the official "term" for their worldview or religion. Understanding someone's worldview is important for (at least) two reasons: first, we have not yet determined which worldview, if any, is true (are they all true, are none of them true, or are some of them true?), and second, we need to understand what lies at the core of our friends' beliefs so that we can interact with them and our culture appropriately.

So how do we identify worldviews, and once we have, how do we evaluate them?

Assignments and Discussion Questions

1. What does it mean to give an "apologetic" for something? Do you think that people only give apologetics for religious matters, or does it occur in other areas too? In what other areas might this occur?
2. Has anyone ever asked you to give a reason why you believe something? What did you say, and what was the reaction you received?
3. What does apologetics CPR stand for? Find an example of each type of statement in a book, magazine, or article.
4. What is the biblical evidence for doing apologetics? Remember, we're not currently trying to show that Christianity is true. However, we do need to show that *doing* apologetics is consistent with Christianity. Choose one of the biblical examples of apologetics referenced earlier or find your own and read through the account. Can you identify all three parts of CPR in these accounts? Why do you think some accounts may focus more heavily on one aspect rather than another?
5. With your teacher's approval, read through *How Do We Know There Is a God?* by Dr. John Warwick Montgomery. Have you ever heard anyone ask these questions before? Have *you* ever asked anyone these questions? Choose one or two of the questions to write down in your notebook to investigate throughout your studies in this handbook. Why did you choose those questions?

6. With your teacher's guidance, choose one fiction book and one nonfiction book from this unit's book-list. You will read these two books throughout the rest of this unit.

Notes

1 The term for someone who does apologetics.

2 Craig Parton, *The Defense Never Rests: A Lawyer among the Theologians* (St. Louis: Concordia, 2015), 20.

3 "627.apologia," *Bible Hub*, accessed July, 30, 2017, http://biblehub.com/greek/627.htm.

4 For a thorough treatment of these three parts, read "Christian Apologetics in the Light of the Lutheran Confessions" by Dr. John Warwick Montgomery. You will find it in *Christ as Centre and Circumference*, one of the books in this unit's suggested reading list.

5 "[Magisterial reason is] the idea that fallen man's rational reflection could be a source of religious truth apart from the Bible . . . reason trying to pronounce on divine things independently of Scripture." J. I. Packer, "'Sola Scriptura' in History and Today," ed. John Warwick Montgomery, *God's Inerrant Word* (Minneapolis: Bethany Fellowship, 1974), 44.

6 John Warwick Montgomery, *Faith Founded on Fact*, 18th printing (Newburgh: Trinity Press, 2003), 130.

7 Ibid., 132.

8 You can find it reprinted in John Warwick Montgomery, *Christ as Centre and Circumference*, 147–63.

9 By "confessional Lutherans," I am referring to those who adhere to the Lutheran confessions—namely, the "conservative" synods of the WELS (Wisconsin Evangelical Lutheran Synod), ELS (Evangelical Lutheran Synod), LCMS (Lutheran Church–Missouri Synod), and some other smaller church bodies.

10 John Warwick Montgomery, "Apologetics for the 21st Century," reprinted in *Christ as Centre and Circumference*, 137.

11 Title of a work by Francis Schaeffer.

12 See Parton, *Religion on Trial*, 29. We will unpack this concept later on in this handbook.

13 This used to be a fairly popular catchphrase and bumper sticker in midwestern evangelicalism.

14 See Parton, *Religion on Trial*, chapters 2 and 3.

15 Preface, p. xi.

16 Parton, *Religion on Trial*, xiii.

17 Ibid., xi.

18 Quoted in Nancy Pearcey, *Total Truth* (Wheaton: Crossway, 2004), 11.

CHAPTER 2

MESH-AGE and You

> A worldview is like a mental map that tells us how to navigate the world effectively.
>
> —Nancy Pearcey, *Total Truth*[1]

Renowned author and scholar Nancy Pearcey offers a grid of three guiding principles to identify when one is trying to determine a worldview. David Noebel, the founder of Summit Ministries, in his work *Understanding the Times*, delves into six of the world's foremost religions in great detail, and it is an excellent resource for the student who wishes to investigate different worldviews in more depth. For the purposes of this handbook, I shall not evaluate each worldview. As apologist Craig Parton says, if we did that we should be here for a very long time—there are in excess of ten thousand "religions, cults, and isms" in the world today.[2] For now, I will focus on what a worldview has to say about **MESH-AGE**.

MESH-AGE is an acronym for how a worldview understands "man, evil, salvation, history, authority, God, and ethics (or morality)."[3] In other words, all worldviews address the following seven questions:

Man: What does the worldview say about human kind and its destiny?
Evil: What does the worldview say about evil in the world?
Salvation: What does the worldview say about rescue or reprieve from suffering?
History: What does the worldview say about the course of world events?

Authority: What does the worldview adhere to as its source of truth?
God: What does the worldview say about the existence of a divine being?
Ethics/(Morality): What does the worldview say is acceptable moral conduct?

Think of each of the previous seven areas as parts of the "mesh," or connections between chinks in a knight's armor, or as points of impact on a knight's shield. The answer to each of these seven questions will determine how you view the world and how you interact with others at a personal, national, and global level. Is the chainmail tight enough to protect the knight (i.e., help you explain the way the world is) but fluid enough to allow him to move (i.e., somehow fill a personal need that you have)?

Think of this unit as a shield. In ancient times, warriors needed strong, durable shields to protect them as they went into battle. If we are to give a strong defense for our faith, we need a strong and dependable shield. Like most analogies, this one can break down quite easily, as our friends who know a thing or two about ancient armor can tell us!

We cannot go over *every* worldview and evaluate them in this manner. The beauty of MESH-AGE is that it can be applied to any worldview (and offshoot) and you will get a pretty good idea of what an individual believes. Once we know that, we can begin to understand why someone would act, say, or think the way that he does—and how that influences the world around him.

But wait! Don't all religions say basically the same thing anyway? Won't the answer to MESH-AGE stay fairly consistent from Buddhism to Christianity to Zoroastrianism? Let's do a brief comparison of a handful of worldviews using MESH-AGE in order to find out.

Man: What Do Worldviews Say about Humankind and Its Destiny?

What are human beings? How did we get here? Do we have a purpose? Are we naturally good, naturally evil, or somehow cosmically neutral? Do we have a purpose and meaning in life? Let's take a brief look at some possible answers to these questions.

Naturalism is the belief that everything can be explained in terms of natural causes.[4] In other words, physical matter is all there is. This means that, according to naturalism, "human beings are complex 'machines'; personality is an interrelation of chemical and physical properties we do not yet fully understand."[5] In other words, "The cosmos is all that is or ever was or ever will be," and humans are simply a part of that cosmos.[6] There's nothing spiritual about the way humans came into being: "Man arose as a result of the operation of organic evolution and his being and activities are also materialistic, but the human species has properties unique to itself among all forms of life, superadded to the properties unique to life among all forms of matter and of action. Man's intellectual, social, and spiritual natures are exceptional among animals in degree, but they arose by organic evolution."[7] According to naturalism, human beings are flesh and blood but not soul and spirit.

New Age spirituality, also called new spirituality, is "a worldview that teaches everything and everyone are connected through divine consciousness."[8] I'm god, you're god, and that tree over there is god. There is a new age coming for the human race, an "evolution of the human mind" and a "quantum leap in the progress of mankind."[9] As we gain a clearer understanding of our states of consciousness—which can be achieved to some extent through meditation, mind-altering drugs, and biological and psychological evolution—we will realize our godhood as "creators of worlds, capable of Genesis [creation]."[10]

Whew! Are you overwhelmed yet? Let's blow quickly through two more religious explanations of human beings. **Islam** says human beings were created out of clay by Allah.[11] They are distinct from animals, and human beings are born without sin. **Eastern religions** like Confucianism and Taoism think that humans are basically good and don't require any type of salvation.[12] Some don't even distinguish between good and evil, and some see the body as a hindrance to us that must somehow be cast off.

Even from these much simplified explanations, we can see that we have run into what logic calls **contradictions** (or **contraries**)—or, put another way, "The religions of the world are mutually exclusive; the basic tenets of one contradict the fundamental convictions of the others, so all of them cannot possibly be correct."[13] Even just taking their views of humankind, we can see that we have a problem here. Islam says that human beings were created by Allah, naturalism says that we are complex machines evolved by purely mechanical and unguided processes, and various Eastern religions and New Age thinking posit that we are gods (or at least god-like) in our souls and that our physical bodies are hindrances. Though these beliefs could all be false, they could *not* all be true.

Logic (Clarity)

"Logic!" exclaims Professor Kirk in *The Lion, the Witch, and the Wardrobe*. "Why don't they teach logic at these schools?"[14] Logic has gone out of style in today's world—or, at the very least, it has often been reduced to what *you* want it to be at any given point. In many cases, it is dismissed as cold, hard, and unfeeling, a vice of those who live without empathy or beauty.

Logic is a framework for how you interact with and organize statements about the world. The frame of a house shows you how different pieces of a structure will fit together and relate to one another. It will tell you what can consistently fit inside this structure, but it will *not* tell you *what* the structure is made of or what you should put into it. Likewise, logic represents the "scaffolding" of the world, and it can help you make sense of the world around you, but it cannot tell you any of the *facts* or details about how the world truly is.[15]

I'm not going to provide you with an exhaustive survey of logic. That would go beyond the scope of this course. I do, however, want to give you a brief overview and provide some key definitions.

Logic deals with *arguments*. An argument, far from being a shouting match, is a collection of *statements*. A statement is a sentence that is either true or false.[16] Claims that are neither true nor false are known as "technically meaningless."[17]

At the core of logic is something called the "law of contradiction" (also, confusingly, known as the "law of *non*contradiction"). This law states that "something cannot both exist and not exist at the same time."[18] Any meaningful discussion rests on this law, partially because I myself either exist or I do not, and because I cannot both be telling you the truth about the law of contradiction and lie about it at the same time! Without the law of contradiction, it would be impossible to derive any meaning from a statement because the statement would blend with its opposite.[19] Consider the following example: "Jesus Christ is God in the flesh and the savior of the world" and "Jesus Christ is *not* God in the flesh and *not* the savior of the world." Without the law of contradiction, those statements would blend together and become meaningless.

Why do we need this law? Because it's necessary. Without it, we couldn't understand anything. Logic provides a framework for how facts relate to each other. You don't *have* to be logical, but if you deny the law of contradiction, you will have grave difficulty with everyday tasks. Crossing the street, for example, necessitates a strict adherence to logic. If you don't look both ways before crossing to avoid stepping out in front of a bus, you will experience firsthand the perils of acting contrary to logic. Automotive vehicles will quite literally pound the concept of *exclusive or* into you—either you cross the street safely *or* you do not; either you are hit by a bus *or* you are not.

Let me explain that a little bit with an example. Find your favorite optical illusion. Perhaps it is Ruben's goblet, where you can see a goblet or two faces. Notice the use of the word *or*. Let's unpack this word a bit.

In logic, there are two very different uses for the word *or*: the **inclusive** and the **exclusive**. The **inclusive or** is what I am using when I ask, "Do you see a goblet or two faces in this optical illusion?" It is possible that you see *both*—likewise, my question includes the possibility that you can answer "Both." Both possibilities can be true, one can be true, or neither can be true. If it's Thanksgiving and your grandmother asks you if you would like pumpkin pie or ice cream, can you get away with answering "Yes"? Possibly, depending on your grandmother's judgment about your dietary requirements! However, if you are in the front seat giving me directions while I drive and, upon coming to a T-intersection, I ask, "Which direction do I turn—right or left?" it would not be appropriate to reply "Yes." This is what we call the **exclusive or:** it means that "one or the other but not both" options can be true.[20] If you asked me, "Are you married or single?" I could not respond that I was *both*—both states of being (the state of being married and the state of being single) cannot be true for the same person at the exact same time in the same way. I am either one or the other.

Many people seem to treat worldviews in the *inclusive or* sense. You will find individuals who would answer "Is Christianity true or is Islam true?" with "Yes." They would view the conjunction *or* as being in an *inclusive* state. Like an optical illusion, both can be equally true. You and I can look at the same image and see a pair of faces or a goblet, and we would both be equally correct. Isn't that what happens when you and I look at the world too? We may see different things, but we're both equally right, aren't we? It isn't worth arguing over who sees a goblet and who sees two faces, so how can it be worth it to argue over worldviews?

What is the outcome of viewing an optical illusion? Psychology can tell us many interesting things—perhaps what you see is influenced by your mental state or vice versa. In the end, does it really matter? Will you live your life differently depending on whether you see two faces or a goblet? Perhaps, but it is unlikely. I am willing to hazard that you could live your life in much the same way whether you see one or the other or both images. The same cannot be said of worldviews. It will drastically impact your day-to-day life academically, socially, politically, and religiously. Some worldviews claim that it will even impact you eternally.

Beyond Analytics

"At some point, you're going to have to stop analyzing." I laughed sheepishly at my dad's raised eyebrows. He knew me well enough to know that I would continue to agonize over a decision I had spent months investigating, and he was right that the time had come to move beyond my analysis paralysis. What my dad was saying was that my overly analytical mind was chugging away at a problem that had gone beyond the scope of logic. I needed to focus on the *facts* I was fitting into my problem-solving framework. If my facts couldn't stand up to scrutiny, my framework, no matter how logical, would be a burned-out, heartless skeleton.

Logic is crucially important, but it never takes the stage alone. Many people pride themselves on being logical or thinking logically. Just thinking that you are being logical does not mean that you actually *are* logical. Furthermore, the *content* of beliefs—the "stuff" that logic can't tell us—must be evaluated too. A worldview must also fit the facts of how the world truly is. A sound framework is vitally important, but you cannot live in it until you have discerned the correct materials that you need for building a solid and beautiful house. We need another method for that.

You may be wondering why we should investigate Christianity first out of all other religions. Are we simply assuming that it's true? Far from it, we are investigating Christianity first because it claims that Jesus Christ is the only way of salvation and that He physically rose from the dead.[21] We don't need to believe that claim in order to investigate it. If the claim is true, according to the law of contradiction, *every* other religion in the world is false. There cannot be multiple ways or means of salvation. In addition, as we shall see, the claims of Christianity *do* have truth-values. They are testable. That's why we spend so much time focusing on Christianity—not because we are assuming it is true but because investigating its truth claim will give us an answer to the question of which worldview—if any—is true. If Christianity is false, we can look elsewhere for truth. If it is true, all other worldviews not only are incorrect but are leading people to eternal damnation. Such a strong statement warrants sober and thorough investigation to discern if eternal life truly does hang in the balance.

Recap: What does MESH-AGE stand for? How can we use it to evaluate and understand worldviews? What is logic? How is a worldview like chainmail? Why can't all worldviews be true? What has to be true in order for something to be a contradiction? Why is Christianity the first religion one should attempt to investigate when examining worldviews?

Postmodernism: Inclusive to the Core?

> This new set of assumptions about reality—which goes far beyond mere relativism—is gaining dominance throughout the culture. The average person who believes that there are no absolutes may never have heard of the academic exercise of "deconstruction." The intellectual establishment may disdain the electronic world of television. Contemporary politicians may be unaware of *avant garde* art. Nevertheless, these are all inter-connected and comprise a distinctly postmodernist worldview.
>
> —Gene Edward Veith Jr., *Postmodern Times*[22]

After reading the preceding paragraphs, this comment will inevitably arise: "I have a friend/relative/peer/instructor who doesn't believe any of the stuff we just studied. In fact, when you ask him about what he believes, his answer may change. He talks a lot about his 'truth' and my 'truth,' and sometimes he doesn't even like to use the word truth at all." My friends, welcome to the postmodern age.

The popular view in our world today is that there are no absolutes. "Fragmentation, indeterminacy, and intense distrust of all universal or 'totalizing' discourses (to use the favored phrase) are the hallmark of postmodern thought."[23] There is no truth, and what works for you may not work for me. You will typically find that postmodernists are extremely "inclusive" and "tolerant" of other worldviews, with the noted exception of Christianity. Why?

Christianity makes strong and unapologetic claims on two points that make postmodernists uncomfortable: one, that there is absolute truth that is independent of personal experience and two, that absolute truth is knowable.

"Postmodernism," by contrast, "is a worldview that denies all worldviews."[24] In other words, postmodernism rejects "'foundationalism,' defined as 'the idea that knowledge is the reflection of truth and that we can discover a stable foundation for it in God, History, or Reason.'"[25] Reason and logic are rejected—or the attempt is made to reject them. This makes postmodernism difficult to evaluate based on our prior MESH-AGE acronym. Postmodernism contends that it has no authority to which it subscribes—"'Performance, not truth,' is the only criterion."[26] Does it work for you? If so, do it. "Right" and "wrong" may depend on the current situation in which you find yourself.

Postmodernism embraces storytelling. Worldviews, scientific theories, historical anecdotes, and legal precedents are viewed in the same light: useful fictions but not absolute truth.[27] We are no longer concerned with whether something is true. We are concerned with whether something "works" for us or if it fits our agenda, whether this is a political, religious, social, or personal need.

You could say, perhaps, that the thing postmodernism most excludes is the *exclusive or*. There is no room for outdated notions of truth, morality, or objectivity in this framework. The key to recognizing postmodern thinking is to recognize the lack of absolutes and the emphasis on personal or subjective experience—as you can see by looking at the world around you, this "antiworldview" is permeating our society today.

Assignments and Discussion Questions

1. What is a worldview? How does understanding worldviews help you respond to the person who says, "I don't have a religion"? (Read through the preface and chapter 1 of Craig Parton's *Religion on Trial* for more help.)
2. Evaluate a worldview by using the MESH-AGE acronym. You can evaluate a religion that you saw in a TV show, book, movie, or newspaper article. You must evaluate a worldview other than the one that you personally hold. Work with your teacher to decide on a format for this assignment (whether that be a paper, a presentation, or some other format). In your handbook notebook, note which worldview you chose and why you chose to evaluate it.
3. Which aspect of MESH-AGE do most people focus on in our world today? In other words, what appears to be their main concern or question in life? Is there an aspect of MESH-AGE that people want to ignore (e.g., God)? Why do you think that is?
4. Think about a fictional book that you have read recently. What (if any) postmodern elements did it contain? Were there characters who blurred the lines between right and wrong? Was it a subtle element or a driving theme of the book? (If you need help, consider reading *The Magician's Nephew* by C. S. Lewis or *Princess Academy* and its sequel, *Palace of Stone*, by Shannon Hale.)
5. What is the danger of treating worldviews like optical illusions? What can (and can't) optical illusions teach us about apologetics? Write a brief paper (three pages maximum) explaining your answer.
6. Give an example of a statement that contains an *inclusive or* and one that contains an *exclusive or*.

What would happen if your *exclusive or* statement was treated as if it were inclusive?

Nonnegotiable: Creedal Christianity

We typically say that apologetics is a defense of **creedal Christianity**. By this we mean that we are defending the Christian faith as detailed in the three ecumenical creeds (Apostles', Nicene, and Athanasian). In so doing, we are getting to the heart of Christianity—what some theologians, such as C. S. Lewis, have called "mere Christianity." This is not to say that other points the Bible makes are insignificant. It just means that we are providing a defense for those matters that are at the heart of Christianity. And of course, at the heart of Christianity is Christ. Our goal is to get people as quickly as possible to the cross of Christ and bring them up short before their Savior. The details—such as, for example, the historical fact that Ruth was a Moabitess[28]—can be dealt with later.

It is important to note that we are *not* interested in defending religion, the concept of a god in general, or the peculiarities of one's own ideas about what being a good person should look like. Religion without Christ, to the Christian worldview, is not only false but eternally harmful. We need to look at *what* Christianity says, and then we can begin our evaluation of worldviews.

The Christian MESH-AGE

Remember, the gospel is "'Christ died for sinners and [you qualify].'"[29] How does creedal Christianity answer our seven guiding questions? This will be our worldview, our "mere" Christianity.

Man: Humans were directly created by God in the garden of Eden (Genesis). Adam and Eve were the first man and first woman. They were endowed with something called the "image" of God—that is, with attributes that are a reflection of Him (Gen. 1:26). God has been interested in humanity since the creation of the world, and He is concerned about our eternal welfare (1 Tim. 2:1–7).

Evil: Evil is a real presence in this world. Sin has separated us from God. Adam and Eve were originally sinless until an event called "the fall" happened. Adam and Eve chose to disobey God, and because of this first sin, evil entered the world (Gen. 3). Evil is not created by God. Because of the fall, all humans are now born with *original sin*—no one is perfect (Eph. 2; Ps. 51:5; Rom. 3:23). There are three major forces of evil: the devil, also known as Satan, a fallen angel who is the prince of darkness and father of lies, and there is no truth in him (John 8:44)—he hates those who bear the name of Christ and seeks to destroy them (1 Pet. 5:8); the "world," meaning the earthly pleasures and sins that tempt us to doubt and be misled, for because of the curse the world hates the name of Christ (John 15:19); and our own sinful natures, the inheritance of all human beings since Adam and Eve. Every inclination of our hearts is sinful from the start because of this original sin (Matt. 15:19).

Salvation: Because sin has separated us from God, we are not able to keep His holy law and we are in danger of spending an eternity apart from God in hell, a place that was created for wicked angels and Satan. Everyone who sins is condemned to death, and all have sinned (Rom. 3:23; Ezek. 18:4). We are not able to save ourselves—we need a Savior who has kept the law perfectly and has paid the price of sin, which is death (Rom. 6:23), and who has broken the curse of the grave (Rom. 5). There is only one way to be saved: by grace through faith in Jesus Christ, who paid the debt of our sin and rose again to win for us salvation (Rom. 3:21–26).

History: "Christianity sees history as linear, focusing on the past coming of Christ and His death for the sins of the world. Christianity also promises an end to the history of this world, culminating in the second return of Jesus Christ in judgment of both individuals and nations and the transformation of the heavens and earth."[30] Human history had a definite beginning (in the garden of Eden), and this world will be destroyed at the end of time and a new heaven and new earth will be created (Rev. 21:1).

Authority: The Old and New Testaments are the inspired and infallible word of God (John 5:39). Jesus Christ is the incarnate Word of God, and He is the final authority and judge of the living and the dead.

God: God is Triune, absolute, and good; the second person of the Trinity, Jesus Christ, came down from heaven and was incarnate of the Holy Spirit and born to the virgin Mary. The first person of the Trinity is God the Father, and the third person is God the Holy Spirit.

Ethics/Morality: Christianity has a definite standard of behavior. Our good works cannot save us (Eph. 2:8–9), but we should defend others, speak well of them, and help and support others in Christian love.[31]

That's a lot to wrap your head around! Now you may be thinking, "Yes, yes, I know all of this—I know the truth." But not everyone accepts the truth of Christianity, do they? If they did, we wouldn't have to provide a defense for it!

So just what is truth, and what things do people look to in order to find it? Why does it matter?

Assignments and Discussion Questions

1. Review the Apostles', Nicene, and Athanasian Creeds. Choose one aspect of the MESH-AGE explanation of Christianity to expand upon using the creeds, Luther's explanations, and Bible verses. For example, you may decide to investigate more thoroughly what the Christian worldview says about ethics and morality. With your teacher's help, write an explanation of the aspect and relate it back to the other six aspects of MESH-AGE.
2. If you get into an argument with your friend over whether or not oak trees grew in first-century

Jerusalem, are you providing a Christ-centered apologetic for the faith? Why or why not?

3. Some people think that Christianity says that the God of the Bible is also the god worshipped by other religions. Is this what Christianity says? Does the Christian's source of authority (the Bible) say that there are many paths to God? Did Jesus really claim to be God and the only way to heaven?
4. With your teacher's approval, investigate C. S. Lewis' *Mere Christianity*. (Your teacher may wish to choose sections for you to read or to read sections aloud to you.) What does he mean by the word "mere"? What is the apologetic danger in saying, "We have no creed but Christ"? (Hint: How do we *know* who Christ *is*?)

Notes

1 Ibid., 23.

2 Parton, *Religion on Trial*, 19.

3 Yes, we could term it MESSAGE (which is admittedly easier to say) by swapping "Story" for "History," but I didn't for reasons I will discuss later.

4 Jeff Myers and David Noebel, *Understanding the Times* (Manitou Springs, CO: Summit Ministries, 2015), 490.

5 James Sire, *The Universe Next Door* (Downers Grove: InterVarsity, 1997), 56.

6 Carl Sagan, quoted in ibid., 54.

7 G. G. Simpson, quoted in ibid., 60.

8 Myers and Noebel, *Understanding the Times*, 490.

9 Sire, *The Universe Next Door*, 139.

10 Ibid.

11 See Sadaf Farooqi, "The Creation of Man as Mentioned in the Quran," *Muslim Matters*, last modified February 3, 2012, http://muslimmatters.org/2012/02/03/the-creation-of-man-as-mentioned-in-the-quran/.

12 Parton, *Religion on Trial*, 5.

13 John Warwick Montgomery, ed., *Christianity for the Tough Minded* (Minneapolis: Bethany Fellowship, 1973), 11.

14 C. S. Lewis, *The Lion, the Witch, and the Wardrobe*, First Harper Trophy Edition (New York: HarperCollins, 2000), 182.

15 Ludwig Wittgenstein refers to logic as a "scaffolding." Quoted in Montgomery, *Tractatus Logico-Theologicus*, 34.

16 Robert Johnson, *A Logic Book*, 5th ed. (Belmont: Thomson Wadsworth, 2007), 1–2, 379, 385. We will explore how we determine the so-called truth value of a statement in this book.

17 Parton, *Religion on Trial*, 63. This topic will be addressed in more detail in unit two.

18 Ibid., 22.

19 Montgomery, *Tractatus Logico-Theologicus*, 33.

20 Johnson, *A Logic Book*, 384.

21 See John 14:6, Acts 4:12, and 1 Corinthians 15.

22 Veith, *Postmodern Times*, 19.

23 David Harvey quoted in Veith, *Postmodern Times*, 42.

24 Ibid., 49.

25 Patricia Waugh quoted in ibid., 50.

26 Ibid.

27 Ibid., 57.

28 Anecdote frequently mentioned in presentations by noted apologist Dr. John Warwick Montgomery.

29 Parton, *The Defense Never Rests*, 20.

30 Parton, *Religion on Trial*, 6.

31 Luther, *Luther's Small Catechism with Explanation*, 10–11. See Luther's explanation to the 5th, 8th, 9th, and 10th commandments.

CHAPTER 3

"What Is Truth?"

Pilate said to [Jesus], "What is truth?"

—John 18:38.

The Merriam-Webster dictionary defines truth as "the property (as of a statement) of being in accord with fact or reality" and "the real facts about something: the things that are true."[1] This, at first glance, seems fairly straightforward. True statements are those that line up with reality and how the world is. Upon closer inspection, we have a problem. We just spent the previous pages dealing with *worldviews*: different ways that religions and individuals view the world and reality as a whole. How can we possibly decide what is true if not everyone agrees on what reality is? How do we determine what truth is? Do we follow our hearts, rely on the sincerity of our beliefs, or subscribe to "common sense"?[2]

My Truth, Your Truth, Whose Truth?

If you listen to popular music at all, you have very likely heard a song with lyrics like "listen to your heart," "follow your heart," "stay true to yourself," and so on. The emphasis is on your happiness, your feelings, and your viewpoint (sound familiar?). What you believe doesn't have to mesh with anyone else's beliefs, and anyone who challenges you is an intolerable hypocrite who should be ashamed of himself for being so closed-minded.

I have previously discussed the *exclusive or* as it relates to religions. How are we to know which exclusive or is correct? Have you ever had a friend say to you that you cannot criticize her religion or spirituality because you've never tried it? How do we discern what is true?

Emotions

People can appeal to feelings, emotions, and beliefs to validate themselves. For example, even the contemporary Christian artist TobyMac sings in one of his recent hits:

> Oh, I feel it in my heart
> I feel it in my soul
> That's how I know . . .
> Everybody talkin' like they need some proof
> But what more do I need than to feel You?
> Everybody talkin' like they need some proof
> But what more do I need than to feel You?[3]

The singer feels that his own feelings are more than enough to validate a radical adherence to the knowledge that the object of his worship is true. A brief listen to any contemporary Christian radio station will quickly reveal many sentiments of this nature.

This seems chillingly reminiscent of the admonition I received at one point during my college career to "let go" and become wildly drunk on the basis of how good it feels to have absolutely no worries in the world. It should be noted that the offer was declined and that several of the encouragers spent the evening falling unconscious on the way home—with no memory of what had happened and a tremendous hangover the next morning. They assured me repeatedly that they had a marvelous time—if only they could remember it.

It is possible to get a spiritual-seeming, euphoric high in many ways. Yoga, walking a meditative labyrinth, spending Hanukkah with family, or experiencing Mecca for the first time as a devout Muslim can excite the emotions in the same way as a particularly upbeat pop song or eye contact from that special someone. The difficulty lies in the fact that everyone seems to be able to experience this euphoria by different means. Because of our study of MESH-AGE, we know that these worldviews are incompatible. Feeling something strongly does not make it true, and failure to remember this can leave one passed out on the metaphysical road after an emotionally intoxicating experience.

But surely the sincerity of one's belief counts for something? I can believe with all my heart that I am the president of the United States. This, however, is a testable claim. One can go back through the records to see who exactly was sworn in as president after the last election and determine through testing if I am that person. Or I can sincerely believe that the cure for migraine headaches is to stare at the sun for six hours each day. In both cases, my belief does not change the facts—but in the second case, it could impact my health and wellbeing.

Consider an example from the cult classic film *The Princess Bride* in which the brave Westley is bound and determined to adventure through the Fire Swamp. His lady, Buttercup, expresses alarm concerning the fearsome ROUSes (Rodents of Unusual Size) that haunt the forest. Westley shakes his head and confidently states, "Rodents of Unusual Size? I don't think they exist." As soon as he finishes speaking, he is promptly pounced upon by one of the creatures. Your belief does not determine what is real, but if you keep repeating to yourself that the ROUSes of life (the hard questions, doubts, etc.) do not exist, you may find yourself surprised when they attack you with unexpected vigor.

In other words, "Faith [is] a relational term, always involving an object of belief."[4] If I drink from a cup containing arsenic, but I fervently believe it is water from the Fountain of Youth, I will die nevertheless unless I receive immediate intervention. The **object** of my faith, in this case the arsenic, does not change into water simply because I believe it is H_2O. Worldviews, as I have discussed, deal with matters of life and death. It would be well if we tested what waters we are drinking.

Can emotions discover what is real? Consider professions where life and death are on the line. In the field of medicine, one would not expect a physician, when faced with a patient who complains of an ingrown toenail, to respond, "Well, I feel that the best way to heal your toe is to amputate your right arm." Likewise, the lawyer of a client accused of murder whose defense consists of the sentimental "I feel a deep peace radiating forth from this person and therefore, your honor, can say with the utmost confidence that he is innocent" will soon find himself in search of other employment.

Ignorance

"I think the multiverse is a distinct possibility," Derek said as he fanned the pages of his science textbook.

Mona raised her eyebrow. "The *what?*"

Derek gave an exaggerated sigh and rolled his eyes. "The *multiverse*. You know, the theory that there are an unlimited number of parallel universes. Anything is possible. There could be an exact replica of me in another universe that's out slaying dragons or something."

"Again, *what?*" Mona shook her head. "How could we possibly know that?"

"We don't know for certain that it isn't true." He shrugged. "And there's no evidence that it *isn't* true."

In theory, Derek is correct: anything is possible. However, that doesn't mean that anything is *probable*, and it doesn't mean that anything should be accepted simply because it hasn't been disproven. That fact that we don't know something doesn't automatically make that something a *probability*. In logic, this is called an "argument from ignorance."[5]

Arguments from ignorance are almost always untestable. For example, if I believe in fairies who live in my backyard and disappear every time a human tries to find them, this isn't a testable claim. If you say to me that you can find no evidence for the fairies' existence, I will reply, "Of course you can't! The fairies are clever. You'll never find any proof that they *don't* exist, though, so you can't say I'm wrong." If the fairies are completely indiscernible to humans, there is no way you are ever going to find evidence of either their existence or their nonexistence.

This argument is "technically meaningless."[6] It cannot be tested or verified in any sort of objective way. It has no truth value (either true or false), and even more than that, it relies on "facts" that are completely untestable.

If I believe in something because it is impossible to disprove it, I am believing in something that has no truth-value. Even more than that, I am forsaking ever having a relationship or connection to the thing in which I believe. If the fairies will never leave evidence for humans or intervene to help me in any sort of tangible way, what exactly is my connection to them? I can't know them. How can they solve the problems of life for me or interact with me if they won't enter tangibly into my life?

Is this the best way possible to back up our claims, or is there another method we can use?

Authority

Every worldview has an ultimate source of authority, or something that answers the continual question (to avoid infinite regress) "Yes, but *why* is it like this instead of like that?" with a final "Because 'I' said so." This "I" can take many shapes and forms. Materialists—those who adhere to the principle that physical matter is all there is—unabashedly say that physics, the branch of science that deals with "matter, energy, and force," is "the ultimate explainer" of life, reality, and our existence.[7] Some worldviews that contain New Age spiritual thought place the brunt of truth—sometimes referred to as the "prime reality"—onto the individual person, the self that creates its own reality and is its own source of authority and truth.[8] "Because of its absolute subjectivity, the I-am-God or I-am-the-Kosmos position remains beyond any criticism external to the subject."[9] If *I* am the source of my own reality and the author of my own authority, you cannot criticize me because *you* are not *me*.

With so many different sources of authority, how can we know which one is true? Both the Koran and the Bible claim to be revelations from God, and Joseph Smith—the founder of Mormonism—believed that he was visited by an angel who gave him direct revelation from God in the form of golden tablets from heaven. Is there some way to test authority claims? That's what we'll investigate later on in this handbook.

Assignments and Discussion Questions

1. Where do most people look for truth in our world today? (See, for example, chapter 2 in *Religion on Trial.*) Find an example in a book, newspaper, or online article that illustrates someone's source of truth. Is it a good source of truth? Why or why not?

How do you determine what *is* a good source of truth?

2. A small boy is at the checkout counter at the local grocery store. His mother asks him if he would like to have a Brand A candy bar or Brand B. The boy immediately grabs both. His mother frowns and makes him put one of them back. What happened? Think of another situation with a similar type of mix-up and either write, draw, or act out the scenario (and its explanation).
3. Which part of this unit was most challenging to you? In your handbook notebook, write down something that you don't understand and investigate it with your teacher. Which part was easy to understand and why? Which part do you think will help you most in developing your defense of the faith?
4. Choose one of the following unit resources to investigate and read with your teacher. How can learning more about worldviews aid you in doing apologetics? What does the Bible say about investigating other viewpoints (cf. 1 John 4)?
5. Why do we say that apologetics is a *defensive* art form? What does it mean to "give a reason for the hope that is within you"?
6. Read "Part Three: How Critical Thinking Saves Faith" in Nancy Pearcey's *Finding Truth*. Read through the study questions on pages 367–69. What does it mean to think critically? How can you practice critical thinking in both your academic and everyday life?
7. Pretend that someone has asked you why you're reading this book. What's the big deal with apologetics, anyway? In your course notebook, write answers to the "Five *W*" questions: *What* is apologetics, *Who* should do it, *Where* can it be done, *When* should it be used, and *Why* does it matter? (If you have trouble answering all of these questions, investigate the unit resources with your teacher.) Leave a space and

write "*How* can I do apologetics?" You'll write down some ideas for this later in the course.

Notes

1 "Truth," *Merriam-Webster*, https://www.merriam-webster.com/dictionary/truth.
2 Parton, *Religion on Trial*, 12.
3 TobyMac (recording artist), *Feel It*, Compact Disc (Forefront Records, 2015).
4 Montgomery, *Tractatus Logico-Theologicus*, 26.
5 Johnson, *A Logic Book*, 382.
6 Parton, *Religion on Trial*, 29. We will reexamine this type of statement in a later unit.
7 Nancy Pearcey, *Finding Truth* (Colorado Springs: David C. Cook, 2015), 70. See also "physics," *Dictionary.com*, http://www.dictionary.com/browse/physics?s=t.
8 Sire, *The Universe Next Door*, 146.
9 Ibid., 148.

Unit One Review

Review Questions

1. What does the term "apologetics" mean?
2. Why should Christians in general (and Lutherans in particular) be concerned with doing apologetics? Is giving a defense of the faith a biblical concept or not?
3. Why can't all religions be true? Can't we all just live and let live?
4. What does MESH-AGE stand for? What does it have to do with apologetics?
5. What do we mean when we say that we are defending "creedal Christianity"? Why is it "nonnegotiable"?
6. Why do many people today talk about "truths" instead of "truth"? Isn't it arrogant to think that truth can be knowable?
7. What are some ways that people decide what is true?
8. This unit was loosely based on a medieval concept of the transcendental "True."[1] How does understanding something correlate to the concept of it being true? How does truth act upon understanding and vice versa? Why is this important for apologetics?
9. What was one surprising thing that you learned in this unit? Why was it surprising?

Vocabulary List

apologetics: The act of providing a defense and giving reasons one believes something.

apologist: One who does apologetics.

clarification: The act of using definitions and coherent language to clear up misunderstandings about a subject or event.

contradiction: Two facts that cannot both be true at the same time and in the same way.

creedal Christianity: The core beliefs of Christianity as contained in the Apostles', Nicene, and Athanasian Creeds.

exclusive or: A statement that contains two conclusions that could not both be true.

inclusive or: A statement that contains two conclusions that could both be true.

logic: A framework for how one reasons and organizes information.

MESH-AGE: The seven core components of a worldview—a worldview's stance on "man, evil, salvation, history, authority, God, and ethics/morality."

positive evidences: The reasons and facts offered by a worldview as to why one should accept that worldview in preference to other religions.

postmodernism: An "antiworldview" that rejects the notion of absolute and knowable truth.

refutation: The act of pointing out flaws and fallacies in contradicting worldviews.

worldview: The religion one holds—whether privately or publically—that determines how one approaches life and answers the seven "big" life issues (MESH-AGE).

Resources

The following are suggested resources for this unit. This is a starting point for further study and should not be considered a comprehensive list. Many of these books contain challenging material that may be difficult to understand—don't let this discourage you. If you are studying this book with a mentor or instructor, ask him or her for help in selecting which books to investigate.

Nonfiction

The Bible.
Rationale: Cf. 2 Timothy 3:16–17.

Lewis, C. S. *Mere Christianity*. New York: HarperOne, 2000.
Rationale: Lewis has a beautiful writing style and confronts questions in a clear, fluid manner. Although some Lutherans wish he were more solid on grace *alone* and the distinction between law and gospel, Lewis provides a gentle introduction to Christianity that is worth reading.

Luther, Martin. *Luther's Small Catechism with Explanation*. St. Louis: Concordia, 1986.
Rationale: A concise overview of Christianity.

Montgomery, John Warwick. *Christ as Centre and Circumference*. Hamburg: VKW, 2012.
Rationale: This volume is worth the price tag. Featuring a collection of essays by Dr. Montgomery, it provides a springboard for further apologetical research. The essay "Christian Apologetics in the Light of the Lutheran Confessions" furnished the three-part definition of apologetics that I introduce in this unit.

———. *Christianity for the Tough Minded*. Edmonton: Canadian Institute for Law, Theology, and Public Policy, 2001.
Rationale: The self-described book of "essays written by a group of young scholars who are totally convinced that a spiritual commitment is intellectually defensible" may appear daunting at first, but it contains essays on several vital topics. From philosophy to literature, ethics to psychology, this book provides an overview of the intellectual validity of Christianity.

———. *How Do We Know There Is a God?* Bloomington: Bethany House, 1973.

Rationale: A handy pocket guide to important questions deemed "inappropriate in polite society."

———. *Tractatus Logico-Theologicus*, 5th ed. Eugene: Wipf & Stock, 2013.

Rationale: A diamond among apologetical literature, this book may admittedly be difficult to read. While it isn't light bedtime reading, it is an invaluable resource that should be available to you as a reference if nothing else, though I would encourage you to challenge yourself by reading at least portions of it.

Myers, Jeff, and David Noebel. *Understanding the Times*. Manitou Springs, CO: Summit Ministries, 2015.

Rationale: A thought-provoking investigation into worldviews and their consequences. Should be a must-read for everyone who desires to live in the world but not of it.

Parton, Craig. *The Defense Never Rests: A Lawyer among the Theologians*. St Louis: Concordia, 2015.

Rationale: A must-read for everyone. Instruction, encouragement, and sound apologetics all in one book. Note: a revised version is available.

———. *Religion on Trial*. Eugene: Wipf & Stock, 2008.

Rationale: This book is Montgomery's *Tractatus Logico-Theologicus* lite. Parton's clear style and firm grasp of Montgomery's thesis make this a book that you will reference over and over again. A must-have for any apologetics library. Note: a revised version is available.

Pearcey, Nancy. *Finding Truth*. Colorado Springs: David C. Cook, 2015.

Rationale: Although this book is aimed at older students, it expertly deals with identifying and responding to multiple worldviews. The discussion questions, study guide, and sample exam are extremely helpful for the serious student who desires to dig deeper into apologetics.

Veith, Gene Edward, Jr. *Postmodern Times*. Wheaton: Crossway, 1994.

Rationale: What exactly is "postmodernism"? Although written in 1994, this book is still shockingly relevant today for those who desire to see how our culture has changed (and is changing).

Fiction

Fiction can often provide us with a new way of seeing things. The following books may help you begin to discern worldviews and competing truth-claims in the world around you. **Note:** Most of these works are written with a worldview other than Christianity at their base. Your challenge as the reader is to sift through the worldviews and discern what is at the heart of the characters' decisions, actions, and thoughts.

DuPrau, Jeanne. *City of Ember.*
Rationale: Postapocalyptic literature that deals with surprisingly deep themes of life, death, and how we determine what is true.

Goldman, William. *The Princess Bride.*
Rationale: A cheeky oddity that subtly pokes fun at a number of philosophical themes. Also a classic film, in the author's opinion.

Grahame, Kenneth. *The Wind in the Willows.*
Rationale: A delightful excursion into deeper philosophical themes (with a water rat, and who doesn't enjoy aquatic rodents?).

Hale, Shannon. *Princess Academy* and its sequel *Palace of Stone.*
Rationale: Both books present a unique worldview that doesn't shy away from investigating *how* we know whether something is true or not.

Henry, Marguerite. *King of the Wind.*
Rationale: A captivating story that shows how one's worldview can impact surprising aspects of one's life.

Lewis, C. S. *The Lion, the Witch, and the Wardrobe* and *The Magician's Nephew.*
Rationale: Lewis is both masterful storyteller and sincere apologist, and his Chronicles of Narnia are a delightful study in both.

Tolkien, J. R. R. *The Hobbit.*
Rationale: A classic that is both beautiful and powerful, and an excellent introduction to Tolkien's Middle-Earth.

Note

1 For a very complicated explanation, see Goris and Aertsen, "Medieval Theories of Transcendentals."

Unit Two

Focus on Judgment ("Goodness")

> [Jesus answered them,] "Do not judge by appearances, but judge with right judgment."
>
> —John 7:24

In this unit, I will examine what it means to be tough-minded or tender-minded, and I will begin an interdisciplinary exploration of apologetics with sections on mathematics and computer science. All subject areas I will discuss can be paired with *both* tough-minded and tender-minded apologetics, which you will see as you go along, but some subjects lend themselves more easily to one area of apologetics than to another. Before we get started, let's take a look at what *tough-minded* and *tender-minded* actually mean.

CHAPTER 1

Distinguishing Tough-Minded and Tender-Minded

> The tough-minded and the tender-minded, as William James described them so brilliantly, are perennial types, perennially antagonistic . . . Respect for the facts of experience, open-mindedness, an experimental trial-and-error attitude, and the capacity for working within the frame of an incomplete unfinished world view distinguish [the tough minded] from the more impatient, imaginative, and often aprioristic thinkers in the tender-minded camp.
>
> —Herbert Feigel, *Logical Empiricism*[1]

Tough-Minded

> Now Thomas, one of the Twelve, called the Twin, was not with them when Jesus came. So the other disciples told him, "We have seen the Lord." But he said to them, "Unless I see in his hands the mark of the nails, and place my finger into the mark of the nails, and place my hand into his side, I will never believe."
>
> —John 20:24–25

When you think of apologetics, chances are you think of hard facts put forth to answer or address tough questions. After all, I've already covered in unit one why all religions can't be true, and I used logic—formal reasoning—to do it. This involves critical thinking and aims to give a firm answer to a skeptical question posed by someone who is concerned with the "intellectual" reliability of Christianity.[2] Tough-minded Christianity involves "respect for the facts of experience," and the case for Christianity "hinge[s] explicitly and entirely" on the central truth claim of 1 Corinthians 15:17.[3] If the fact of the resurrection of Christ is false, our faith is false.

Tough-minded apologetics seek to address the concerns of the skeptic by supplying "deductions on the basis of sound evidence, even when the conclusions are either astonishing or disturbing."[4] The disciple Thomas demanded hard, physical evidence before he would believe in anything so astonishing as the resurrection of a man from the dead. Craig Parton, a leading apologist and noted trial lawyer, outlines an apologetic for the tough-minded in his book *The Defense Never Rests*.[5] He sets forth four guiding questions for making the case for a tough-minded Christianity. I highly recommend that you read his exposition. I won't reinvent the wheel by restating it here.

Resources for tough-minded apologetics abound, largely because prior to postmodernism, most honest skeptics were tough-minded. Like good detectives, they were (and still are) interested in facts, figures, and evidence. Though tough-minded individuals remain in our society, the postmodern world is trending toward being a tender-minded realm.

Tender-Minded

> The heart has its reasons of which reason knows nothing.
>
> —Blaise Pascal, *Pensées*[6]

"That's one of the things my mom struggles with the most," the young man said. He shook his head, a slight frown creasing his forehead. "How could God forsake His own Son? How could any parent do that?" From her own experience as a parent, his mother could not imagine abandoning her child to death on a cross. Her heart rebelled at such a foreign concept, and her emotions could not accept the idea that a loving and perfect Father would willingly choose to strike down His Son. It wasn't so much that she didn't believe what the Bible said, the young man explained, or that she didn't understand *why* Jesus had to die, but rather that she could not grasp the emotional weight of abandonment and ascribe that to a God of love, peace, and harmony. She could not reconcile the image of Jesus being held on Mary's lap with Jesus screaming in agony on the cross, an agony that His Father was able to prevent.

In other words, she was not concerned with the evidence of the crucifixion. She was not repeating Thomas' request for cold, hard facts. She was looking for a personal spirituality that conveyed her type of truth. Her heart had a reason for believing as it did that was entirely separate from her mind's knowledge and acceptance of the facts. She wasn't tough-minded. She was tender-minded.

"Tender-minded individuals" are "those persons whose sensitivities and ultimate concerns lie in the areas of music, art, literature, and the theater."[7] Tender-minded persons tend to gravitate toward subjects and ideas that move them deeply. Their experiences of truth are governed by their *subjective* or personal experiences. In their words, truth is often a product of one's own interpretation. Tender-minded individuals are drawn to beauty as they experience and interact with it. Although they are less concerned with concrete facts and objective evidence, their responses to such evidence are "often not hostile—the evidences simply do not penetrate to the level of serious consideration."[8]

For some people, this can be a difficult concept to grasp. For others it makes perfect sense. A gothic cathedral, Beethoven sonata, and midnight sky full of stars will call strongly to the tender-minded. They are the imaginative thinkers—or, as Irish poet Arthur O'Shaughnessy observed, they would be the ones proudly stating:

> We are the music-makers,
> And we are the dreamers of dreams,
> Wandering by lone sea-breakers,
> And sitting by desolate streams;
> World-losers and world-forsakers,
> On whom the pale moon gleams;
> Yet we are the movers and shakers
> Of the world for ever, it seems.[9]

How do we reach such individuals? Is there a way to offer a reason for the hope that is in us that is personal, beautiful, and meaningful to a tender-minded soul?

Tell Me a Story

> Stories never really end . . . even if the books like to pretend they do. Stories always go on. They don't end on the last page, any more than they begin on the first page.
>
> —Cornelia Funke, *Inkspell*[10]

The best-selling Inkworld trilogy, by author Cornelia Funke, takes the reader on a journey that blurs the line between fiction and fact. Characters known as "silvertongues" have the ability to read characters out of books—or real-life people into them. Storytelling, imagination, and reality meet and fuse together throughout the three-book series in a truly enchanting way.

For the tender-minded person, stories have incredible power. Silvertongues, far from being confined to the pages of books, are those who create beautiful, meaningful, imaginative ideas, whether through art, music, the theater, or the written word.

Many individuals of this mind-set often appear genuinely happy if you subscribe to a different worldview, uttering such encouragement as, "I'm so happy that works for you!" The allure of sharing one's beliefs, dreams, and ideas in the form of one's life story is very important to them.[11] Everyone's story may look different, the tender-minded soul says, but if you can find mystery and spiritual enlightenment, *there* is a story worth living.

This focus on storytelling and longing for something personal and yet sacred provides an opening for an apologetic that is both objectively true (based on fact) and subjectively touching (based on the needs of the heart).

Assignments and Discussion Questions

1. What does it mean to be "tough-minded"? What does it mean to be "tender-minded"? Which one do you consider yourself to be and why?

2. Read the preface and introduction in *Faith Founded on Fact* by John Warwick Montgomery. With your instructor's help, skim chapter 1, paying special attention to the rebuttal statements brought against Christianity. How is Christianity uniquely equipped to deal with tough-minded questions?
3. Do you think that it is easier to give a tough-minded apologetic or a tender-minded one? Why? Why is it important to be ready to give a defense to *anyone* who asks the reason for the hope that is within us?
4. Read chapters 7–9 in *The Defense Never Rests*. Choose one of the mentioned "apologists" to investigate (C. S. Lewis, J. S. Bach, Dorothy Sayers, or any other name mentioned). Did this apologist deal with primarily tough-minded or tender-minded issues? (Note to teachers: assist your student in researching and, as always, use your discretion as to the maturity level of your child when choosing an apologist to study.)
5. With your teacher's approval, choose one of the following movies to watch: *Cinderella* (2015), *Oz the Great and Powerful* (2013), *Inkheart* (2008), or *Beauty and the Beast* (1991). Other movies can be substituted in at your instructor's discretion. Are the characters predominantly tough-minded or tender-minded? Is adherence to facts presented in a positive, negative, or neutral light? What is the movie's MESH-AGE? Do you think that visual art forms (like movies) lean toward being more tough-minded or more tender-minded? Why?
6. With your teacher's approval, read the essay "Christian Apologetics" by C. S. Lewis in *God in the Dock* (or have your teacher read portions of it aloud to you). What does Lewis mean when he says, "What we want is not more little books about Christianity, but more little books by Christians on other subjects—with their Christianity latent"?[12] How can we best write

"little books" on "other subjects," and why is this vital for Christian apologists today? Is this a tough-minded or a tender-minded endeavor, or is it both? Why? How can you write little books to further a Christ-centered apologetic? (Hint: It doesn't have to involve actual writing!)

Notes

1. Herbert Feigel, flyleaf to John Warwick Montgomery, *Christianity for the Tough Minded* (Edmonton: Canadian Institute for Law, Theology, and Public Policy, 2001).
2. Parton, *The Defense Never Rests*, 135.
3. Ibid., 119.
4. Ibid.
5. See chapter 7 especially.
6. Blaise Pascal, *Pensées* (London: Penguin, 1995), 127.
7. Parton, *The Defense Never Rests*, 136.
8. Ibid.
9. John Matthews, ed., *The Book of Celtic Verse* (New York: Metro Books, 2010), 209.
10. Cornelia Funke, *Inkspell* (New York: The Chicken House, 2005), 45.
11. Parton, *The Defense Never Rests*, 134.
12. C. S. Lewis, *God in the Dock* (Grand Rapids: Eerdmans, 1970), 93.

CHAPTER 2

Mathematics

From Wonder to Wisdom[1]

And He [Christ] is before all things, and in Him all things hold together.

—Colossians 1:17

A Note to Instructors

In the traditional quadrivium, two "math" areas are typically taught: arithmetic and geometry. For the sake of this handbook, these have been combined into one general "mathematics" area. This is not to say that arithmetic and geometry do not bring their own distinct nuances to the table, but since our prime objective is apologetics, both provide a similar lens through which we can focus our attention. Mathematics, for our purposes, will deal primarily with relationships between numbers and certain properties of the numbers, along with examples.

Some of the math topics discussed here may be advanced, depending on the maturity level of your child, or they may be basic review. The purpose here is to help your child become more familiar and comfortable with an interdisciplinary approach to learning concepts in apologetics. If a concept needs to be reviewed several times, I would encourage you to spend more time investigating it with your child. There are many books and resources to aid you. A list of resources can be found at the end of this section. Do not be discouraged by the breadth or depth of the information presented here. The important thing is that we avoid the trap of compartmentalization, with "religious studies" being in a separate truth-category from the rest of knowledge. "All truth is God's truth, wherever it is found."[2]

If you are teaching your child at home, I would encourage you to think creatively when integrating this section with the mathematics curriculum you are currently using. Mathematics, especially for the middle school student, should be presented not as a chore but as a journey. Let your child explore concepts that interest her. Vocabulary introduced in this section should be reviewed as part of a holistic overview. In other words, the goal is not only that the child can correctly define "analytical statement" but that he can identify it, begin to see how it applies to other subject areas, and grasp how it is used in apologetics.

Dr. Gene Edward Veith Jr. recommends that "math and science [be] taught mimetically."[3] The process of imitation and repetition works, he says, because it "guides students to meditate on models or types in order to present ideas in concrete form so students can understand an idea or truth and then apply it."[4] In this section, your child will be introduced to ideas dealing with infinity, Mandelbrot sets, and concepts of numbers themselves. The student at this stage of learning will want to know "why"—why this instead of that, why is it like this, and why should I care?

There is no need for you as the instructor to know everything about both mathematics and apologetics before introducing this section. The beauty of this type of handbook is that you are able to *learn alongside* your child. There is no shame in not knowing the answer to your child's question about a particular concept. The problem arises when you do not know and do not care to find out, unless you are comfortable with letting your child reply "idk" ("I don't know") as an answer to puzzling questions.

The unit resources at the end of this section provide you with a starting point for further investigation. As always, the nebulous Internet is available for perusing, but exercise discretion and ensure that your sources are reliable. Sources should always be read critically; that is, one should constantly be questioning the source and extrapolating the author's worldview from his writings (remember MESH-AGE? Use it!). Wikipedia, while thoroughly entertaining at times, should not be relied upon with any degree of certainty—although it may at times reference reliable sources that may be of use.

Speaking of references, this section on mathematics was influenced heavily by the work of Dr. Jason Lisle. Every attempt has been made to cite his work appropriately and comprehensively. The discerning reader is encouraged to investigate his work more thoroughly.

A Note to Students

Christianity is a holistic worldview. Holistic means "relating to or concerned with wholes or with complete systems rather than with the analysis of, treatment of, or dissection into parts."[5] As Lutherans, we believe in the separation of the two kingdoms—the secular kingdom of the left hand and the sacred kingdom of the right hand—but our worldview is not something that we pull out and use one day a week and then set aside until next Sunday. Christ Jesus came to earth and became fully human. We are called to mirror this incarnation on a *much* smaller (and sin-tainted) scale by living our faith in every aspect of our life. We understand the difference between *natural revelation* (sometimes also called *general revelation*)—the revelation concerning God that is apparent in creation and the "book of nature"—and *special revelation*—the complete story of how Christ Jesus is God incarnate come to earth to save us from our sins as revealed in Holy Scripture alone.[6]

Natural revelation, on its own, is not enough. We are not defending the idea of religion or a somewhat transcendental feeling that we experience while viewing a particularly lovely sunset or enjoying an especially good chocolate cupcake. However, if we have a deity who is so far above our world and our experiences that he has left no echo of Himself in our world, we fall back on *presuppositional* arguments and nonsense. Christianity proclaims that the material world, while sin-cursed and fallen, is still the creation of a personal God who will one day restore it to perfection.

Natural revelation is indeed insufficient for apologetics, but we must be careful not to dismiss it entirely. In addition to developing our own appreciation for the created order of the world in which we live, natural revelation often can meet both the tough-minded and the tender-minded person close to where they live and think.

The tough-minded person wants facts about how the world really is. The tender-minded individual longs for meaning, beauty, and purpose to life, and he will often seek out a worldview that speaks to those deep needs and that will fulfill his longing for a sense of unity.

What we term "subjects" or "areas of study" are simply parts of the same whole—the overall body of knowledge of reality. A falsehood in any one area can affect the body, either directly as an error in the model itself or indirectly in its uses ("a little leaven leavens the whole lump," as St. Paul said). Some of these errors will be more intense than others, and I am by no means suggesting that only Christians can understand mathematics or that Christians will always, by definition, have the correct understanding of any given subject area. Objective truth is true whether one believes it or not—or, as one student has said, "Would a nonbeliever get a different answer for 1 + 1? Objective truth is true no matter what worldview is taught!"[7]

Why should we even bother to integrate different subjects into our study of apologetics? Am I saying that you can only understand secular topics if you are a Christian? No—and this is a very important point. Some individuals and church bodies believe that it is not possible for a non-Christian to recognize the truth of Christianity before conversion. Unbelievers, they say, are so blinded that they cannot begin to grasp any reasonable argument offered by the believer, and therefore it is a silly waste of time to do apologetics at all. This is a type of *presuppositionalism*.[8] Some presuppositionalists also believe that unbelievers cannot understand *secular* facts about the world around them.[9] One such man, Cornelius Van Til, summed it up with the phrase "all is yellow to the jaundiced eye," and this yellow lens through which the world is viewed "controls without exception all forms of non-Christian philosophy."[10]

Dr. Calvin Jongsma, former professor of mathematics at Dordt College, responds indirectly to such claims with the mundane example of tooth brushing. Tooth brushing, the professor says, can be (and is) performed by believers and unbelievers alike. There isn't a "Christian" way to brush your teeth that an unbeliever is incapable of understanding.[11] The motivation for brushing your teeth may be slightly different for Christians—a desire to be a godly steward of the body God has given you, for example—but the technique remains largely the same. My personal physician is not a Christian, and yet she knows more about medicine and the human body than I ever will.

In the same way, Christianity is not a special realm of mystical knowledge that an unbeliever is incapable of understanding. Some Christian presuppositionalists claim that this understanding of apologetics is unbiblical—yet the Bible is filled with examples that show that fallen man is still capable of using his mind. Adam and Eve, after eating the forbidden fruit, recognized the voice of God and were able to respond to His call (Gen. 3); pagan King Darius recognized that the God of Daniel was the one true God after seeing the miraculous taming of the lions (Dan. 6); and disbelieving Thomas received his skeptical wish and professed "My Lord and my God!" after touching the nail wounds in Jesus' physical, resurrected body (John 20).

By studying different subject areas, we are not claiming that in order to gain any type of knowledge one must be a Christian. What we are saying is that truth is knowable and that there is no speech, nor language, nor subject matter where the echoes of that truth are not heard.[12] If there is a personal God who is both Redeemer and Creator of our world, we would expect there to be echoes (however faint) of this in the created order of the world. I have discussed how the splintering of knowledge into subjects is for our own benefit and that each of these subjects has something to say about reality as a whole. All worldviews say *something* about the reality (or nonreality) of life, thus it is not unreasonable to expect that every subject, no matter how seemingly far afield of "religious" matters it may be, has something to contribute to the discussion of and defense for a worldview.

We must never forget our focus in doing apologetics: taking the questioner to the cross of Christ and the empty tomb and bringing him face-to-face with Mary's son, our Creator and Redeemer. The following sections contain suggestions for ways of incorporating subjects of study into one's apologetic. Think of them as perpetual medieval pages who will not advance to knighthood: they aren't doing the heavy lifting, nor are they the stars of the show, but they have been commissioned by the King to aid His soldiers in the field.[13]

Recap: What does it mean to be "tough-minded" or "tender-minded"? What do we mean by "natural" vs. "special" revelation? What is "presuppositionalism"?

Show Me the Facts

How can mathematics aid us in doing apologetics? Surely apologetics is purely religious and math is purely secular, right? Wrong! There is much that we can learn from this subject that can aid us in our defense of the faith.

When most people think of mathematics, they instinctively think of "tough-minded" people. The stereotypical mathematician is focused on cold, hard, unfeeling facts and strict logic. Like practically all stereotypes, this only gives us half of the picture—and a very poor half, at that. Just as there are many ways math can be applied to create, describe, or discover various things, so it can be used in many ways in apologetics—and not only apologetics for the tough-minded.

Tender-minded individuals are interested in meaning, beauty, and the "holism" that I have been discussing throughout this handbook. They want to see the unity in things, events, and individuals, and they are quick to see patterns in thoughts and ideas. They're eager to find spiritual dimensions in everyday life.

Spiritual dimensions? In math? That sounds a little crazy, doesn't it? Not really, according to Dr. Jongsma, who views mathematics as a part of God's desire to reconcile all things to Himself. "All aspects of life are touched by God's act of salvation, including mathematics," Dr. Jongsma explains. "In one sense redemption makes all things new, but in another sense it doesn't. It frees things to be themselves once again; it doesn't add a spiritual dimension that was previously missing."[14]

In other words, mathematics and spirituality are not at odds with each other. Mathematics can open our eyes to incredible beauty in the created universe around us. It can help us subcreate amazing wonders of technology. It can also help us start a conversation with both tough-minded and tender-minded individuals.

To quote Dr. Jongsma again, "Whatever has mathematical features, which is just about everything, can benefit from mathematical knowledge, offered in the context of a kingdom vision and a broad understanding of how these features fit into the whole."[15] Tough-minded people want to know the facts that are available to us from the "hard" sciences. Tender-minded people want to see how all of life is connected into one coherent concept. Mathematics can offer us the best of both worlds.

I encourage you to use this section in tandem with whatever mathematics curriculum you are currently studying in your general schooling. See if you can find any overlap between it and this section. Remember, mathematics and spirituality are not at odds with each other any more than natural revelation is at odds with special revelation—but also remember that general revelation can never be the complete answer. And as we'll see later on, not even the toughest critic would want that to be the case.

A Glimpse of Eternity

When you think of "mathematics," what do you think of? Multiplication tables, calculators, geeks wearing glasses and acing exams? What about beauty, power, and wonder? Are mathematics and spirituality in conflict, or are they somehow woven into the frame of our reality?

How exactly would you define "mathematics"? It's a difficult question, isn't it? Dr. Jason Lisle, noted mathematician, astronomer, and astrophysicist, says it simply: "Mathematics is the study of the relationships and properties of numbers."[16] We're narrowing down our definition, but what, then, are numbers?

Numbers are not material objects that you can touch and observe like plants, animals, or people. If you don't believe me, try using a number as your answer the next time you are called upon to play Twenty Questions. After your friends have asked if it is an animal, vegetable, person, place, or object, you're already a fourth of the way to winning the game. If they happen to ask if "it" is an idea, as some tricky questioners are wont to do, what are you to say? Are numbers "concepts" like ideas?[17]

Numbers can be represented in many different ways. We are probably most familiar with the typical Arabic numerals: 0, 1, 2, and so on. Take 3 for example. The number that you see on this page is a representation of a concept: you are not looking at the "actual number three."

Suppose that there was a king of a certain country who decided to outlaw mathematics. Perhaps he had a bad experience in math class as a child, or perhaps he simply was tired of having to count his fabulous wealth day after day after day. This king—we'll call him Edgar—decided that the best way to outlaw mathematics was to hunt down and destroy all numbers. He realized that this would take an incredibly long time, so he decided to have his scribes write down only the numbers 0 through 9. "After all," the king thought to himself as he stroked his beard, "all numbers are combinations of those digits." His scribes wrote down the perfectly formed numbers on a scroll and presented it to King Edgar. He marched to the town square where, with a flourish of his wrist, he cried, "This is the end of all numbers!" and threw the scroll into a huge bonfire.

Unfortunately—or perhaps fortunately, as we will see—Edgar had not destroyed the numbers, and he had not destroyed the study of the relationships between numbers. Edgar did not have his scribe write down *numbers*. He had them write down *numerals*, the representations of the numbers. Numbers themselves are nonphysical concepts with unusual properties.

Numbers: What a Concept!

Numbers, unlike the world we see around us every day, are nonphysical. As our tongue-in-cheek example of King Edgar shows, numbers can take physical representations in the shape of numerals, but destroying a numeral does not destroy a number. The creation of different ways of representing numerals can be traced back to different civilizations throughout history, but the concept of numbers appears to be something that humans have not created, and numbers are not restricted to describing physical things around us.

It is possible to speak of nine billion people, but according to the current world census, nine billion people do not exist.[18] Or take an extremely small example: have you ever seen 0.0003 trees in a forest or fish in a river? Yet we use numbers like these every day, and we are able to think of and use the numbers in different ways.

Due in part to the conceptual nature of numbers, mathematics is not always readily apparent to us. Most people do not focus on the mathematical properties of their smart phones, computers, cars, houses, or garages. That does not mean that mathematics is not "there" or was not involved in the object's creation or sustainment. It simply means that mathematics is **abstract**, which means that it "relat[es] to or involve[es] general ideas or qualities rather than specific people, objects, or actions."[19] Math is not confined to physical structures.

In order for something to be a Mustang convertible, it must be an automobile that is made by Ford and has a retractable roof (along with whatever else it needs to be a Mustang—Ford manufacturers would know this better than I!). Using these criteria, we can quickly identify which cars whizzing past us on the highway are Mustangs and which are something else. We can say that the sky-blue Mustang is a **concrete** instance of the concept of a Mustang. Just as there can be many different sky-blue Mustangs out on the road, so there can be many numerals.[20]

The abstract nature of numbers often makes them difficult to recognize in the real world. When I walk down the street, I can easily identify telephone poles, cars, and traffic lights. I can't see the numbers that were involved in creating them. They're there—in the architectural design, the circuitry, and the dimensions of the objects—but they're hidden in the physical objects. Dr. Jongsma notes that "there has thus developed a stark disparity between the reality of mathematics' presence in society and the public's perception and understanding of this fact. Those who look more closely, however, find mathematics nearly everywhere."[21]

How do we look more closely? What do we find when we do? What on earth does all this have to do with apologetics? Let's keep going to find out!

Beauty in Pure Numbers

When you think of mathematics, do you think of beauty? You should.

The Fibonacci sequence[22] occurs in nature (shells), Pascal's triangle (a concept dealing with probability), art (in the golden mean), and more. In the ancient quadrivium—the four subject areas traditionally taught to complete a well-rounded education—mathematics was described as the study of "pure number."[23] The student was expected to understand numbers in their pure form before mathematics was applied to other disciplines and subject areas. However, mathematics was taught alongside other subjects to encourage a holistic approach to knowledge—and to encourage the pursuit of that which is true, good, and beautiful.

Mathematics is a subject teeming with beauty. Although the reason *why* it is beautiful is contested among mathematicians, scientists, and philosophers (the evolutionary model, for example, has a very difficult time understanding this[24]), most people today agree that this discipline contains an elusive quality that intrigues and delights an inquisitive mind.

One concept in mathematics in particular has been named a "haunting beauty": Mandelbrot sets.[25] Let's take a look at this unique concept in order to continue our discussion of mathematics.

Mandelbrot Sets

A "set" is "a group of numbers that all have a common property."[26] You have seen mathematical sets before: the set of odd numbers contains, for example, 1, 3, and 5 but not 2, 4, and 6. The Mandelbrot set contains numbers defined by a specific formula. If we create a graph of the numbers contained in the Mandelbrot set, something interesting happens.

A graphed Mandelbrot set displays an intricately complex shape. The black points in the following image represent numbers that are in the Mandelbrot set, and the other colors distinguish those that are not.[27] A Mandelbrot set is called a **fractal**, which means that it "has an infinite number of its own shape built into it."[28] As you can see, there are spirals and squiggles coming off the main black shapes. If you zoom in closer, you will discover intricate spirals and yet more iterations of the Mandelbrot set. If you zoom out on the number line, you can see another, smaller object further down the line. In the image below, this object is surrounded by a green box.

If you zoom in on the object, you will discover another shape like the larger one at the right. It's a "baby" Mandelbrot set! This one, like its larger "parent," contains the same squiggle patterns—the same infinite number of its own shape built into it. And all these images appear because of graphing numbers on a chart!

Let's back up for a moment and talk about infinity. Infinity is an interesting concept, and it is also one that is difficult to grasp for humans. It means "the quality of having no limits or end."[29] By zooming in and zooming out of our graphed set of numbers, we can begin to see how the shapes repeat *ad infinitum*—to infinity. Fractals can aid us by giving us a visual representation of what it means to be infinite. In other words, "eternal" numbers help finite

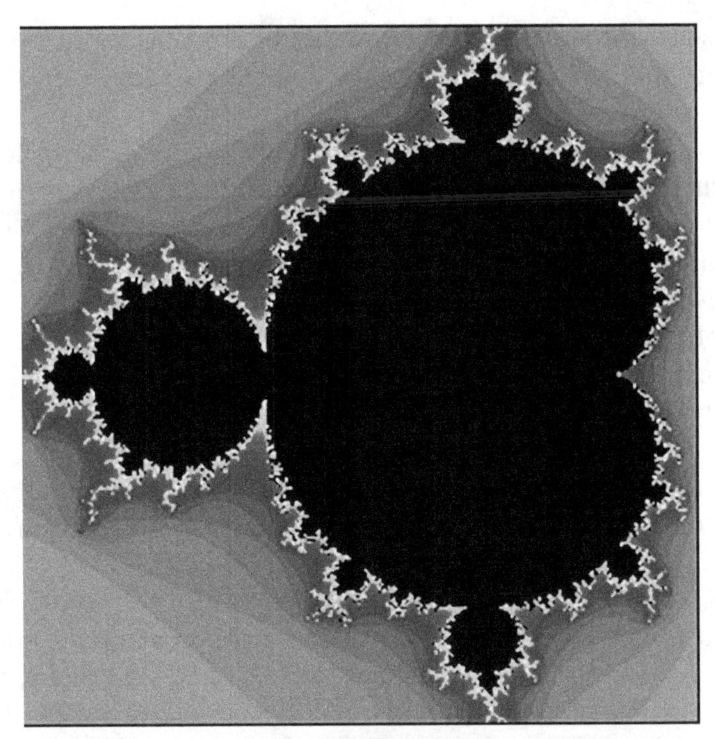

30

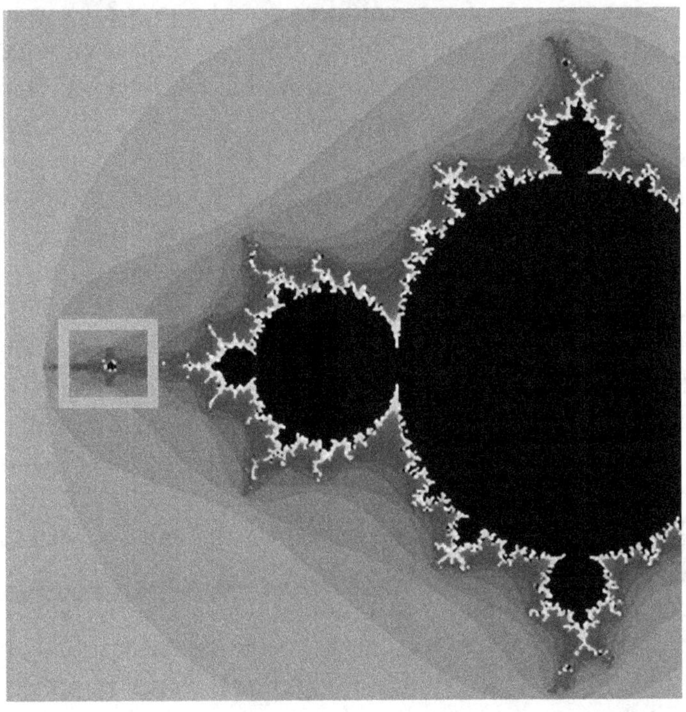

minds understand as best they can the concept of eternity.[31] We can describe it as best we can, though we do not have a full grasp of what it truly means to be infinite.

Some people carry this difficult concept even further. They say that there is no way for something that is finite (like humans) to truly understand something that is infinite (one example being eternal numbers). This doesn't just apply to mathematics. *Finitum non est capax infiniti* is the fancy Latin phrase for the belief that the finite cannot contain the infinite.[32] Some philosophers have extended this phrase to say that if an infinite God exists, he could not reveal himself using any sort of finite means (such as human history). (Side note: We will examine this view more thoroughly when we reach the section on history.) While it is true that we cannot understand everything about that which is infinite, the fancy Latin phrase is actually an incredibly outlandish assertion. Why?

To say that the infinite cannot do something would be to assume that we know everything there is to know about the infinite. By the *finitum* principle, though, we are finite and not infinite, so we *can't* know everything there is to know. How could we possibly know what the infinite (e.g., God) could or could not do? As writer and apologist G. K. Chesterton quipped, "We don't know enough about the unknown to know that it is unknowable"![33] However, there does appear to remain some kind of disconnect between what is finite and what is infinite.

Seventeenth-century philosopher and mathematician Gottfried Leibniz wondered, "Why is there something rather than nothing?"[34] In other words, why does something (such as the universe, our planet, or you yourself) exist rather than not exist? It is possible to look at mathematics and wonder much the same thing. Why does something exist that seems to be without limits? Why is it possible to physically represent a Mandelbrot set in a way that is visually pleasing to humans? To take it one step further, why is there beauty, and why are we able to recognize it?

These questions cannot be answered analytically. Mathematics cannot explain its own existence. Knowing *that* a certain formula produces numbers that, when graphed, display mind-blowing and infinite complexity does not tell you *why* this conceptual set produces something so beautiful in the physical world. In other words, this appears to be an example of **Einstein's Gulf:** the term given to the logical gap "which separates the world of sensory experiences from the world of concepts and propositions."[35]

Einstein's Gulf says there is a gaping chasm between the physical ("concrete") world of objects and the nonphysical ("abstract") world of concepts and ideas. Most scientists who are interested in Einstein's Gulf are interested in how something physical (e.g., humans) developed something nonphysical (e.g., abstract thought).[36] It appears to muddy the water a bit if we speak of abstract concepts displaying physical beauty. We're crossing the gulf, but we're going in the opposite direction—from the abstract to the concrete instead of vice versa.

There are everyday examples of this occurring, however. You do it every time you write down a numeral: a physical representation of a *number*, a nonphysical entity. The difficulty is that the numeral you wrote down would not write itself. In other words, the number seven would not suddenly one day decide to write the numeral 7 across the sky in jet-trails. In the same manner, the numeral 7 that you can write down on a sticky note could not suddenly become the conceptual number seven (remember King Edgar and his failed attempt at destroying numbers). There is a gulf separating the two.

Why is Einstein's Gulf problematic? The problem is that material objects don't transform themselves into abstract concepts (the numeral 7 won't one day turn into the number seven) and that, in order for concepts to become physical things, *something* needs to help them bridge the gap.[37] This is especially an issue for the evolutionary model of origins that holds that matter (like the human body) existed prior to—and somehow gave rise to—nonmatter (like the human mind and consciousness).[38] Taking Mandelbrot sets as an example, some evolutionary mathematicians and scientists attempt to explain the crossing of the gulf with the idea that the formulas for calculating the Mandelbrot set are extremely simple. Thus, they say, we have an example of something very simple (a formula) giving us something very complex (the graphed set) in the same way that humans evolved from very simple forms into very complex ones.[39] In other words, they essentially disregard the gulf altogether.

This could perhaps be a more plausible explanation if we could show that mathematics was dreamed up by some ancient shepherd who wanted to differentiate between his sheep. Different representations of mathematics (numerals, words, etc.) have been used throughout history by various people groups. Numbers and mathematics, however, do not appear to be have been created by humans. Numbers do not change. Numerals have changed over the course of time, but numbers and the laws that govern them have not. One plus one equaled two at the time of Queen Victoria, and the same is still true today.

"But how can numbers not be created by humans?" you may wonder. After all, the assumption of math teachers everywhere is that we are able to represent numbers in a concrete form and use them to build concrete objects. Mathematics can be a way of "subcreating," or using our abilities to invent, rearrange, and repurpose something that is created. Mathematicians Blaise Pascal (in the seventeenth century) and Wilhelm Schickard (in the sixteenth) both created calculating machines that were physical objects. We use physical devices that interact with numbers every day when we pick up our cell phones, power on our computers, or whip out our calculators. These physical objects were all created by humans. Human beings can use math to subcreate and arrange numbers in different ways. For example, computer programs often interact with mathematical properties to solve unique problems. It's possible to be extremely creative in the application and manipulation of numbers—but the numbers were already there. We didn't invent them. We discovered them.

Mathematics cannot explain its own existence. Mathematics can raise interesting questions and pose fascinating thought problems, but it can't enlighten us about its mysterious nature. We wouldn't expect general revelation to reveal this to us—that's the realm of special revelation (and, consequently, why all apologetics must be wholly centered on Christ, the Word incarnate). That's what we will examine next: the limitations of mathematics and what can be done about it.

Limitations of Mathematics and Logic

> Mathematics needs a context . . . mathematics is *always important* but *never enough*.[40]
>
> —Calvin Jongsma, Emeritus Professor of Mathematics, Dordt College

Mathematics interlocks with its sister subject area **logic** in several ways, but perhaps the most important is their mutual certainty level in and adherence to a verifiability principle. Formal logic and pure mathematics can be absolutely, 100 percent certain. Put another way, "A statement of logic or mathematics is a statement true by definition."[41] One plus one is two, three squared is nine, and three unicorns plus three unicorns equals six unicorns. Whether or not unicorns exist is irrelevant to the discussions posed by creative mathematicians constructing word problems; you do not need to travel to Camelot to search for unicorns in order to solve it.

Absolute certainty can be a wonderful thing. Odd as it may sound to you, there are people who are immensely comforted by the fact that there are problems that have definitely true answers. The math problems you encounter in your schooling at this point in your life contain **analytical statements**, which means that they are true by definition.[42] You don't have to investigate it, compare differing authorities, or hypothesize for yourself. If you were to ask three math teachers from the United States, South Korea, and Germany what 1 + 1 is, you would receive the same answer of 2 (although, perhaps, in different languages or representations). There isn't *my* view of 1 + 1 versus *your* view of 1 + 1, assuming that we are both using the symbol "+" and the numeral "1" in the way that is normal for middle school mathematics.[43] If we can be 100 percent certain in mathematics, can't we carry it over to apologetics and be 100 percent certain about our faith in the exact same way that we know that 1 + 1 equals 2?

Analytical statements, to put it bluntly, tell us absolutely nothing about the factual nature of the world around us.[44] The word problem in the preceding paragraph does not tell me if unicorns exist or if they're imaginary and what possible implications that could have for me, especially if I have just purchased a living, breathing unicorn via the Internet from a salesman in Poland. It tells me nothing about what historians and writers have said about unicorns, what my two-year-old nephew believes concerning them, or whether I should start worshipping a unicorn deity who currently holds residence on Pluto and demands that I daily apply a rainbow temporary tattoo to my forehead.

Mathematics, indeed, is *always important* but *never enough.*

The beauty of Fibonacci numbers, the sequences in the Mandelbrot set, the concept of infinity, and the idea of subcreation are all beautiful—none are sufficient. Are they worth studying and exploring? Absolutely. Can we expect the same certainty we have concerning them to be obtainable in all areas of life? No.

I once read a novel where one of the supporting characters was a math instructor. At some point in the storyline, it was mentioned in an offhand description that she believed and trusted in nothing unless she could manipulate it the same way she could manipulate calculations. That negatively impacted the story for me. Why? Because even for that tough-minded, no-nonsense character, it simply was not a true statement.

All of us trust in something—oftentimes many things throughout the course of a day—of which we are not analytically certain. Were you absolutely certain that your bed would hold your weight when you went to sleep last night? Were you utterly convinced that the candy bar you bought from the store was not secretly laced with spinach and beets? More important, what do you turn to when something is drastically wrong in your life? When a friendship isn't working out, do you derive happiness from the knowledge that 1 + 1 is 2? Perhaps you have seen a family member contract a serious illness, or maybe you have experienced one yourself. In the midst of pain and uncertainty, is your source of comfort a mathematical formula?

It cannot be. An analytical statement can tell you nothing about the facts of the world: what your illness is, what your diagnosis is, and the other details. Nor can it tell you what you should do about your illness: how you should seek treatment, what comfort you can gain from some source, and so on. Most if not all worldviews make claims about **is** and **ought**. Buddhism claims that there **is** no "god," and one **ought** to separate oneself from the world and deny all desires.[45] These statements cannot be reached by analytical thinking.

Writer and anthropologist John Donohue puts it succinctly: "All people, even the most practical, speculate on questions of ultimate meaning and spiritual development."[46] We live in a factual world where analytical statements cannot help us with the most important questions we face in life: questions of meaning, suffering, and death. The kind of god that could be defined mathematically could be downloaded as an application to your smart phone, but it would have no personal connection to you. That sort of god would provide no answers to your questions of ultimate meaning and would have no interest in the factual, synthetic world in which we live, suffer, and, eventually, die.[47]

Analytical statements of mathematics can mimic attributes of God and can be seen in the incredible design of the world around us. However, like other areas such as weather patterns and origin science, not everyone agrees that mathematics contains examples of design and beauty. Some individuals think, as I briefly mentioned, that Mandelbrot sets are consistent with chaos theory in evolution. Can minds be touched by the discovery of design in surprising areas? Of course. It happens every day. We are surrounded by an incredibly complex world filled with odd, exciting, and mysterious things, such as intricate designs in humble sea creature shells.

This does not mean that it would be an efficient use of our time to argue that Mandelbrot sets prove the Bible is true. They don't, and we would not expect an analytical statement to prove a **synthetic statement**, or a statement of fact that can be verified in some way.[48] The other subject areas I will discuss will deal more thoroughly with synthetic statements and their role in apologetics. Any subject area discussed here is *always important* but *never enough*—however, any subject can serve as an entry point to introduce seekers to the One who is both infinitely important and wholly sufficient.

Assignments and Discussion Questions

The following assignments are suggestions only. Be creative and think of your own ways to investigate mathematics and apologetics with your instructor's approval.

1. What is Einstein's Gulf? How does it relate to things that are "abstract" and things that are "concrete"?
2. What can fractals help us to understand? Why?

3. Give an example of both an analytical statement and a synthetic statement. How are they different from each other? In what ways are they similar?
4. Choose an aspect of mathematics to investigate on your own (possible ideas include Fibonacci sequences, Mandelbrot sets, Pascal's triangle, infinity). With your teacher's input, create an assignment based on your chosen aspect. This can be a paper, an art display, a documentary video, or anything else you can think of. While doing your investigation, keep in mind the following questions:
   a. How is this aspect related to apologetics? Can it be used primarily for tough-minded or tender-minded discussion (or both) and why?
   b. Natural revelation, while exciting and meaningful, is not enough to do apologetics. Describe what natural revelation is and why you should not base your apologetic on it.
5. Investigate the differing views people hold on Mandelbrot sets. For example, some evolutionary scientists view them as consistent with chaos theory. Many creation scientists view them as evidence of intelligent design. Compare and contrast the views.
6. What are some ways that the tough-minded intersects with the tender-minded in mathematics? (Hint: think of the Fibonacci sequence in nature and in man-made creations such as poems where each stanza contains a number of syllables in a sequence.)
7. Investigate different worldviews and their views on mathematics. Surprisingly, many religions have statements about mathematics—choose one to examine in detail. How does the religion fit mathematics into its MESH-AGE? Why would this matter for "meeting people where they're at" while still providing a solid apologetic?
8. Investigate different mathematicians and determine how their worldviews influenced their work.

9. Investigate the impact of Christian mathematicians in history (possible starting points being Pascal and Schickard). Did their worldviews influence their contributions to mathematics? If so, how?
10. In a postmodern culture, some still cling to the belief that "math/science" can hold the answers to society's problems. Investigate a current news article that reflects this thinking and respond to it from an apologetics standpoint.

Unit Resources: Mathematics

The following are resources for you and your child to investigate. As you explore mathematics, keep an eye out for apologetic implications! All resources should be read critically, especially those that deal with reformed thinking. In addition, some of the resources may be difficult for young students. Exercise discretion and select resources that are best for you and your child.

Bishop, Steve. "Beliefs Shape Mathematics." *Spectrum* 28, no. 2 (1996): 131–41. Accessed February 18, 2016. http://citeseerx.ist.psu.edu/viewdoc/download?doi=10.1.1.364.2861&rep=rep1&type=pdf.

Charis Mathematics. Accessed February 18, 2016. http://www.johnshortt.org/Pages/CharisMathematics.aspx.

Chase, Gene B. "How Has Christian Theology Furthered Mathematics?" In *Facets of Faith and Science*, vol. 2: *The Role of Beliefs in Mathematics and the Natural Sciences: An Augustinian Perspective*, edited by Jitse M. van der Meer. Lanham: University Press of America, 1996. Accessed February 18, 2016. http://home.messiah.edu/~chase/articles/Facets/index.htm.

Jongsma, Calvin. "Mathematics: Always Important, Never Enough: A Christian Perspective on Mathematics and Mathematics Education." *Journal of the Association of Christians in the Mathematical Sciences* (2006). Accessed December 27, 2015. http://www.acmsonline.org/journal/2006/Jongsma.pdf.

Journal of the Association of Christians in the Mathematical Sciences. Back issues available on the web. Accessed February 18, 2016. http://www.acmsonline.org/journal/index.html.

MacKenzie, Pamela. *Entry Points*. London: CARE for Education, 1997. Accessed February 18, 2016. https://www.calvin.edu/kuyers/read/entryPoints.pdf.

Mandelbrot sets. For more information on Mandelbrot sets from a creation-science perspective, refer to the work done by Dr. Jason Lisle of the Institute for Creation Research. Visit http://www.icr.org/ for more information.

Neuhouser, David. "The Role of Mathematics in the Spiritual Journey of George MacDonald." *Zondervan Library at Taylor University*. Accessed February 18, 2016. https://library.taylor.edu/dotAsset/a34250e8-8d4b-4675-b6d2-61133bbffe03.pdf.

Oller, John W., Jr. "Adding Abstract to Formal and Content Schemata: Results of Recent Work in Peircean Semiotics." *Applied Linguistics* 16, no. 3 (1995): 273–306. Accessed February 18, 2016. http://www.iupui.edu/~arisbe/menu/library/aboutcsp/oller/SCHEMATA.HTM.

———. "Einstein's Gulf: Can Evolution Cross It?" *Acts & Facts* 29, no. 9 (2000). Accessed February 18, 2016. http://www.icr.org/article/einsteins-gulf-can-evolution-cross-it/.

Rogalsky, Tim. "Distinctively Christian Mathematical Instruction: A Hopeful Imagination." *Direction* 37, no. 1 (Spring 2008): 71–81. Accessed February 18, 2016. http://www.directionjournal.org/37/1/distinctively-christian-mathematical.html.

Notes

1 Veith, *Classical Education*, 18.

2 Pearcey, *Finding Truth*, 90. A paraphrase of St. Augustine's quote in "On Christian Doctrine."

3 Veith, *Classical Education*, 118.

4 Ibid., 119.

5 "Holistic," *Merriam-Webster*.

6 Myers and Noebel, *Understanding the Times*, 184, 185.

7 Cheryl Swope, *A Handbook for Classical Lutheran Education* (CreateSpace Independent Publishing Platform, 2013), 71.

8 What is presuppositionalism? "A Christian presuppositionalist presupposes [assumes] God's existence and argues from that perspective to show the validity of Christian theism.

This position also presupposes the truth of the Christian Scriptures and relies on the validity and power of the gospel to change lives (Rom. 1:16). From the Scriptures, we see that the unbeliever is sinful in his mind (Rom. 1:18–32) and unable to understand spiritual things (1 Cor. 2:14). This means that no matter how convincing the evidence or good the logic, an unbeliever cannot come to the faith because his fallen nature will distort how he perceives the truth. The only thing that can ultimately change him is regeneration. To this end, the presuppositionalist seeks to change a person's presuppositions to be in conformity with biblical revelation." Matt Slick, "Presuppositional Apologetics," *Christian Apologetics & Research Ministry*, accessed February 18, 2016, https://carm.org/presuppositional-apologetics.

9 Parton, *The Defense Never Rests*, 72–74.

10 Cornelius Van Til, *The Defense of the Faith*, 4th ed. (Phillipsburg, NJ: P&R 2008), 100–101. Quoted in Scott K. Oliphint, "Van Til the Evangelist," *Ordained Servant Online*, accessed February 18, 2016, http://opc.org/os.html?article_id=118.

11 Calvin Jongsma, "Mathematics: Always Important, Never Enough," *Journal of the Association of Christians in Mathematical Sciences* (2006): 11, accessed February 18, 2016, http://www.acmsonline.org/journal/2006/Jongsma.pdf.

12 Psalm 19:4 (NKJV).

13 Astute historians of medieval times will undoubtedly tell me that this is *not* how medieval pages were commissioned. I salute your keen perceptions and beg pardon for the sake of analogy!

14 Jongsma, "Mathematics," 10.

15 Ibid., 11.

16 Jason Lisle, "Evolutionary Math?," *Acts & Facts* 41 (2012): 11–13, accessed February 18, 2016, http://www.icr.org/article/evolutionary-math.

17 The definition of an idea is an interesting philosophical question that is a bit too involved to enter into here . . . To serve the purposes of this discussion, using the term "idea" almost presupposes that *someone* has a concept floating around his/

her/its mind. Some writers use "idea" and "concept" interchangeably. For the sake of our discussion on mathematics, we will adhere to the term "concept" when dealing with numbers.

18 See http://www.census.gov/popclock/.

19 "Abstract," *Merriam-Webster.*

20 This analogy, like all examples, breaks down if it's poked too severely. For one thing, there is really only *one* number seven (or eight, nine, ten, etc.). It's difficult to say the same thing for the concept of a Mustang.

21 Jongsma, "Mathematics," 8.

22 "An infinite sequence . . . of which the first two terms are 1 and 1 and each succeeding term is the sum of the two immediately preceding." "Fibonacci," *Merriam-Webster.*

23 Jackquelyn Veith, "Teaching the Quadrivium," quoted in Swope, *Classical Lutheran Education*, 70.

24 For one example, see Dan Reich, "The Fibonacci Sequence, Spirals, and the Golden Mean," *Department of Mathematics, Temple University*, accessed February 18, 2016, https://math.temple.edu/~reich/Fib/fibo.html.

25 John Briggs, *Fractals: The Patterns of Chaos* (New York: Simon and Schuster, 1992), 74.

26 Jason Lisle, "Fractals," *Answers Magazine* (January–March 2007): 52–55, accessed February 18, 2016, https://answersingenesis.org/mathematics/fractals/.

27 Different colors and variations of shading are used to highlight the outline of those numbers which *are* in the set.

28 Lisle, "Fractals," 52–55.

29 "Infinity," *Merriam-Webster*, https://www.merriam-webster.com/dictionary/infinity. "Countable" vs. "uncountable" infinity are concepts beyond the scope of this handbook, so this section has been simplified accordingly.

30 Generated at "Mandelbrot Set Generator," *Easy Fractal Generator*, accessed February 18, 2016, http://www.easyfractalgenerator.com/mandelbrot-set-generator.aspx.

31 Pamela MacKenzie, *Entry Points* (London: CARE for Education, 1997), 133ff. It should be noted that there is a distinction between infinity and eternity and that not everyone defines "infinity" or the "infinite" in the same way.

32 Montgomery, *Tractatus Logico-Theologicus*, 68.

33 Ibid., 69.

34 G. W. Leibniz, "The Principles of Nature and of Grace, Based on Reason," in *Leibniz Selections*, ed. Philip P. Wiener, *The Modern Student's Library* (New York: Charles Scribner's Sons, 1951), p. 527, accessed February 18, 2016, http://www.reasonablefaith.org/the-existence-of-god-and-the-beginning-of-the-universe#ixzz40YncwAZ5.

35 Quoted in J. W. Oller Jr., "Einstein's Gulf: Can Evolution Cross It?," *Acts & Facts* 29, no. 9 (2000), accessed February 18, 2016, http://www.icr.org/article/einsteins-gulf-can-evolution-cross-it/.

36 The assumption in this argument is that the "physicalness" of humans was present before their "nonphysical" attributes, as is assumed in the evolutionary model of origins.

37 Oller Jr., "Einstein's Gulf."

38 Ibid.

39 "Fractal Evolution," *Leading Edge Research Group*, 1995, accessed February 18, 2016, http://www.fractal.org/Bewustzijns-Besturings-Model/Fractal-Evolution.htm.

40 Jongsma, "Mathematics," 15.

41 Parton, *Religion on Trial*, 29.

42 Ibid.

43 That is, assuming that "+" means "plus" and that "1" is in ordinary base 10.

44 Parton, *Religion on Trial*, 29.

45 Ibid., 3, 9.

46 John Donohue, *Herding the Ox* (Wethersfield: Turtle Press, 1998), 40.

47 Parton, *Religion on Trial*, 31, 34.

48 Ibid., 30.

CHAPTER 3

Computer Science

An Apologist's Paradigm

> Walk in wisdom toward outsiders, making the best use of the time. Let your speech always be gracious, seasoned with salt, so that you may know how you ought to answer each person.
>
> —Colossians 4:5–6.

A Note to Instructors

In the traditional quadrivium, this would be a section on astronomy. It isn't for three key reasons: First, astronomy curricula have already been done—and done quite well—by numerous individuals and organizations.[1] Second, computer science is a subject that is not typically taught to middle school students (and *especially* not in conjunction with apologetics). Oh, STEM initiatives for increasingly younger ages are entering our school systems, and computer literacy programs are everywhere. Coding games flood the Internet, promising to teach your child programming in an hour or less. There may well be a place for all of these activities in our twenty-first-century, tech-heavy world, but none of these adequately grasp what computer science *is*. Third, and perhaps more important for our purposes, computer science is the modern equivalent to the role astronomy filled in the quadrivium.

The quadrivium carried with it the idea that foundation should precede specialization. One of the dangers of an increasingly technophilian culture is that we are inundated by new technology every day.

We become enchanted by the end result—a flashy new application, a mobile-friendly website, a million followers on social media—and too quickly forget (or never understand in the first place) the concepts behind it. Few people would agree that if you want to be a successful chef at a Michelin-starred restaurant you should attempt to perfect your *filet de boeuf* without an understanding of the ingredients, the visual aesthetic of the dish, and the basic tenets of food preparation. Teaching children to code does not mean that we are teaching them computer science.

How does this correlate with apologetics? Perhaps a better question would be, How does this *not* correlate with apologetics? Apologetics does not share the same cultural pedestal with computer science—within or without Christendom—and even when it *is* seen as an important aspect of our faith, it is very often misunderstood. There is also a type of thinking—which noted computer scientist Don Knuth terms "the computer science perspective"—that is extremely helpful to apologetics, as we shall see next.

This section is necessarily vocabulary heavy. Part of the reason for this is the nature of the computer science beast, and the other part is that my undergraduate degree was in information technology with a minor in computer science. I am admittedly biased toward this discipline. Much of my knowledge in this section is due to the excellent instruction by the computer science department at Concordia University Wisconsin and the insight of my father, Dr. Gary Locklair, who is chair of that department. Every effort has been made to cite resources appropriately. For the mature child (or interested parent) who wants to learn more about computer science, I have included some solid resources for further study at the end of this section.

A Note to Students

I want you to forget everything you think you know about computer science. Round up all that floating knowledge—from Internet memes, TV and movie nerds, and any programming or coding you may have gleaned—and shove it into the back closet in your brain. Those unruly bits of knowledge aren't allowed to come out until I say so. Order them a pizza and let them chill while I discuss computer science.

You see, this section of this handbook won't teach you the newest buzzwords you can use to impress your friends. You won't be a stellar programmer by the time you finish it. We're really not interested in the latest iWhatever or tablet that just came on the market that will be obsolete in six months anyway. Our primary goal is apologetics and how we can best uncover new ways to polish our armor and ready our defenses for attacks on our faith. We're concerned with how a computer science mentality aids us in developing a strong apologetic—primarily for the tough-minded but also for the tender-minded. This section will focus more on *how* to do apologetics than on evidences for tough- or tender-minded individuals.

Think of this section as a knight's training hall. You'll be practicing how to use defensive techniques and develop a strategy for a coming battle. Gregory Koukl, a well-known apologist and author, calls this "the ambassador model," an approach based on friendly conversation instead of confrontational "fightin' words."[2] Koukl's approach, based on key "tactics," will be extremely useful to us as we investigate apologetics in light of computer science.

Computer Science Mentality

> One of the main characteristics of a computer science mentality is the ability to jump very quickly between levels of abstraction, between a low level and a high level, almost unconsciously.
>
> —Don Knuth, *Things a Computer Scientist Rarely Talks About*[3]

Computer science, succinctly, is problem solving.[4] We're often misled into believing that computer science applies only to technology, first because of the word *computer* in its name, and second because we often only see the end products of this discipline. A computer is a tool that we can use to solve a problem. We often think of sci-fi movies where robots interact with humans using technology that has advanced so far that it begins to look like magic, but in reality, computer science serves a very practical purpose. It may surprise you to know that there was a time when cell phones, the Internet, and automatic garage doors did not exist. Although all technology can be misused for bad purposes, advances in modern technology have, for the most part, contributed to solving problems for people. I'd much rather have my car break down on a country road today, where I can easily call for help, than thirty years ago when cell phones were all but unheard of!

How do people fit into this, and how does any of this fit into apologetics? I've said that a computer is a tool for solving problems. A computer *system*, however, contains something beyond just the nuts and bolts of an electronic device, and this concept parallels surprisingly well with apologetics.

A computer system, according to Dr. Locklair, has three components: **hardware, software**, and **people**.[5] Hardware is the physical stuff of a computer: the chips, boards, and components. The main hardware piece is the central processing unit, or CPU, a small, typically square chip that actually does the stuff that a computer program tells it to do. Computer programs that give the CPU instructions are called **software**. Software isn't physical like hardware. Some examples of software that you may encounter are software application packages (often called "apps") that run on your phone, tablet, or computer. You can download a game app to your phone and play it, or you can use a word processing app like Microsoft Word to type up a paper for school.[6]

I've covered two of the three components of a computer system, and I've saved the best for last. Computer science is problem solving, and in the quote at the beginning of this section we saw a word called "abstraction." What does this have to do with a computer system? So far we've looked at the techy parts of computer science. Now let's take a look at its heart.

The final component of a computer system is **people**. This can refer to the people who are using a computer system ("users") and it can refer to those who create or manage computer systems for other people.[7] People provide the intelligence of a computer system. They interpret and apply information to the problem they wish to solve.[8] This application of intelligence is part of what Dr. Don Knuth termed a "computer science mentality" in the quote we read earlier. A computer scientist has a unique way of thinking about the problems that need a solution. There are many aspects of being an effective problem solver, but one of these abilities is uniquely primed for an apologetics application. Dr. Knuth is right—one of the key elements of a computer science (problem solving) mind-set is the ability to deal with various levels of **abstraction**.

"Abstraction" refers to something that is simplified. High levels of abstraction have very few details about the object in question. Low levels of abstraction have many details and reveal much of the complexity of an object. If I told you that I live in a house, you would say my statement has a high level of abstraction. You may get a general idea of what kind of dwelling my house might be, but you won't have any of the details. If I told you that I live in a red-roofed, two-story farmhouse in rural Wisconsin, you would have some of the details—I've peeled back a layer of abstraction. If I gave you the square footage of my house, all of its dimensions, and the street address, we'd be closing in on a *low level* of abstraction.

What is the point of abstraction? It can break knowledge up into manageable chunks of information that you can use to do other things. If I was too hung up on the electrical components of my keyboard, the way it is powered, and how touching the keys sends signals, I may never get around to using the keyboard to actually type this. It is useful to present a high-level view of a concept that then spirals into a more in-depth examination of the subject.

However, if I had such a high level of abstraction that I merely thought of the keyboard as a *thing*, this could end very badly for me. If I don't recognize that the keyboard is an *electronic* thing, I may be tempted to clean it with soap and water. I may even put it in the washing machine with the rest of my *things* or in the dishwasher with those other *things*. There are important distinctions concerning the keyboard that I need to be aware of in order to use it as a tool that can help me do useful things, like write this handbook.

Computer scientists deal with abstraction daily. Ask your tech support cousin how many times a day she hears a phrase like "I can't log in," "My computer won't start," or "Printing doesn't work." These phrases contain a high level of abstraction. The technician's job will be to politely get the user to a lower level of abstraction. She may ask questions like, "What happens when you try to log in? What does the screen look like when you try to print? What does it look like when your computer doesn't start?" She needs more details before she can solve the problem. Assuming that there has been a catastrophic hardware failure when the *real* problem is an unplugged cord wastes time, causes frustration, and annoys the user.

This can also happen in apologetics. Think about it: what is someone *really* saying when he says, "There's no evidence that God exists"? We're missing the details of that statement, and we're missing the train of thought that led him to make such a statement. Abstraction requires awareness and an unwavering focus on the topic—the *heart* of the problem—at hand. When we give a defense for our faith, we need this same focus on Christ crucified, and we also need an awareness and sensitivity to the person who is questioning us. Let's see how another computer science concept can help us with this.

The Problem-Solving Paradigm

A **paradigm** is "a theory or a group of ideas about how something should be done, made, or thought about."[9] The problem-solving paradigm, then, is a model of how a computer scientist should go about the process of solving a problem. It's a unique way of approaching a problem. The paradigm consists of four steps: understand the problem, plan the solution, implement the solution, and test and maintain the solution. If you think about it, this is a downward spiral of abstraction. We've taken a concept—the act of problem solving—and divided it up into pieces, revealing details that we might have otherwise overlooked.

Let's take a look at the problem-solving paradigm stage by stage. Although each phase can be repeated more than once, we'll examine the typical flow of the stages and how this provides us with a framework for solving our apologetics problems.[10]

Understand the Problem

> To know wisdom and instruction,
> to understand words of insight,
> to receive instruction in wise dealing,
> in righteousness, justice, and equity;
> to give prudence to the simple,
> knowledge and discretion to the youth—

> Let the wise hear and increase in learning,
> and the one who understands obtain guidance,
> to understand a proverb and a saying,
> the words of the wise and their riddles.
>
> —Proverbs 1:2–6

The first step in our problem-solving paradigm is to understand the problem.[11] This requires some level of abstraction. The true heart of the problem is often not as clear as you might think. If something has too high a level of abstraction, it will be difficult to diagnose the problem—and computer scientists are keenly aware of this fact.

Imagine that your friend comes up to you and hands you a single sheet of white paper.[12] "I need an airplane," your friend says. You willingly agree and take the sheet of paper. Your friend leaves the room to get a soda and you feverishly begin creating your airplane by folding, rotating, and flipping the sheet of paper. By the time your friend returns, your masterpiece is completed.

"Here it is—probably the best paper airplane I've ever made," you say proudly as you hand over the delicate aircraft. Instead of being delighted with your work, your friend frowns.

"No, I needed a drawing of an airplane for a poster I'm creating."

What happened? The level of detail was unclear, leading to miscommunication and frustration. Your friend had one airplane in mind—a hand-drawn Boeing 757, perhaps—and you had quite a different concept. The same thing can happen when a computer scientist begins work on a new software application.

Imagine what would happen if you said to a software engineer, "I need you to create an airplane application for me." Would the software engineer immediately lock himself in his basement with a bottle of Mountain Dew, throw on his headphones, and begin coding? He certainly wouldn't be a very good software engineer if he did! Before he can solve the problem, he needs to understand it. What do you mean by "airplane application"? Do you mean an airplane simulator to use in virtual reality environments, a mobile device game to pass the time, or specialized software for pilots and airlines to track important flight data? The software engineer simply does not have enough information to launch into solving the problem. He doesn't know what the **output**, or end result, of the solution should be, so how can he possibly know how to create it?

The same miscommunications and frustrations can occur in apologetics. Sometimes people ask questions that contain a very high level of abstraction or that are quite vague. It can be challenging to see what exactly is at the heart of the person's question. If we don't understand the question—or the challenge posed—we may waste time and energy in the way we answer, and we risk adding to the confusion and miscommunication.

For example, maybe you've heard one of these questions or statements before:

"God doesn't condemn anyone just because they aren't perfect. Hell is something people made up to scare their kids into behaving."

"Christians are so intolerant. How can you be a part of a religion that's so closed-minded?"

"It's irrational to believe in a god. There's no proof that any kind of higher power exists."

What is at the heart of each of the above statements? What is the true output? It might be something radically different than what it seems. There is actually a high level of abstraction in the statements above. We don't have the details about the concepts that are being discussed. What does the first speaker mean by "God" (the God of the Bible, a bodiless life-force, some other religion's god)? What about the second question: what is meant by "intolerant" and "closed-minded" (is it intolerant to say that only those who have purchased tickets can view a film in a movie theater)? *What*, specifically, is irrational about believing in God—and are we talking about the God of the Bible or one of the Hindu deities?[13] It can be tempting to jump on any of these statements with guns blazing, ready to defend the truth—but if you charge full steam ahead without any further information, you risk creating a beautiful paper airplane instead of the hand drawing that is actually needed. We don't want to shut down the conversation—we want to encourage communication. We also need to recognize the high level of abstraction and encourage the speaker to flesh out her concepts. We can do this by asking questions that are focused on *understanding the problem*.

Koukl puts it this way:

> Asking questions enables you to escape the charge, "You're twisting my words." A question is a request for clarification specifically so that you **don't** twist their words. When I ask a clarification question, my goal is to **understand** a person's view [and its consequences], not to **distort** it [*emphasis his*].[14]

What questions can we ask? After all, prattling, "Your statement is far too abstract. Would you please elucidate?" while entertaining, will get you nowhere. You don't want to talk down to the speaker, and you yourself need to encourage the lower levels of abstraction. You're the software engineer whose client needs an airplane app. What do you do?

Koukl suggests three guiding questions that can be used to "develop a game plan for discussing your Christian convictions."[15] We'll examine the first one now and the other two later.

It's such a simple question, yet it carries huge weight: "What do you mean by that?"[16]

There are various ways to apply this question. For example, "What do you mean by that?" can take the form of "Could you give me an example of ___?" or "What makes you think that?" Remember that you are not trying to humiliate or embarrass the other person by asking him a question! You are trying to understand his viewpoint so that you can *understand his problem*. If you don't understand the problem, you won't understand how to give an appropriate response.

It's important to practice good listening skills. This means that you need to pay attention to the response you get, and if you don't understand the response, keep at it—politely and winsomely!—until you feel that you *do* understand. "Sincere questions are friendly and flattering," Koukl says, and most people are more than willing to talk about their own ideas.[17] You can accomplish this in a few different ways. You could say, for example, "Let me see if I understand you on this: in your opinion, god lives inside all of us, and this force cannot reject anyone. Is that right?"[18] Be polite and be genuinely interested in the response. No one likes to feel like his view is being overlooked or shunned. Remember that we are trying to understand at this stage in the game. You don't have to agree with someone else's view in order to understand it. You *do* need to understand it in order to effectively defend the truth.

Top-Level Abstraction: Apologetics in Focus

Let's spiral outward for a moment and examine this phase of the problem-solving paradigm at a higher level of abstraction. Do we understand the problem that we need to be solving in apologetics? Do we understand what our output should look like?

To recap, our problem is that we need to "always [be] prepared to make a defense to anyone who asks [us] for a reason for the hope that is in [us]; yet [we need to] do it with gentleness and respect."[19] So we need to (1) be prepared, (2) give a defense, (3) understand the hope that is in us well enough to give a reason for it, and (4) do it with gentleness and respect. Never lose sight of the fact that our hope is in the life, death, and resurrection of Jesus Christ.

Be careful not to give in to the temptation of having to "win" every argument. It is the Holy Spirit's job to convert. Your calling is to be ready to engage in conversation "in season and out," when you expect it and when you do not.[20] You don't have to be "successful" in your defense, but you do need to be willing to discuss your faith and the reasons you have for it. Our expected output is not dramatic conversions but honest, thoughtful conversations. Koukl says it best: "You don't need to hit home runs. You don't even need to get on base. Just getting up to bat—engaging others in friendly conversation—will do."[21]

Plan the Solution

> Many are the plans in the mind of a man, but it is the purpose of the LORD that will stand.
>
> —Proverbs 19:21

The next step in the problem-solving paradigm is to plan the solution. At this stage, we know *what* the problem is. The software engineer now understands that "airplane app" means a game that can be played on a mobile device in which a user navigates an airplane through a series of maze trials in order to get the passengers to their destinations on time. At the end of each maze, the user has to solve a math problem.[22] In our apologetic discussion, we should now understand the question or statement that we intend to answer. We now need to plan our solution (our defense). But how? Let's take a cue from the software engineer and explore how to use this stage to our advantage.

Pseudocode is one of my favorite words. It sounds awesome and techy, and it stands for an often-overlooked tool that is indispensable for problem solving, both within computer science and outside of it. **Pseudocode** (pronounced "sue-doe-code") is a type of abstraction, and it refers to an algorithm that is written in plain English (or another human language).[23] That's great, you say, but what's an algorithm?

An **algorithm** is an unambiguous, general-purpose set of instructions for solving a problem.[24] You can use algorithms for all sorts of things. We use algorithmic procedures all the time. For example, here is an algorithm for multiplying fractions together:

- Multiply the numerators together.
- Multiply the denominators together.
- Reduce the answer to the lowest terms.[25]
    - This is the answer to the problem.

The procedure above is written in pseudocode. It is in words that we can understand, and it is general purpose because it does not tell us what the numerators and the denominators are. We can use this for any combination of numerators and denominators. Believe it or not, the algorithm I've just shown is very abstract from a computer scientist's point of view!

Let's say that this is the first math problem our software engineer is going to have in his airplane game. Remember that one of the hallmarks of a computer science mind-set is the ability to switch back and forth between levels of abstraction. Our software engineer realizes that the three-step algorithm above is too abstract because it is missing steps in the procedure. Humans often subconsciously fill in these missed steps, but computers can't think like we do. The software engineer needs to change the way he thinks about the problem so he can appropriately plan the solution. He needs a more detailed algorithm, and if he is recalling the way he solved this problem in school, his pseudocode might look something like:

- Arrange the fractions to be multiplied in a straight line.

- Multiply all the numerators together.
    - Write the answer of this multiplication down to the right of the fractions and to the right of an equals sign.
- Multiply all the denominators together.
    - Write the answer of this multiplication down to the right of the fractions, to the right of an equals sign, and below the answer of the numerator multiplication.
- Reduce the answer fraction to its lowest terms.
    - Find the greatest common divisor (GCD) of the numerator and the denominator.
    - Divide the numerator by the GCD and write down the number to the right of the previous answer.
    - Divide the denominator by the GCD and write down the number to the right of the previous answer and below the numerator that was found in the previous step.
        - This is the answer to the problem.

Phew! That's a lot of work. And this algorithm is not even as detailed as it could be!

A computer scientist uses pseudocode to keep track of planning his solution. He knows that it will need to be translated into something called a programming language in the next step of the problem-solving paradigm, but for this stage, he's just fine with having a procedure written down in English.

How in the world do algorithms and pseudocode help us in apologetics? Let's take a look at Koukl's next guiding question: "How did you come to that conclusion?"[26]

What? What does this question have to do with pseudocode and algorithms? Koukl explains that asking this question "helps you know *why* [a questioner] thinks the way he does. It charitably assumes he has actually come to a conclusion—that he has reasons for his views and not merely strong feelings about it. It will give him a chance to express his rationale, if he has any. It will also give you more material to work with in addressing his objections."[27]

In this way, you are subtly shifting the burden of proof onto the other person. You are asking for reasons the person believes the way she does. If someone says that the Bible has so many errors in it that it can't possibly be true, you can respond, "That's an interesting view. How do you know that?" You are not attempting to prove him wrong. You are attempting to get him to offer solid reasons for believing what he does.

You're looking for the breadcrumbs of belief, in other words. You're searching for the road the speaker has followed to arrive at his destination. You are searching for his algorithm, the conceptual set of instructions he considers sufficient to explain the belief he holds.

Now, an astute reader with a memory of the section on mathematics might pause here. Wait a minute, you may be thinking. The algorithm we looked at dealt with analytical or mathematical statements. Someone's statements of belief are going to be synthetic, or based on facts that can be verified. Can we still use algorithms as an analogy?

The answer is yes. All analogies are imperfect and will break down if we carry them too far, but that doesn't mean that they are of no use to us at all. Remember, computer science is a mind-set as well as a subject area. Algorithms are useful ways to organize procedural information. It is true that beliefs do not necessarily follow a set procedure ("first I'll believe in a bunch of gods, then I'll believe in reincarnation, and then I'll sum it all together and become a vegetarian"). However, algorithms can be a useful way of testing for gaps in thinking. Remember our first algorithm example earlier? It was missing several key steps that a human would easily be able to infer. When we're dealing with synthetic statements, missing steps may indicate faulty thinking.

For example, suppose that someone—we'll call him Frank—says, "Believing in God is irrational because there is no scientific proof for his existence." We may be tempted to say that his "belief in God" algorithm looks like this: In order to determine if belief in God is rational,

- Consult the natural sciences.
- If science does not give us proof about the existence of God, He does not exist.

This looks like an oversimplification! We must be missing a step or two. First we need to ask Frank what he means—what does he mean that belief is irrational, what kind of God is he saying is irrational, and what does he mean by scientific proof? Is he looking for analytical certainty? (If so, see the section on mathematics!) Once we determine what he means, we can ask him why he believes that. This will help us flesh out our algorithm and gain a clearer understanding of Frank's beliefs.

Never be afraid to ask for more information or to take a step back from the discussion. Koukl says that once you have asked questions in order to understand someone's point of view, it's more than all right to take a step back and say, "Let me think about it. Maybe we can talk more later."[28] If you feel pressured to counter a claim you may not be familiar with, be honest! Express to the person that you don't know everything there is to know about every subject. Take what you have learned so far in your conversation and do more research on the topic of intelligent design, the problem of evil, or whatever question backed you into a corner. Find out the answer so that you'll be prepared next time. In other words, write up your own algorithm.

All right. So if that's how algorithms mesh with both computer science and apologetics, how does pseudocode fit into all this? The answer may surprise you.

Over the course of my life, I have had conversations with presuppositionalists, empiricists, and agnostics, just to name a few.[29] With the possible exception of agnostics, I have very rarely had people say to me in the course of our conversations, "Yes, I'm a (presuppositionalist, empiricist, whatever), and that's why I think this way." Most people do not have labels for why they believe what they believe, and many don't even know that such labels exist. Ordinary, everyday people like you and me tend to use their own type of pseudocode when they talk about their beliefs. The pseudocode is composed in language that they can understand and that makes sense to them—language like "I believe that truth comes from the heart," "No one can know for certain," and "Creation has been disproven by scientists."

Labels can help us get a handle on a belief system, and they can help us develop an apologetic for it—but "in the field," when you're actually conversing with someone, throwing labels around haphazardly will not help you. Listen to the type of language someone uses. Train yourself to abstract meaning from it. Can you see the connection between "That may be true, but I can't accept it" and postmodernism? What tactics can you use to reach out to that speaker? That, my friends, is the importance of pseudocode. Recognize it and learn to speak a language that your questioners can relate to instead of flaunting polysyllabic words that you picked out of the dictionary.

Top-Level Abstraction: Apologetics in Focus

Let's spiral outward once again and look at planning the solution from an overall apologetics perspective. In computer science, planning the solution often entails looking at what input is required. How do we do this in apologetics?

Input often comes in the form of data.[30] Data (singular "datum") are the "raw facts." For example, the letter *w* in the previous word *raw* is data. Data need to be formatted before they convey information.

What is the difference between data and information? Consider the following chart:

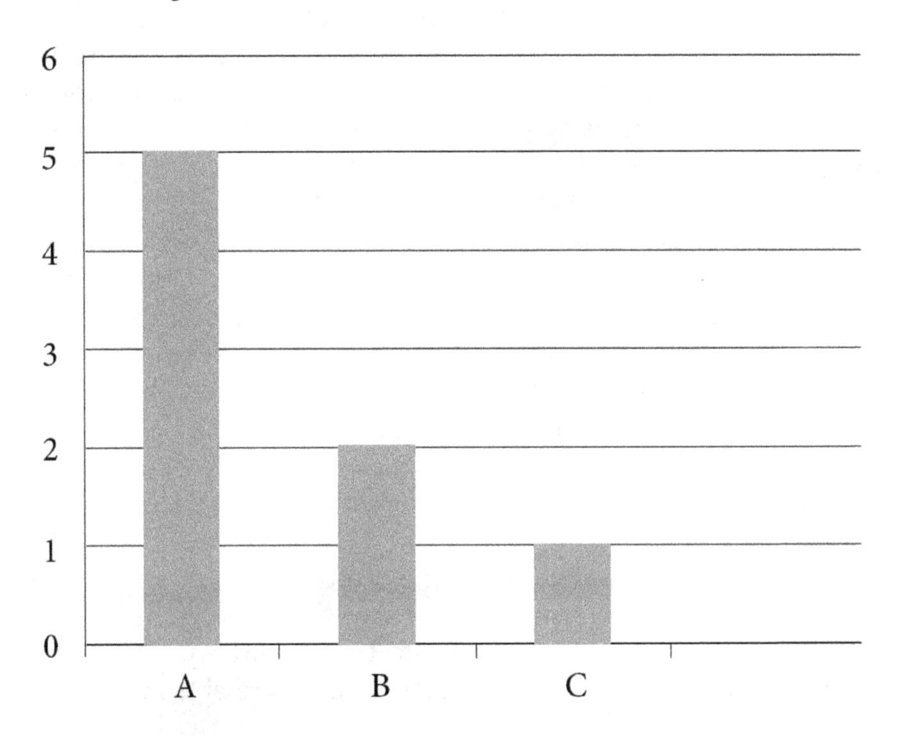

What is going on in this chart? What do the numbers on the left side indicate? Is it number of complaints per day for a certain company? If so, company C is doing the best with only one complaint. Is it thousands of dollars raised for a certain charity by three different people? If so, person A has raised the most—$5,000. This chart contains data, but it lacks any meaningful information.

Dr. Locklair uses the analogy of *knowledge* versus *wisdom* to explain this. Maybe you've heard the quote commonly attributed to twentieth-century writer Miles Kington: "Knowledge is knowing that a tomato is a fruit. Wisdom is not putting it in a fruit salad." Although master chefs may disagree (and the quote is more than a little cutesy!), it brings up an interesting point. In many cases, *knowing* something is not enough—you also need to know how to *apply* it.

For a computer system, this means that data must go through *information processing*, a set of four unique tasks, before it can be formatted as information. For apologetics, the question "How did you come to that conclusion?" helps us process the input we are receiving. *Why* does someone hold the viewpoint that she does? How is she applying knowledge (data) in order to reach her belief (information)? Does she *have* a reason for her beliefs?

Let me insert a side note here. Hypothetical stories, as Koukl points out, are not reasons for belief.[31] Offering an explanation is *not* the same thing as giving an argument or answering someone else's claim. I once had someone—who professed to be a Christian, incidentally—tell me that he didn't *disbelieve* one of the miracles attributed to Jesus in the Koran. In it, a young Jesus is said to have shaped birds out of clay, breathed on them, and caused them to become living animals.[32] The young man with whom I was talking was enchanted by this miracle. When asked why he believed it might be true, he replied that it was such a unique and interesting account, and it sounded like something the Jesus of the Bible might have done. He admitted that it might be true or it might not be true, and he doubted there was any way whatsoever to provide evidence that it actually happened, but he preferred to think that it was true.

That's not a reason for believing something. That's an example of someone giving an explanation of something instead of a reason for it. In addition to that, to say in effect, "You can't say it happened, but you also can't say it didn't happen" is an unverifiable statement.[33]

I discussed in the mathematics section the difference between analytical and synthetic statements. There is another type of statement called "nonsensical" or "technically meaningless," which refers to a statement that can be neither confirmed nor denied—nor held up to any sort of standard of truth.[34] When I call these statements "meaningless," I am not unduly insulting them—the statements can be very interesting and provide insight into a person's thinking and the way a society functions[35]—but I am saying that, from a verifiability standpoint, they have no meaning. The young man did not give a *reason* for believing that Jesus animated clay birds. He gave an unverifiable claim. In addition to that, it's worth noting that he had close friends who were genuine and wonderful people and who happened to be devout Muslims. To his mind, a sincere belief in the Koran (as evidenced, he believed, by a life of community service and friendship) could not be entirely false.

What if questioners simply do *not* give you a reason or evidence? Perhaps they don't have any. Perhaps they don't know where to look. Instead of ridiculing them for their beliefs ("How stupid can you be? You don't have any reasons for believing what you do!"), this is a golden opportunity to share why *you* have reasons for your faith. Remember, we're looking for the input that we will need in order to solve our problem. That input may be adherence to Darwinian evolution, confusion over the existence of evil, or a feeling of the heart.

At this point, it's important to note that we may have to jump back up to the first phase of understanding the problem. If we don't understand the response to our question ("How did you come to that conclusion?"), we may need to take a step back and ask, "What do you mean by that?" If we don't understand the problem, it will be very difficult to solve it. Take the time to understand and plan out solutions in practice, when you aren't under pressure from someone else. Getting into a computer science mentality takes time and practice, but with diligent study, it can become second nature.

Implement the Solution

Ah, now we're actually getting to the heart of things! At this stage, a computer scientist is ready to begin creating a solution to a problem. The software engineer we've been following is now beginning to actually create the airplane game. He has taken what he learned in the first stage and fleshed out in the second stage, and he is ready to embark on the next phase. He has designed his solution, and he is ready to transform it from an idea and implement his solution. He is using tools (a computer, programming languages, and specialized software) to create something new (a software app). At this point in our apologetics discussion, we are ready to take the next step. We understand the other person's point of view and we have an idea of how he got there—now we're ready to guide the conversation where we want it to go.

This is an extremely interesting stage. Did you catch something unusual in the previous paragraph? The software engineer is ready to take an idea (a concept) and turn it into an app (something concrete). Now you may be thinking that an app, as software, cannot be something concrete. Isn't software conceptual? In a way, yes it is—but an application, like our airplane game, is an example of something that bridges the gap between a concept and something concrete. It's software, so it's not physical—and yet there is something new that was not there before, something that can be interacted with and put to use to solve a problem. Like all analogies, this one will break down if we poke it enough—if you prefer, you can think of a hardware designer instead of a software engineer. Either way, it still brings up an interesting point for our discussion on apologetics.

I'm going to break trend and discuss the high-level implications of this before we dig back into the details. Hang on to your hats: we're going up a level of abstraction.

Bridging Einstein's Gulf

Do you remember the section on mathematics where I discussed Einstein's Gulf? That's the name given to the problem of the gaping chasm between the physical ("concrete") world of objects and the nonphysical ("abstract") world of concepts and ideas. In the section on mathematics, I brought up the idea of the gulf and gave an example of something that appears to cross it (numbers). I didn't discuss *how* something bridges it. Perhaps I can use an analogy here.

In addition to following the general problem-solving paradigm, the software engineer follows a process to develop his software.

There are different processes used by different companies, but most people have the same basic framework of what is called the software development life cycle.[36] Like the problem-solving paradigm, the SDLC has phases that a software developer follows. There are five phases—requirements, design, implementation, validation, and support—that do not necessarily occur in order. These phases fit into the general problem-solving paradigm in two categories: *analysis* and *synthesis*. This is roughly what it looks like:

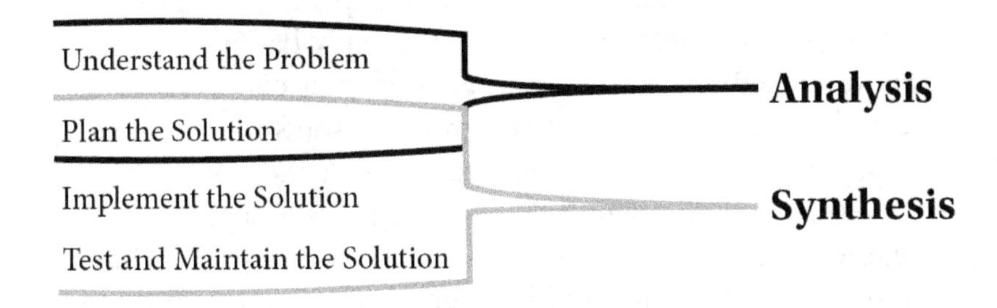

During the analysis portion, the focus is on breaking down information in order to understand it. The dictionary defines analysis as "a careful study of something to learn about its parts, what they do, and how they are related to each other."[37] Think of it as aiming for a very low level of abstraction—we *want* to see the details so that we can appropriately understand and plan. Synthesis, on the other hand, is "something that is made by combining different things (such as ideas, styles, etc.)."[38] In synthesis we are focusing on how we can bring all the necessary components together in order to build up and create something new.[39] We want to take the pieces we've identified in the analysis stage and integrate them into a solution.

How do we do this? How exactly do we move from planning to implementing? There is obviously some overlap there. Could it be that this is another example of Einstein's Gulf?

Think about it. Yes, it's true—in the previous two stages (understanding and planning), you have been writing, drawing, and making physical marks that represent your ideas. However, your solution is still very much conceptual. It's an *idea*. No matter how clearly defined you see it in your mind's eye, you as a software engineer could not go to the client and say, "The app you asked me to make is fully functional in my mind, so I'd like my payment now, please." It doesn't work that way! You haven't delivered a finished product that exists outside of your thoughts. So how do you move from idea to implementation?

The software engineer has a secret weapon: the second phase of the software development life cycle, *design*. The design process, according to Dr. Locklair, is the "heart of software engineering."[40] It is the essence of software development and the bridge between idea and implementation. What is design? Where does it come from?

Design is conscious, deliberate, and complex. It means "to create, fashion, execute, or construct according to plan."[41] Design conveys *information* (not just *data*), and it doesn't simply happen. According to computer scientist Fred Brooks, "great design comes from great designers."[42] When asked how to improve software engineering, Dr. Brooks replied that people—designers—were the key to improvement.[43] Design isn't something that spontaneously happens in software engineering. It takes hours upon hours of work by intelligent, creative people in order to produce a good design. Design converts the question "What do we need?" into "How do we do it?"[44] Practically speaking, this requires additional planning for more algorithms (and things called data structures) as well as an ability to think about order.

In short, design is a lot of work. It's a creative process, and creative processes, according to noted writer and brilliant thinker Dorothy Sayers, contain three components: *idea, energy*, and *power*.[45] Dr. Locklair fleshes this trinity out into the computer science concepts of *idea, implementation*, and *interaction*.[46] We are concerned with the *implementation* that corresponds to Sayers' *energy*.

As you can see, analysis contains the stages of "understanding the problem" and "planning the solution." Synthesis overlaps slightly with analysis because "planning the solution" can also occur in this category. Synthesis also exclusively contains "implementing the solution" and "testing and maintaining the solution." To move from planning to implementation requires the energy behind the act of designing. Dorothy Sayers, using the analogy of a writer, says that "[the Energy] is dynamic—the sum and process of all the activity which brings the book into temporal and spatial existence . . . It is the Energy that is the creator in the sense in which the common man understands the word, because it brings about an expression in temporal form of the eternal and immutable Idea . . . it is something that is distinct from the Idea itself, though it is the only thing that can make the Idea known to itself or to others."[47] This *energy*—which Sayers also called the *activity*—can exist even if it does not take a physical form. When it *does* take a material form, it is the energy that drives the design, the crossing of the bridge from thought to written word or created app. It is a passionate concept that contains "feeling, thought, toil, trouble, difficulty, choice, [and] triumph."[48] The activity is a synthesis, a bringing together of the former idea and plans, which is then made available to others. Without energy, we could not know the idea. Without the implementation of a software app, we could not know the problem it is capable of solving or the idea it conveys.

We've traversed Einstein's Gulf—or at the very least, we see a way across it. If energy, a.k.a. design or activity, is the bridge in computer science, what is it in other areas of life? How do we distinguish between a sturdy, dependable bridge and an imaginary path?

Test and Maintain the Solution

The *final* phase of the problem-solving paradigm is to test and maintain the solution. I purposefully emphasized the word *final* with italics because this phase should occur throughout the problem-solving process. A good software engineer knows that waiting until the end to test his app is a very bad idea. During my time as a system administrator for the computer science department at a university, I regularly saw frantic students attempting to fix all of the problems with their apps on the day before a huge assignment was due. Some of this last-minute panic is unavoidable, but if testing had been performed throughout the creation process, some of the issues would not have come as such shocks!

Software engineers distinguish between two types of testing: validation and verification. **Validation** occurs before all of the software development life cycle phases and asks the question, "Are we doing the correct thing?"[49] For example, before the requirements phase (during "understanding the problem"), we want to make sure that we are correctly understanding what is expected of us. Remember my paper airplane example earlier? We could have saved time and effort if, when handed a piece of paper and instructed to make an airplane, we had asked, "Excuse me, would you like a paper airplane or a hand-drawn one? What kind of airplane would you like?" This would have either validated or negated our idea of what kind of airplane we should be making.

Verification occurs at the end of a phase and asks, "Did we do the thing correctly?"[50] It compares our result with what was expected. We could take a hand-drawn picture of an airplane to our friend and ask, "Is this the type of airplane you had in mind?" He could then tell us if the plane was too big or too small, if it should be a different type of plane entirely, or if it should be colored in.

In addition to validation and verification, a software engineer must develop a test plan. Traditionally, this plan lists inputs and expected outputs.[51] For example, let's say your grandparents gifted you with a generous check of $5,000 they would like you to invest over a period of ten years and then withdraw to use either toward a college education or starting a business. You've done some research and you've found a place that will pay you 9 percent interest on your $5,000 as long as you keep your money with them for ten years. (If you ever find such a place, please let me know. Look up current bank interest rates if you need help understanding why.) You're extremely excited because you have just created a calculator app that will help you figure out how much money you will earn. You give your app the input of your starting value ($5,000), the interest rate (9 percent), and how long it accumulates (ten years). Your app gives you the output of $550. "Wow!" you think to yourself, racing to tell your parents. "This is great!"

There's just one problem. The app didn't give you the correct output. It *looked* correct because it didn't give you an outrageous value like $9,087,231 or $0.10, but it wasn't right. In order to test something, you should know what the expected output is so that you aren't fooled by correct-looking results!

Testing looks for errors in a software app. Testing does *not* improve the product—it simply tells you that there is something wrong with it.[52] Testing must always occur against some standard. That's why it's vital to understand the problem—if we don't know what our app is supposed to do, how can we know if it's doing it or not?

How can testing be applied to apologetics? How do we test both how we interact with people and whether or not we have crossed Einstein's Gulf?

In life you will hear many things that sound true but really aren't. The Bible tells us that we are to test the spirits in order to discern what is true and what is false.[53] Isn't there some way in which we can test such things? Yes, there is; we looked at it briefly in unit one, and we will delve into it in more detail in the next unit. For now, remember that testing always implies a *standard.* A software engineer who does not believe in standards will not get very far in her profession.

What about Einstein's Gulf? If it's possible to cross it in software engineering—which it appears to be—is it possible to cross it in other areas of life? What's the big deal about Einstein's Gulf, anyway? Hold on to those questions—we'll be examining them in more detail very soon. For now, let's take a final look at how we can maintain our conversation with an apologetic questioner.

Has It Ever Occurred to You That You Might Be Wrong?

I vividly remember the day I learned that Charles Schulz, beloved cartoonist and creator of Charlie Brown and Snoopy, passed away. I was less than ten years old, and I didn't quite grasp the full significance, but I remember being deeply sad. As I grew older, I read more of his classic comic strips. Many years later, when I was in college, I came across one of his comic strips that has stuck with me ever since. In it Charlie Brown hears that his beagle, Snoopy, is writing a book on theology (Snoopy is a prolific author, so this comes as no surprise to Peanuts fans). Charlie Brown muses that Snoopy better have a good title for his newest tome. Snoopy, awash in cool confidence, thinks to himself, "I have the perfect title. 'Has It Ever Occurred to You That You Might Be Wrong?'"

I don't know about you, but I hear this question (or its sister question "How do you know you're right?") all the time. The tricky thing is that, very often, the people who ask this question *are not* looking for an answer. They usually don't want to hear about your reasons as much as they want to accuse you of being an arrogant bigot. People who ask this question are often looking for fireworks.

In other words, this is not the best question you can use when you engage in discussion with someone. People become very uncomfortable—and understandably so—when they feel that you are attacking *them* personally. (Note how easy it is to ask this question in a sarcastic, belittling tone.) However, the thought behind "Has it ever occurred to you that you might be wrong?" isn't wrong in and of itself, and it can still serve a useful conversational purpose.

Koukl, after reminding us of Jesus' admonition to be as "wise as serpents and innocent as doves" (Matt. 10:16), suggests a gentler way of turning the tide of a conversation: "Have you ever considered (insert idea here)" or "Can you help me understand (this concept you hold)?"[54]

The point of testing in computer science is to uncover errors. The point of Koukl's questions is to "gently [question] a person's beliefs or [confront] a weakness with his argument."[55] We're trying to politely show folks the errors or gaps in their beliefs.

For example, "Have you considered that the existence of evil is actually evidence for the existence of God, not evidence against it?" is a gentler way to broach an often emotionally charged subject.[56] You aren't directly poking holes in your friend's beliefs. You're holding up those beliefs to the light and encouraging your friend to identify the holes himself. Does this actually "work" in the real world?

I had the opportunity to use this while discussing Genesis with a "bad Christian" (his words, not mine). He admitted that he didn't adhere to many of the doctrines of his church body, and he wasn't too sure about the Bible either, but he liked the spiritual feeling that he gained from attending a gorgeous, cathedral-like church. He asked me why Genesis was so important and why I believed it didn't mesh with the idea that God used Darwinian evolution to create the world. I knew from previous conversations that this particular man would question practically everything said to him and that he was even willing to play devil's advocate (argue for a view that he did not personally hold) if it kept a discussion and debate going. I asked him if he would agree that the "secrets" or keys to evolution were time and death, and he said yes, that made sense to him.[57] I then asked him if it had occurred to him that if macroevolution was true, then there was death before the fall into sin. He stared at me, his eyes slightly widened.

"I never thought of that before," he admitted. He paused, seemed about to speak, then said, "I have to think about that."

That was all I wanted. I didn't want to win an argument for intelligent design or have him experience a road-to-Damascus conversion. I simply wanted him to examine a hole in his system of belief that didn't fit.[58] A gentle "Has it occurred to you?" opened the door, at least momentarily, for reflection upon the coherency of his belief system.

The same holds true for the question "Can you help me understand this?" As I've discussed before, most people are not compelled to examine their beliefs regularly. Gradually leading the conversation in the direction you want it to go is part of giving a defense "with gentleness and respect."[59] Never forget that we are dealing with eternal souls, souls that we desire to join us one day with their Creator.

Validation and verification can help keep us honest in our dialogue with skeptics. Part of being a good computer scientist—and a good apologist—is self-awareness, the ability to monitor your actions and thoughts and adjust them as needed. Scripture itself says that we are to take every thought captive to Christ.[60] We must always be ready to engage in discussion, and in order to do this, we need to be focused on the *correct thing*.

Medieval knights had a code of conduct—often referred to as a code of chivalry—that outlined what was the right and honorable thing for a knight to do. Their actions had to adhere to a specific standard. At the top of most of the codes of chivalry was the admonition to fear God and serve the king. Software engineers, in much the same way, are guided not only by the needs of their clients but also by governing boards that set out ethical guidelines for computing (see, for example, the ACM and IEEE organizations' codes of ethics). Christian apologists know of a higher code that exists.

Now, lest you caution me that I'm falling back into presuppositionalism, let me explain. I am not at this moment discussing our defense for the standard that we have (I've dealt with this a bit already, and I will deal with it more in coming sections). What I'm saying is that we *have* a standard. How do you know if you're doing apologetics correctly? Check the standard. Check the Source—and note the capital S. Our apologetic must be grounded firmly in Jesus Christ. If it isn't, we aren't truly Christ-centered, and we have no more foundation for our faith than any other religious practitioners have for theirs (more on that later).

It's extremely difficult to test your own apologetic—and your own faith—if you don't understand either. Don't neglect reading your source material, the Bible. Read it. Read it again and again and again, and if you have questions, dedicate yourself to finding the answers. No one will do apologetics perfectly, and that isn't the point. The point is that, by grace through faith, our King Jesus has summoned you to be a knight in His Church Militant. His grace called you and His grace will support you. Don't be overwhelmed by the task ahead. Hold fast to the standard, test the spirits, prepare yourself for battle, and remember who it is that trains your hands for war.[61] Be ready to engage in dialogue with anyone who approaches you, and develop the mindset of a computer scientist, able to abstract, discern, and understand as you learn how to more deeply love your God with all your mind.

Assignments and Discussion Questions

1. Investigate the following unit resources and choose one or two to delve into more deeply. With your teacher's approval, write a paper, give a presentation, or otherwise incorporate what you have learned into your study of apologetics. Your assignment should somehow address this theme: "Why Christ-Centered Problem Solving Is Needed in Apologetics Today."
2. Investigate famous Christian computer scientists (see Dr. Montgomery's resource below for a starting point). Did their faith influence their scientific discoveries and if so, how?
3. Write your own algorithm for *planning* your defense of the faith. What resources can you use? How can you find more information? Plan it out!
4. How does Einstein's Gulf aid us in giving a Christ-centered apologetic that's both tough-minded and tender-minded? Can something be both factually true and aesthetically beautiful, and how does this mirror our apologetic task?
5. What is "abstraction" and why does it matter for apologetics? Why should a computer scientist's "mentality" also be an apologist's mentality?
6. Computer science can help you with apologetics. How might a strong background in apologetics be helpful in computer science? In what ways are the two related?
   a. A note to teachers: There are several (secular) resources that can help you investigate this. Not all material contained in them will be appropriate for young readers, but for talking points, you

may want to consider the following books: *Moral Machines* (Wendell Wallach and Colin Allen) and *Robot Ethics* (edited by Patrick Lin, Keith Abney, and George Bekey).

7. Find the section of your course notebook where you wrote down the "Five *W*" questions. After the question "*How* can I do apologetics?" write down some ideas that you have learned from my discussion of computer science and Gregory Koukl's guiding questions. If you need help, investigate Koukl's book *Tactics* with your teacher.

Unit Resources: Computer Science

The following are resource suggestions for you to investigate with your instructor. Many of the following resources are available online—try using your favorite search engine and see if you can find them.

Brooks, Frederick. "The Computer Scientist as Toolsmith." *Communications of the ACM* 39, no. 3 (March 1996): 61–68.

———. "No Silver Bullet." Reproduced from: Brooks, Frederick P., *The Mythical Man-Month* anniversary edition with four new chapters. Reading: Addison-Wesley, 1995.

Knuth, Donald. *Things a Computer Scientist Rarely Talks About.* Stanford: CSLI Publications, 2001.

Koukl, Gregory. *Tactics*. Grand Rapids: Zondervan, 2009.

Montgomery, John Warwick. "Computer Origins and the Defense of the Faith." *Perspectives on Science and Christian Faith: The Journal of the American Scientific Affiliation* 56, no. 3 (September 2004): 189–203.

Sayers, Dorothy. *The Mind of the Maker*. Edited by Susan Howatch. London: Continuum, 2004.

Notes

1 See, for example, works by Dr. Don DeYoung, Dr. Jason Lisle, Dr. Danny Faulkner, and so on. The Institute for Creation Research (http://www.icr.org/) is a good starting resource.

2 Gregory Koukl, *Tactics* (Grand Rapids: Zondervan, 2009), 20.
3 Ibid., 13.
4 Donald Knuth, *Things a Computer Scientist Rarely Talks About* (Stanford: CSLI Publications, 2001), 13.
5 Gary Locklair, "CSC 150: Information Processing I" (lecture, Concordia University Wisconsin, Mequon, WI, September 19, 2011).
6 There are other types of software—for example, systems software—that are more in-depth than the scope of this handbook.
7 Typically system creation is attributed to *computer scientists* and system management is attributed to *information technologists*, or "IT guys." For the sake of this handbook, we'll take a high-level view and not worry about this distinction.
8 Locklair, "CSC 150: Information Processing I."
9 "Paradigm," *Merriam-Webster*.
10 There are many different frameworks that can be used, and many professional computer scientists use some version of the software development life cycle. We are abstracting these models into the general problem-solving paradigm.
11 Gary Locklair, "CSC 150" (lecture, Concordia University Wisconsin, Mequon, WI, November 2, 2011).
12 Analogy adapted from Dr. Locklair.
13 Koukl, *Tactics*, 54.
14 Ibid., 45.
15 Ibid., (subtitle).
16 The first of the "Columbo Tactics" is covered in chapter 3 of *Tactics*.
17 Koukl, *Tactics*, 47.
18 See ibid., 52.
19 1 Peter 3:15.
20 2 Timothy 4:2.
21 Koukl, *Tactics*, 15.
22 There is obviously a *lot* more information that is needed to fulfill the requirements of this project. We'll "abstract" our analogies here for the sake of space.
23 John Dalbey, "Pseudocode Standard," *California Polytechnic State University*, last modified December 2, 2003, accessed

February 19, 2016, http://users.csc.calpoly.edu/~jdalbey/SWE/pdl_std.html.

24 See "Algorithm," *Merriam-Webster*.

25 "How Do You Multiply Fractions?," *Virtual Nerd*, accessed February 19, 2016, http://www.virtualnerd.com/middle-math/multiplying-dividing-fractions/multiply/multiply-fractions-definition.

26 Koukl, *Tactics*, 61.

27 Ibid.

28 Ibid., 69.

29 An empiricist is someone who believes that "all knowledge is derived from sense experience" or what can be observed and tested with the five senses (see "Empiricist," *Dictionary.com*). An agnostic is "a person who does not have a definite belief about whether God exists or not" (see "Agnostic," *Merriam-Webster*).

30 Input can also come in the form of commands issued by a user, but we will focus on data for this discussion.

31 Koukl, *Tactics*, 62.

32 Surah 3:49, 5:110. Referenced in Sam Shamoun, "Mohammed's Attempt of Damage Control," *Answering Islam*, accessed February 19, 2016, http://www.answering-islam.org/Shamoun/sura3_7.htm.

33 Montgomery, *Tractatus Logico-Theologicus*, 64. See also the discussion on arguments from ignorance in unit one.

34 Ibid., 63.

35 Ibid.

36 Gary Locklair, "CSC 370: Software Engineering" (lecture, Concordia University Wisconsin, Mequon, WI, February 5, 2013).

37 "Analysis," *Merriam-Webster*.

38 "Synthesis," *Merriam-Webster*.

39 Gary Locklair, "CSC 370: Software Engineering" (lecture, Concordia University Wisconsin, Mequon, WI, February 21, 2013).

40 Gary Locklair, "CSC 370: Design Process" (lecture, Concordia University Wisconsin, Mequon, WI, March 19, 2013).

41 "Analysis," *Merriam-Webster*.

42 Frederick P. Brooks, "No Silver Bullet," accessed February 19, 2016, http://worrydream.com/refs/Brooks-NoSilverBullet.pdf, 15. Reproduced from: Frederick P. Brooks, *The Mythical Man-Month*, anniversary edition with four new chapters (Reading: Addison-Wesley, 1995).

43 Ibid., 15.

44 Locklair, "CSC 370: Design Process."

45 Dorothy Sayers, *The Mind of the Maker* (New York: Continuum, 2004), 25–37.

46 Gary Locklair, "CSC 370: Design" (lecture, Concordia University Wisconsin, Mequon, WI, March 5, 2013).

47 Sayers, *The Mind of the Maker*, 80.

48 Ibid., 80.

49 Gary Locklair, "CSC 370: Testing" (lecture, Concordia University Wisconsin, Mequon, WI, April 16, 2013).

50 Ibid.

51 Ibid.

52 Ibid.

53 1 John 4:1.

54 Koukl, *Tactics*, 84–85.

55 Ibid., 84.

56 Ibid.

57 A catchphrase popularized by evolution advocate Carl Sagan.

58 This conversation could be classified as a *dogmatic* conversation (in other words, a discussion of doctrine between people who hold to the same teaching), but I've included it here because his reluctance to classify the Bible as inerrant is important. However, the fact that my question—which referenced the Bible he wasn't sure he believed—brought him up short is evidence that, at some level, he could grant for the sake of argument that the Bible should be treated as a holistic entity. Be aware of these types of situations, where the line between defending the reason for the faith within you and drawing evidence from the *source* of your faith overlap.

59 1 Peter 3:15.

60 2 Corinthians 10:5.

61 Psalm 18, Psalm 144.

CHAPTER 4

Introverts and Extroverts

"Come on, come on, let's go!" Annie skipped ahead, waving her hand impatiently for Clara to follow. "It's music time!" She bounded into the sanctuary and marched up to the first pew, flopping down so hard that her brown curls bounced furiously in their pigtails. Clara paused in the doorway and clutched her folder to her chest. The sanctuary was almost full of chattering, laughing children, more children than the small church ever saw on a typical Sunday. Clara knew that Vacation Bible School drew in a large crowd from the community, but she hadn't realized how *large it was. She glanced over at her family's typical Sunday morning pew. Being so far back from the front of the sanctuary, it was still empty. It had the best view of the beautiful artwork on the ceiling above the altar—a blue sky filled with flaming angels and, at the very center, Jesus shining with the sun rising behind Him, His arms stretched out in blessing. Clara began edging her way toward the safety of her pew.*

"Clara, come up here!" Annie yelled, thumping the pew next to her. Clara winced as dozens of heads turned to stare at her curiously. She felt her cheeks burn as she stumbled up to sit next to Annie. "This is the perfect seat," her friend proclaimed. "Now we can volunteer to stand with the music leaders!" Clara sank down into the pew and sighed. It was going to be a very long day.

—

Carter arrived early for catechism class. Pastor Wright was in the office making copies of the night's exam, and Carter waved at him as he entered the fellowship hall. That quiet boy was already there, sitting close to the corner of the room, his head propped up on one hand and his Bible open in front of him. He had kept to himself all year, sometimes asking a question here and there but mostly scribbling furiously in a notebook. It seemed impossible that anyone could write that fast or find that much to write about during a catechism class. Carter set his Bible down next to the boy.

"Hitting the books already, eh? Overachiever!" He elbowed the other boy with a grin and scooted his chair closer to him. "What's your name again?"

"Peter," the other boy said, so quietly that Carter almost missed it. He gave a small smile and moved his Bible slightly away from Carter.

"Isn't that the guy who denied he ever knew Jesus?" Carter leaned over to look at Peter's Bible. "Hey, you're reading about him, right?" He pointed to a word on the page.

"No—well, yes." Peter ran his finger over the edge of the Bible. He bit his lip and frowned. "Why—why did Jesus call him that?"

"Call him what?" Carter rummaged around in his backpack and popped a piece of gum into his mouth. "Peter? Wasn't that his name or whatever?"

"No. 'Satan.'" Peter shuddered and rubbed his arms. "What a horrible thing to say to someone—to anyone. *But it says so right here: 'Get behind me, Satan.'"*

"I dunno." Carter shrugged. "Were we supposed to read that part?"

"No, but—"

"Then quit worrying. It won't be on tonight's exam. Hey, do you have a pencil I can borrow?"

—

Have you ever met anyone like the characters in the stories above? Perhaps others have noticed that you are "quiet" or "outgoing." Maybe a teacher has told you that you are a natural leader or a grateful friend has been encouraged by the way you listen to her problems. Adults may suggest possible goals for you based on your personality: "You did so well speaking in church today! You should consider becoming a presenter." We tend to think that certain personality types may lead to different careers or vocations because of perceived strengths and weaknesses. Could this affect the way we do apologetics with others as well?

If you've heard the term "introvert" before, you may have pictured the stereotypical "shy" boy who keeps mostly to himself or the girl who almost never speaks up and who mouths the words to a hymn instead of singing along with the Sunday school choir. However, introverts are not always shy—and shy people aren't always introverts. Psychologists have studied what it means to be an introvert for many years, ever since the terms "introvert" and "extrovert" were popularized in 1921.[1] In this section, we will examine two guiding questions: What does it mean to be an introvert? And why does it matter for apologetics?

What Is an Introvert?

> Introversion is a preference for environments that are not overstimulating.
>
> —Susan Cain, *Quiet: The Power of Introverts in a World That Can't Stop Talking*[2]

There are different ideas about what it means to be an introvert. It is likely that at some point in your life, you will take a personality test—either for a class in school, a future job interview, or simply for fun. Many of the leading personality tests will classify you as either an "introvert" or an "extrovert." Most psychologists today agree on the basic personality traits that make up introverts and extroverts, and this can give us insight into understanding how we—and those around us—process information and see the world.

Introverts are individuals who "feel just right" with *less stimulation* in their everyday environments.[3] Stimulation can be anything that you perceive with your senses: sight, hearing, taste, touch, and smell. For example, the act of reading a book by yourself while a spring rain gently falls on the roof has very low external stimulation on you. Contrast that with a birthday party at a roller skating rink: dozens of people, flashing strobe lights, pulsing music, and the scent of floor wax and cheddar-dipped pretzels combine to flood a person's senses with an overload of stimulation. An introvert may still enjoy the birthday party, but she could be extremely tired afterwards—why? Her emotions and personality are very sensitive to outside stimulation like noise, activity, light, and sound. I once had a conversation with a gentleman whose grandson was quiet, withdrawn, and seemed more than a little lost in a large group of children. He confided in me that the six-year-old boy would come home from school—a place teeming with stimulation—and go down into his basement alone. There he would spend hours quietly constructing huge cities, mountains, and landscapes made out of colorful building bricks. "That's how he decompresses," his grandfather told me. "It's as if he's an adult who needs to find a way to relax after a long day at work."

For introverts, this need to unwind and breathe is very common. They often have incredible focus and prefer to concentrate on one task at a time, often preferring to work alone.[4] However, introverts are often quite good at interacting with other people and maintaining strong friendships. The differences are that they generally prefer to have a few close friends rather than belong to a large group, they are more interested in listening to others than in speaking, and many introverts are more comfortable with writing than they are with speaking.[5] In the story at the beginning of this section, Peter was more interested in taking written notes than he was in participating in class discussions. Many introverts feel the same way.

Not every introvert will fit the descriptions I have provided. In the words of writer Susan Cain, human beings are "gloriously complex individuals" who are capable of acting in many different ways depending on the circumstances in which we find ourselves.[6] Most people do not speak to infants and adults in the same manner, for example. I am not claiming to explain *everything* about how an individual will act in *every* circumstance but to provide a framework for recognizing key traits of introverts.

To summarize, introverts are often classified as *thinkers*, *dreamers*, and *idealists*.[7] The dictionary defines an idealist as "a person who cherishes or pursues high or noble principles, purposes, [or] goals."[8] Sometimes these people are called *perfectionists*, or those who strive for perfection in everything they do. Introverts are often writers, artists, and readers—or at the very least, they have a deep appreciation for such things. They are sensitive to things they consider beautiful, and they are often very sensitive to other people. An introvert will be concerned if someone in her life has a problem or appears to feel left out. The highly sensitive person will often have a very strong conscience and sense of "right" and "wrong"—but at the same time, he sincerely dislikes conflict.[9]

Thinker, dreamer, idealist, perfectionist, sensitive to others . . . haven't we heard terms like these before? Yes, we have. Before we examine where and why, let's briefly take a look at the introvert's opposite: the extrovert.

What Is an Extrovert?

> The archetypal extrovert prefers action to contemplation, risk-taking to heed-taking, certainty to doubt. He favors quick decisions, even at the risk of being wrong. She works well in teams and socializes in groups . . . Extroverts enjoy the extra bang that comes from activities like meeting new people, skiing slippery slopes, and cranking up the stereo.
>
> —Susan Cain, *Quiet: The Power of Introverts in a World That Can't Stop Talking*[10]

When you think of extroverts, do you think of a bounding, panting, tail-wagging golden retriever who will bowl you over in his excitement to see you? The stereotypical extroverted human is, in many ways, similar to the outgoing Fido—he craves attention, being in the spotlight, and is happiest when he is in high-energy situations with lots and lots of stimulation. He is often classified approvingly as "outgoing" or "a real leader," and he's an expert at getting teammates pumped up before a big game. Extroverts draw their energy from sources outside of themselves and are especially drawn to high-stimulation environments.

Human beings, however, often don't fit into stereotypes. Many extroverts are frustrated when people think of them as less intelligent or sensitive than their introverted counterparts. Extroverts can still be shut down by being told to talk more quietly or ask fewer questions. Extroverts need to interact with others for longer periods of time than introverts require (or often understand!).

Now, I don't want to gloss over extroverts as if they were somehow below par or not as desirable as introverts. That isn't what I mean at all! However, for the sake of this handbook, we will examine introverts in more depth than we will extroverts. The reason for this is that people seem to have more difficulty understanding introverts (if they themselves aren't introverts) or interacting with others (if they *are* introverts).

Why Does It Matter for Apologetics?

Why should we spend any time at all learning about personality types? That sounds like psychology stuff that high-schoolers do in AP classes. However, learning about introverts and extroverts matters very much to apologetics. You see, the terms I have applied to introverts can also be applied to the tender-minded.

Now, we can't simply say that all introverts are tender-minded and that all tender-minded people are introverts. For one thing, most people are not fully, 100 percent introverted (or tender-minded, for that matter). However, there appears to be a *correlation* between being an introvert and being tender-minded. A correlation means that two or more things are related somehow but that one does *not* have to cause the other.[11] For example, consider a certain town that has more than ten libraries. This same town also has an extremely large number of pet dogs. We could not say that the libraries caused the townspeople to adopt so many dogs! The number of libraries and the number of dogs may have a relationship that is also influenced by another source—for one, the large population of the town.

Apologetics means to give a defense. Will you give the same defense to every question that is asked? Consider an example from the Korean martial art of Taekwon-Do. As with other martial arts, Taekwon-Do has a number of techniques that the student learns: kicks, hand techniques (punches and other types of strikes and thrusts), and a variety of blocks. Taekwon-Do stresses that students *never* start fights, but that they must always be ready to defend themselves if a fight is unavoidable. The student learns many different blocks that can be used for different attacking techniques. A rising block defends against an attack that is coming down toward the student's head. An inner-forearm outward-middle block defends against a middle-level attack, such as a punch toward the student's chest. A low block protects against a low-level attack—the attacker may be doing, for example, a front snap kick.[12]

A Taekwon-Do student who attempts to protect herself from a high-level attack with a low block will find herself completely unprepared for the attack. Different offensive techniques require different defensive skills. You can't block a low front snap kick with a rising block. The kick will bypass your defense, and you won't be in a position where you can effectively retaliate or prepare yourself for the next attack.

The same holds true in apologetics—think about it. We are called to give a verbal defense of our faith. We need to have enough "blocks" in our arsenal to be able to handle questions from a wide range of perspectives. Our stand on Christ crucified and raised from the dead never changes. The manner in which we defend it may.

An introvert may tend to ask questions that are primarily tender-minded—though, of course, it always depends on the individual person. I discussed that introverts dislike conflict; postmodernism seems to fill this need for harmony. If there's no objective truth, there's no need to worry about disagreements! At the same time, introverts often have distinct definitions of right and wrong. That doesn't sound postmodern at all.

Remember that people are individuals who won't fit fully into the mold of "introversion" or "extroversion." Instead of attempting to guess what worldview someone may hold based on her apparent personality, focusing on the individual will provide a clue as to how to proceed with a meaningful conversation. Introverts tend to be highly focused on one thing at a time. They are interested in the *meaning* behind things. The tender-minded person is the same way.

Introverts excel at asking questions and attentively listening to the answers they receive.[13] This means that if they ask you a question about your faith, they will actually want to listen to your answer, if for no other reason than to satisfy their own curiosity about your beliefs. If an introvert is asking you a question, she actually wants to hear the answer—and she will be very sensitive if you try to shut her down. Carter's response to Peter's question in the story earlier—"quit worrying"—will not help Peter. It will simply cause him to look for answers elsewhere.

How can you tell if the person you're interacting with is an introvert (or an extrovert)? You have to get to know him. Spend time with him. Develop and forge a friendship. For most of us, our apologetic task will not be carried out in a public debate. We should, of course, be ready at all times to give an answer to *anyone* who asks. Most people who will ask you questions about your faith at this point in your life will be those you know—a friend, classmate, relative, or teammate.

A word to the wise: be careful of "missionary friendship," or viewing others as merely tasks on a checklist of people that *you* need to convert or change. That's not being a missionary, and it's not being a friend either. Your job is not to convert anybody (that's the job of the Holy Spirit). Your job is not to win arguments or give the most eloquent defense. Dr. Angus Menuge, a prominent professor of philosophy and an adept apologist, sums it up beautifully: "We aren't called to be successful. We're called to be faithful."[14]

Assignments and Discussion Questions

1. Investigate introverts and extroverts with your instructor's help. Do you see yourself as more introverted or more extroverted? What does this mean for how you do apologetics?
2. What are the strengths that extroverts have when engaging in apologetics discussions? What challenges might they face due to their personality type? What strengths do introverts possess when doing apologetics? What tasks might be more difficult for them? Is it possible to use both introvert *and* extrovert strategies when doing apologetics? If so, what strategies might they be?
3. Find someone of the opposite personality type (an extrovert if you're an introvert, or an introvert if you're an extrovert) and select an apologetics subject to discuss. For example, you might choose to discuss why all religions can't be true, or the *infinitum* principle. How does your communication style affect your defensive tactics?

Notes

1. Susan Cain, *Quiet: The Power of Introverts in a World That Can't Stop Talking* (New York: Crown, 2012), 10. Sometimes you will see the spelling "extravert," primarily in research papers and psychological studies. For the purposes of this handbook, I have followed Susan Cain's lead in using "extrovert," the popular spelling of the term.
2. Ibid., 12.
3. Ibid., 11.
4. Ibid.
5. Ibid.
6. Ibid., 14.
7. Ibid., 270.
8. "Idealist," *Dictionary.com.*
9. Cain, *Quiet*, 13, 14.
10. Ibid., 6, 11.
11. "Correlation," *Merriam-Webster.*
12. Taken from the author's personal experience in Taekwon-Do studies under eighth-degree black belt Senior Master Van Hecke.
13. Cain, *Quiet*, 239.
14. Angus Menuge, "The Apologetics of C. S. Lewis" (presentation, International Academy of Apologetics, Evangelism, and Human Rights, Strasbourg, France, July 8–9, 2014).

Unit Two Review

Review Questions

1. What do the terms "tough-minded" and "tender-minded" mean? How do these terms influence our understanding of apologetics?
2. How can mathematics be used in apologetics? What was one key idea that you learned from the mathematics section? Why can't we be 100 percent certain about matters of historical fact?
3. How can computer science be used in apologetics? What was one key idea that you learned from the computer science section? How does the problem-solving paradigm provide a framework for apologetics?
4. What is Einstein's Gulf? Why does it matter for apologetics?
5. What does it mean to be "introverted" or "extroverted"? How can understanding the difference between them aid us in doing apologetics "with gentleness and respect" (1 Pet. 3:15)?
6. This unit was loosely based on a medieval concept of the transcendental "Good."[1] How does goodness correlate to the concept of judging something? In what ways does goodness influence the way we judge things and vice versa? Why is this important for apologetics?
7. What was one surprising thing that you learned in this unit? Why was it surprising?

Vocabulary List

abstract [concept]: Relating to general ideas rather than specific instances. Example: all Mustang convertibles everywhere in the world.

abstraction: Something that is simplified. High-level abstraction (e.g., "I live in a house") is less detailed than low-level abstraction (e.g., "I live in a red-roofed farmhouse in Wisconsin").

algorithm: An unambiguous, general-purpose set of instructions for solving a problem.

analysis: The first two stages of the problem-solving paradigm in which the focus is on breaking down information in order to understand the problem.

analytical statement: A statement that is true by definition.

concrete [instance]: A specific instance of an idea or concept. Example: *your* sky-blue Mustang convertible.

Einstein's Gulf: The term given to the logical gap between the physical (concrete) world of objects and the nonphysical (abstract) world of concepts and ideas.

extrovert: Someone who, in general, prefers more stimulation, requires time with other people in order to recharge, and is likely to be labeled as "outgoing."

fractal: In mathematics, a pattern that contains infinite subpatterns by repeating a relatively simple formula.

hardware: The physical components of a computer.

introvert: Someone who, in general, prefers less stimulation, requires time alone to recharge, and is likely to be labeled as "quiet."

natural revelation: For a Christian, those things that we know about God and ourselves through nature or intuition.

presuppositionalism: A type of apologetics that assumes that Christianity (or another position) is the true starting point of knowledge.

problem-solving paradigm: A method used in computer science throughout the life cycle of creating a solution to a specific problem. Consists of the following phases: understanding the problem, planning the solution, implementing the solution, and maintaining and testing the solution.

pseudocode: An algorithm that is written in plain English or another human language as opposed to a programming language.

software: Nonphysical computer programs that give the central processing unit (CPU) instructions.

special revelation: For a Christian, those things about God and ourselves that have been made known to us through God's word.

synthesis: The last three stages of the problem-solving paradigm in which the focus is on creating a solution to the problem.

synthetic statement: A statement of fact that can be verified in some way.

tender-minded: Term for individuals who desire beautiful, meaningful signs that a position is helpful or subjectively fulfilling before accepting a position.

tough-minded: Term for individuals who desire clear, hard facts and some level of proof before accepting a position.

validation: Ensuring that one is doing the correct task (and correctly understands the problem) before implementing a solution.

verification: Ensuring that one did the task correctly and comparing the resulting solution with what was expected.

Resources

As always, these resources are starting points only. Some works were previously mentioned under the unit one resources.

Nonfiction

The Bible.

Cain, Susan. *Quiet: The Power of Introverts in a World That Can't Stop Talking.* New York: Crown, 2012.

Rationale: Although this book suffers from unfortunate humanist and evolutionary thinking, it is an excellent resource for understanding the "quiet" personality type.

Koukl, Gregory. *Tactics.* Grand Rapids: Zondervan, 2009.

Rationale: A very helpful resource for those interested in starting conversations with a variety of individuals.

Lewis, C. S. *God in the Dock.* Grand Rapids: Eerdmans, 1970.

Rationale: If you read nothing else from this collection of essays, read the one entitled "Christian Apologetics."

Montgomery, John Warwick. *Faith Founded on Fact.* Edmonton: Canadian Institute for Law, Theology, and Public Policy, 2001.

Rationale: A fascinating book that highlights the need for evidential apologetics.

Parton, Craig. *The Defense Never Rests: A Lawyer among the Theologians.* St Louis: Concordia, 2015.

Rationale: See its description under Unit One Resources for more information.

———. *Religion on Trial.* Eugene: Wipf & Stock, 2008.

Rationale: See its description under Unit One Resources for more information.

Veith, Gene Edward, Jr. *Postmodern Times.* Wheaton: Crossway, 1994.

Rationale: See its description under Unit One Resources for more information.

For a humorous take on introverts and extroverts, view "Four Things Introverts Think (but Never Say)," part of the "Messy Mondays" YouTube series by Blimey Cow. https://www.youtube.com/watch?v=FwudkKF7I20.

Fiction

For this unit, I'm going to offer some movie and TV show suggestions for you to investigate. Ask your instructor which ones would be right for you to watch.

Beauty and the Beast (1991, original animated version).
Rationale: This classic film examines discerning truth, looking deeper than the surface, and the consequences of how we relate to one another.
Cinderella (2015, live action).
Rationale: A lovely film that touches on some unique philosophical themes.
The Computer Wore Tennis Shoes (1969).
Rationale: A light-hearted examination of what happens when man becomes too machine-like.
Inkheart (2008).
Rationale: Like the book upon which it is based, this movie examines the power of words, the meaning of reality, and the need for sacrifice.
Oz the Great and Powerful (2013, live action).
Rationale: A quirky, fun film that raises subtle questions about truth and beauty.
Star Trek (ask your instructor for episode recommendations).
Rationale: Oftentimes this TV show (in any season) deals with the conflict between tough-minded and tenderhearted individuals.
Star Wars: A New Hope (1977; other films in the series at your instructor's discretion).
Rationale: Worth watching for many reasons, but don't overlook the subtle (and not so subtle) undertones of Lucas' worldview.
Tron (either the original or the sequel).
Rationale: A film that examines reality in an innovative way and poses some interesting worldview questions in the process.

Note

1 Again, see Goris and Aertsen, "Medieval Theories of Transcendentals."

Unit Three

Focus on Reasoning ("Beauty")

> But in your hearts honor Christ the Lord as holy, always being prepared to make a defense to anyone who asks you for a reason for the hope that is in you; yet do it with gentleness and respect.
>
> —1 Peter 3:15

Welcome to the third unit! It's time to consider the final two subject areas and take a look at some often-overlooked aspects of apologetics. This unit may seem shorter than the previous two, but as always, the same guidelines apply: take your time working through the following sections, and choose areas to investigate more thoroughly on your own. My focus is slightly more tender-minded from here on out. I will attempt to highlight the beauty of truth with creative subject areas and a focus on what happens *after* you begin doing apologetics. Let's dive in with the first subject area: history.

CHAPTER 1

History

An Inheritance from Lessing

Nescire autem quid ante quam natus sis acciderit, id est semper esse puerum.

To be ignorant of what occurred before you were born is to remain always a child.

—Marcus Tullius Cicero, *Orator Ad M. Brutum* (c. 46 BC)

A Note to Instructors

Dr. Ruth Beechick, a distinguished educator and curriculum developer in her own right, says:

> Through stories, children catch on to the idea that people lived in the world before they were born and that their times and doings were in some ways different from ours. They also come to understand that we can learn about the past from books, and from film and other media. At about fourth grade level, most children have reached the information stage of reading, having mastered the mechanics and having built fluency. At this point we become more earnest about history teaching.[1]

This unit won't claim to *teach* your child history as much as it will reinforce how he or she *learns* history. History is most often taught through books in the form of textbooks, historical fiction, and works from the time period studied. Dr. Beechick recommends caution when presenting a child with a textbook and expecting him to learn exclusively from it, especially for history. She notes that textbooks often present a superficial view of the past (*that* something happened instead of investigating why, how, and what it means today) and contain "collections of separate, unrelated topics that, as the children [perceive], may contain only dates, events, and brief vignettes."[2] In other words, history textbooks are often compartmentalized, dumbed down, and present "predigested, prethought, preanalyzed, and presynthesized" information.[3]

This poses a problem not only for the child's academic education but also for his developing worldview. The danger of separating history into neat little compartments of "secular history" and "religious history" does not begin in college, as many people suppose. The seeds are often planted far earlier in a child's life and, if left unchecked, may mature into vicious weeds by the first day of university classes.

Dorothy Sayers, renowned writer and apologist of the twentieth century, addresses this concern in a delightful essay entitled "A Vote of Thanks to Cyrus." In it she details her experience as a child with Cyrus the Persian, a character who lived in the world of tunic-wearing Greeks and Romans "between the pages of a children's magazine [*Tales from Herodotus*]."[4] Later she expresses the shock she experienced upon realizing that Cyrus was *not* confined to his pigeon-holed existence as an imposing figure of classical history, but that he had the nerve to "[march] clean out of our Herodotus and slap into the Bible" as the forewarned doom in Daniel 5.[5] Then, of course, there's the story of Esther and King Ahasuerus, also known as Xerxes—the same Xerxes whom the Greeks famously opposed at the Battle of Thermopylae.[6]

Sayers credits Xerxes and Cyrus for her realization that history is not a compartmentalized buffet but a single, elegant, messy whole. There is not "secular history" and "Bible history," as if the two were divorced from each other. This sad misconception begins in childhood and, in some cases, is never resolved. Sayers notes:

> Most children, I suppose, begin by keeping different bits of history in watertight compartments, of which Bible is the tightest and most impenetrable. But some people seem never to grow

> out of this habit—possibly because of never having really met Cyrus and Ahasuerus (or Xerxes). Bible critics in particular appear to be persons of very leisurely mental growth.[7]

If the life, death, and resurrection of Jesus Christ occurred *not* in history but in the watertight compartment of "Bible history," we are, of all men, to be pitied most. If our salvation occurred not in the time, place, and manner described in the Bible but in a spiritual realm where we cannot test the sources to determine their veracity, then our faith is meaningless. Let's eat, drink, and be merry, for tomorrow we die and stay dead forever.

What, then, can be done? How do we introduce our children to Cyrus and Xerxes and, more important, how do we present a God who has revealed Himself to us in *real* history? We can examine historical and legal methodologies for affirming the truth of Christianity, and we can encourage our children to ask questions (more on that in the note to students).

There are a number of solid resources concerning the interaction between historical methodologies and apologetics. I have attempted to take a unique approach so as to avoid reinventing a wheel that is already well capable of bearing apologetic weight. The resources section will contain works that detail such things as the bibliographical, internal evidence, and external evidence tests, and Simon Greenleaf's *The Testimony of the Evangelists*. There is no need to regurgitate these solid arguments here as they are written elsewhere in a form that, with a little extra application of a curious mind, is well accessible to our target audience.

This section, like the other subject areas, is designed to be used along with whatever history curriculum you are currently using. Give thought to ways of integrating *all* history together—such as timelines that combine biblical events with other events at the same time in history, famous characters from history "marching into the Bible" (and vice versa), and the techniques discussed in this section. For further help, see the resources section at the end of this unit. Especially worth mentioning are Dr. John Warwick Montgomery's *History, Law, and Christianity*, Dorothy Sayer's essays as compiled in *The Whimsical Christian*, and Craig Parton's *The Defense Never Rests*.

A Note to Students

Is history your favorite subject? Perhaps you have a specific time period that you like to investigate. Maybe you're a leading expert on medieval Europe, or you're the go-to person for any questions on the American Revolution. Or perhaps you loathe history and find it dull, boring, and a waste of time.

Regardless of how you feel about history itself, have you ever wondered about the relationship between history and Christianity? Can faith be investigated in the same way that we investigate a fourteenth-century castle or the Boston Tea Party? Why would it even matter whether we can or can't?

It matters a great deal, as we will see. The Roman philosopher Cicero was in many ways correct when he said that "to be ignorant of what occurred before you were born is to remain always a child"—though perhaps not in the way he was thinking. As Christians, Scripture continually admonishes us to "grow up" to a deeper understanding of our Lord Jesus Christ. 2 Peter 3:18 urges us to "grow in the grace and knowledge of our Lord and Savior Jesus Christ"; 1 Peter 2:2 says that we should "long for the pure spiritual milk, that by it [we] may grow up into salvation"; and in 1 Corinthians 13, Paul compares our partial knowledge (how we "see in a mirror dimly") with being a child—the grown-up understanding, the deeper knowledge, will come when we see "face-to-face" He who is to come.

Notice that I am talking about spiritual maturing. Scripture is not advocating that you grow up immediately and become a functioning adult! You'll have plenty of time for that later on. It is important for your spiritual health, however, that you continue to grow in the grace and knowledge of Jesus. Cicero says that ignorance of the past makes one an eternal child. Scripture says that ignorance of the *eternal child* is to be not only a "[child] of wrath" (Eph. 2) but also "dead" (Col. 2:13), "blind" (2 Cor. 4:4), and "[an enemy]" of God (Rom. 5:10).

How do we come to know this child, this Son of Man? Has He revealed Himself to us? Has He entered human history and dwelt among us? The Christian says "Yes." The apologist knows how to share this truth with unbelievers. It's time to grow spiritually and pray that God Almighty would strengthen our hands for the coming war (Ps. 18:34).

Before we dive into this section, I want you to do something for me. I want you to think of two or three (or more) questions that you have or that you think of as you read this segment on history. The questions can be more *abstract* (remember from the computer science section that this means *broad* questions, or those without a whole lot of detail) or more specific. In other words, "What does history have to do with apologetics?" is a legitimate question. Write it down. "Why should I care about history's role in apologetics?" is also fair game. You (or others) might have more questions:

"Is the Bible really a trustworthy historical source?"

"Is it possible to investigate Christian claims in the same way that we investigate historical claims?"

"How does the history curriculum I am using in school relate to apologetics?"[8]

And so on. Be creative. Write the questions down, and if you come across answers to them, write down the answers. If you don't find the answers, consult with your teacher and the resources at the end of this section and keep looking. Remember, it's OK not to know the answer to something! The important thing is that you know where to look for answers and how to discern a good answer from a bad one—and why the answers are important in the first place.

History 101

History is defined as "a branch of knowledge that records and explains past events," or simply "the study of past events."[9] When most people think of history, they think of something that happened a long time ago, like the building of the pyramids in Egypt or the construction of Greek temples. We tend to think of history as something that happened before we were born, unless we're discussing some new event that is "making history." We very rarely think of history as something that occurred earlier in the day. However, as Craig Parton says, "you create history all the time. What you were doing before you began reading this section of this book is now, technically speaking, 'history.'"[10] Life isn't a video game that we can pause and resume when we feel like it. Once a moment is past, it's past.

Some people mistrust history and think that it cannot accurately tell us anything about religious truth. Since we can't know for certain what happened in the past, how could we possibly know for certain anything about religious truth? In other words, it seems we've stumbled across another incarnation of Einstein's Gulf—but this time it's termed something a little bit different. This idea is called Lessing's Ditch, and whether you've heard the term before or not (and I very much doubt you have), it is an idea that is still around today. It carries with it a deep-seated implication for apologetics and the impact it has on history, and vice versa.

Breaking Tradition and Breaking Ground

The year was 1729. The quiet town of Kamenz, Germany, lay muffled under a winter sky in one of the coldest months of the year. The crisp January air hinted at snow. A baby boy was welcomed peacefully into the outside world—or perhaps the scene was less than idyllic and he was screaming at the top of his lungs. Either way, this baby, whose name roughly meant "God's love," would one day become an important thinker, writer, and philosopher.

Gotthold Ephraim Lessing was born at a time in history known as the Enlightenment. The Enlightenment occurred throughout many European countries from roughly the mid-seventeenth century through the eighteenth century and in many ways began with the advancement of natural sciences.[11] I won't delve too deeply into the Enlightenment in this handbook (although I encourage you to explore it on your own! See the end of this section for resource suggestions), but in order to understand Lessing's Ditch, we need to understand what was happening in the world during the time he lived.

What was the Enlightenment? Historian Peter Gay remarks, "the Enlightenment was a volatile mixture of classicism, impiety, and science; the philosophes [social philosophers of the time], in a phrase, were modern pagans . . . [The Enlightenment was] a single army with a single banner."[12] Although there were, of course, differing views of the Enlightenment among its leaders and thinkers—what Prof. Gay would classify as adherents to its "right and left wing[s]"—the North Star that guided thinking at the time, the "single banner" under which the philosophes were united, was deism.[13]

Deism, to quote Dr. John Warwick Montgomery, was "a philosophical religion setting itself against the Theistic belief of classical

Christianity that God had intervened in His own created universe by giving a 'special revelation' through the inspired Scriptures and in the latter days through His own Son. For the Deist, the 'light of Nature' was enough to reveal the permanent standards of moral conduct; man was no fallen sinner in need of special divine guidance, much less a blood Redemption: he had outgrown such primitivism and was on the threshold of a new day of enlightened morality, freedom, and progress."[14] Deism rejected the idea that God had revealed Himself to mankind and that He had become man in the person of Jesus Christ. The deists were enamored of Isaac Newton's discoveries about the "immutable laws" controlling the universe, and they had no doubt that a "master physicist" deity was responsible for its existence.[15] A god capable of such creation would never reveal himself to the "ignorant barbarians" (the Israelites) as the Old Testament claimed, the deists reasoned; nature herself was the revelation of the Maker of the world.[16] No further revelation was necessary or had occurred, and the incarnation was excluded absolutely.

This view, however, caused some problems for a few folks: namely, those who wanted to remain religious (even Christian) and still be at the forefront of Enlightenment progress. A man named Gottfried Leibniz recognized this problem and came up with a solution that, he thought, would allow the rational person to accept Enlightenment thinking while retaining religious belief. It was through "the reconciliation of the mechanical [the immutable laws of the deist] and the teleological [referring to design or purpose in nature] views of the world" that he believed he could unite science with religion, where the two appeared to be at odds.[17]

The answer to this problem, Leibniz figured, was to distinguish between two types of truth, which he termed the "rational" and the "empirical," or what he later called "necessary truth" and "contingent truth."[18] Whew—teleological, empirical, rational, necessary, and contingent? Those are weird words! What exactly does all this mean? It means that we are beginning to see the planting of the seeds of postmodernism, with its rejection of *truth* in favor of truths. It also means that the ground was prepared, as it were, for the digging of Lessing's Ditch.

You see, Lessing was a writer with some big ideas. He lived a troubled and interesting life. His ideas were so unconventional, even for the Enlightenment period, that he didn't publish many of them until after the death of his father, who was a devout Lutheran pastor. When he did publish his ideas, he shook the world up—big time. We're still feeling the aftershocks today. Let's take a look at what exactly happened and how it affects our apologetics nearly 290 years later.

Digging the Trench

Lessing took Leibniz's idea of two separate truths and ran with it. Lessing acknowledged this in his definition of the "ditch":

> If no historical truth can be demonstrated, then nothing can be demonstrated by historical truths. That is: accidental truths of history can never become the proof of necessary truths of reason . . . That, then, is the ugly, broad ditch which I cannot get across, however often and however earnestly I have tried to make the leap.[19]

In other words, Lessing's Ditch is the argument that since we can never achieve 100 percent certainty concerning the truth of historical claims, we cannot gain any degree of religious certainty from historical testimony of the life of Jesus Christ. Why is this? For one, Lessing rejects the notion that "certainty about past events" is attainable based on testimony rather than "firsthand experience."[20] Historical knowledge, to Lessing, falls under the category of contingent truths of fact. This was not enough for his religious certainty. He wanted "truths of reason" to be the basis of something as important as one's religion because "truths of reason are tidy, mathematically certain, and known *a priori*."[21]

Simply put, Lessing wanted *analytical*, absolute certainty for his beliefs. (Remember our friend the *analytical statement* from the section on mathematics?) Historical truths are not analytical, so they cannot provide evidence for believing that Jesus Christ was the Son of God and the truth. "Truths of morals and metaphysics [defined by the dictionary as the fundamental nature of reality]" are confined to their own truth-sphere, safely kept clean of messy, untidy, uncertain historical facts.[22] Lessing saw nothing that could bridge the gap between what is probable and what is certain.

Einstein's Gulf separates the conceptual from the physical. Lessing's Ditch divides the *synthetic* from the *analytical*, or what is probable from what is certain. This view is not just confined to eighteenth-century philosophers. Although it might seem backward, Lessing wanted complete certainty so much that, upon realizing that he could not find it, he rejected the idea that absolute truth was knowable at all. In an effort to find some meaning in his constant struggle with "historical truths" and "truths of reason," Lessing drew a surprising conclusion:

> The worth of a man does not consist in the truth he possesses, or thinks he possesses, but in the pains he has taken to attain that truth. For his powers are extended not through possession but through the search for truth. In this alone his ever-growing perfection consists. Possession makes him lazy, indolent, and proud. If God held all truth in his right hand and in his left the everlasting striving for truth, so that I should always and everlastingly be mistaken, and said to me, "Choose," with humility I would pick on the left hand and say, "Father, grant me that. Absolute truth is for thee alone."[23]

Lessing's god, then, though he might call him "Father" and even "Christ" elsewhere in his writings, is not the God of Scripture but is closer to the god of deism: a deity so far above and beyond human experience that any truth about him is unknown and unknowable. It's the effort that counts, Lessing consoles himself—as long as I'm trying to find the truth, I'm heading in the right direction.

Sound familiar? Our postmodern society has embraced Lessing's Ditch and dug down even deeper. Those who claim to know any sort of absolute truth are seen as intolerant, unspeakably arrogant, and self-righteous. Our society would agree with Lessing; we should humbly seek after truth, not brashly announce that we've found it. No one can find it. It's trying that counts. Behind Lessing's eighteenth-century scholar's vocabulary we find the heart of postmodernism: when it comes to truth, anything goes—as long as you don't claim to have found Truth with a capital *T*.

To Lessing, we can't know that Jesus lived, died, and rose from the dead in the same way that we know Alexander the Great conquered Asia. On the truth of Christ's miracles, including His resurrection and claim to be the Son of God, Lessing remarks that they have "completely ceased to be demonstrable by miracles happening now," which is unsurprising since Lessing lived "in the eighteenth century, in which miracles no longer happen."[24]

In other words, the reports of miracles are not analytically certain, and there is no way to test them since miracles don't happen anymore. We can't be certain, so Christianity is just as probable as Judaism, deism, or Islam, and we should all quit fighting about religion and focus on loving each other.[25] This should sound even more eerily familiar to you. Our world has bought into this idea hook, line, and sinker. (Look back at the brief section on postmodernism and see how closely it lines up with Lessing's ideas!)

How do we respond to the Lessings of our day? Is there a ditch and, if so, is there a way across it? How can we know? Isn't it arrogant to think that we *could* discover truth, if it even exists? Should we abandon all historical knowledge in favor of seeking our own truths? It's time to get our hands dirty and find out.

The Historian and the Lawyer

Lessing craved absolute certainty for the truth claims of Christianity. In the section on mathematics, I mentioned the two types of statements: *analytical* statements of certainty and *synthetic* statements of fact. I remarked that "analytical statements tell us absolutely nothing about the factual nature of the world around us,"[26] and the same holds true for this section. People who claim they desire utter certainty before they can believe Christianity is true do not, in fact, act this way in other areas of life. They couldn't; life simply doesn't work that way.

"Matters of fact," says Parton, "can *never* be 100% certain but that does not prevent us from making decisions which are life and death in nature based on less than certain reasoning."[27] Surgeons perform operations based on less than absolute certainty. Are they analytically certain that a surgery will cure instead of harm the patient? No. They examine the patient's records—her *history*, the record of facts and events in her life that are important medically—and decide based on their research. The patient's history does not exist in a separate "truth category" for the doctors. If they notice that their patient is allergic to a specific type of medicine, they can't say, "Oh, well, this was recorded in the past, so we can't know for certain whether this is true. It's the best medicine on the market for this type of condition, so we should give it to her anyway and hope for the best." That's not how life works for the doctor who, quite literally, holds life and death in his hands on any given day.

Is the doctor who discovers a cancerous tumor arrogant for pointing it out to the patient? Is he implying that the patient is less intelligent than he is or that he is the only one who could have discovered the tumor? Of course not. If the patient chooses not to act on the information since, after all, the doctor is not completely certain, she runs the risk of further harming herself by not acting. She may even die.

There is another area of life where decisions are made without complete certainty, the outcomes of which often deal with life and death. Consider a court room. A legal trial is "really a recreation of history"—indeed, as Parton notes, "our society is built on the idea that history can be understood and 'recreated' through the means of documents, photographs, testimony, etc."[28] While Lessing and his modern day followers may believe that "the realm of historical experience is one of process and flux, the sphere of becoming, not of being," and that "everything in this flowing process of history is relative, nothing absolute,"[29] lawyers would adamantly disagree. People are sent to life imprisonment and, in some cases, even death without analytical certainty.

Legal standards of proof deal with a "preponderance of evidence" for civil cases and the "proof-beyond-a-reasonable-doubt standard" for criminal cases.[30] They also lay out specific guidelines for what constitutes a sound "recreation of history," or what is allowed in a court of law as evidence. This involves examining the source material—in our case, the four New Testament Gospels—and applying certain tests to them. (Note: This would be an excellent assignment for you to tackle on your own. It has been addressed so extensively elsewhere that I won't repeat it here and risk reinventing a perfectly sound wheel!)

What can we learn from our historian and lawyer friends? I'll highlight one key takeaway: "the unbeliever must never be allowed to require a level of proof for matters of fact that in principle are not possible to establish, since matters of fact always involve issues of probability."[31] In other words, if someone asks for absolute certainty, gently point out that the world of facts is not constrained to the realm of analytical certainty. Are you absolutely certain that it is safe to cross that street, eat that apple, ride that skateboard, or get in that car? No. You act on *probabilities* all the time in matters concerning possible life and death—religious claims should be treated no differently.

Finitum non est capax infiniti

More Latin words! How fun is this? Do you remember what this means from my discussion of mathematics? It refers to the belief that the finite cannot contain the infinite. I tied this to Einstein's Gulf and discussed that, at least in computer science, there appears to be a way across this divide. I also briefly mentioned that saying that the finite cannot contain the infinite is an unprovable statement, since how could we who are finite know what is or is not capable of the infinite?

Lessing's Ditch operates under this *axiom*, or presupposed truth, of *finitum non est capax infiniti*. The ditch is, really, a deep chasm between history and eternity. Lessing believed that finite history could never contain the necessary truths of reason, which God alone understands. Lessing has dug down deep in his ditch and widened it so that we are not only cut off from any kind of real truth but also cut off from heaven and anything beyond what our senses can directly perceive. We're earthbound, finite creatures who comfort ourselves by always seeking truth yet never being able to grasp it.

The problem is that we don't live in a closed universe where we always know for certain exactly what can or can't happen. We live in a universe governed by Einsteinian relativity—that is, "the laws of the universe are not an invariable script."[32] The way the universe works is not set in stone. We work with generalizations based on our observations of what occurs in the world around us. History has shown how foolish we look when we grandly say "this must be" or "this must not be" without gathering all the facts about *what actually is*. Let's look at one such example and explore what this means for Lessing's axiom.

The duck-billed platypus has fascinated the world for over two hundred years. If you've never seen a duck-billed platypus, I want you to stop reading this and go look up an image of one (and no, Perry from *Phineas and Ferb* doesn't count!). They are, in my opinion, some of the cutest and strangest looking animals in the known world. Platypuses reside near lakes and streams in eastern Australia. To quote the Oxford dictionary, they are "semiaquatic egg-laying mammal[s] [with] [sensitive, pliable bills] shaped like that of a duck, webbed feet with venomous spurs, and dense fur."[33] A mammal with webbed feet? That lays *eggs*? Preposterous!

That's what the world thought in 1798 when the first platypus skins reached Britain. Its fur, flat beak, and webbed feet were so utterly bizarre that "many in London dismissed the skin as a farce and said the platypus was a hoax."[34] The next year, naturalist George Shaw published a description of the animal in *The Naturalists Miscellany*, vol. X—but Shaw himself was perplexed by this new creature, saying:

> On a subject so extraordinary as the present, a degree of sceptism is not only pardonable, but laudable; and I ought perhaps to acknowledge that I almost doubt the testimony of my own eyes . . . yet must confess that I can perceive no appearance of any deceptive preparation. [Nor] can the most accurate examination of expert anatomists discover any deception in this particular.[35]

The final blow came when European scientists heard the rumors from the native Australian people: the platypus could lay *eggs*. That was the height of absurdity, and obviously the platypus was an elaborate phony based on primitive legends. No self-respecting zoologist could believe such nonsense.

Nearly sixty-five years later, in 1864, in Woods Point, Victoria, a platypus in captivity laid two eggs. Later (or, as some accounts suggest, earlier) dissections of unfortunate platypuses confirmed it: the platypus, the duck-billed mammal with webbed feet, could in fact lay eggs.[36]

Well, that's that, right? That's all very interesting, but what does any of this have to do with infinity, the finite, and apologetics? Sir Norman Anderson, an eminent law professor, explains:

> Great minds refused to accept the platypus' existence and others doubted the claims about what it could do. The problem was

> it did not fit some people's view of how the world operated, so they rejected it and they reached their verdict *even though the weight of evidence said otherwise.* Now the platypus, the animal many said could not be, can be viewed in any Australian zoo.[37]

Instead of going with the facts, some scientists stubbornly held to their presupposed ideas of how things *should* be. Mammals don't nose around riverbanks with duck bills and pad through slimy mud on webbed feet—and they *certainly* don't lay eggs.

Saying the finite cannot contain the infinite is like saying that mammals don't lay eggs. We can't say that the finite cannot contain the infinite in the absence of facts to the contrary—remember way back in unit one, I termed this an "argument from ignorance"—and facts for it abound, as we shall see. You can reject the evidence because it doesn't fit in with your worldview and remain in the dark, but you do so at your own peril. The stakes for Lessing's claim are a bit higher than that of the platypus. If you reject that platypuses are real, you'll most likely only deal with humiliation and teasing from those in the know. If you reject that *the infinite* became finite, you'll have to accept eternal consequences.

The great detective Sherlock Holmes said it best: "When you have eliminated the impossible, whatever remains, however improbable, must be the truth."[38] Holding to outdated notions of reality has kept people in scientific, historical, and spiritual darkness throughout the ages. Lawyers and historians—and apologists—know that sometimes reality is unexpected, unlooked for, and unconventional, but "after careful examination we have to go with the facts even if they support something unusual."[39]

And just what is this "something unusual"? Nothing less than the bridge across Lessing's Ditch—revealed, incarnate, and verified in real history.

The Bridge over Troubled Waters

Lessing was right.

Does that statement surprise you? So far I've discussed issues with his ditch and his conflicting view of truths. We've seen the perils of rejecting historical evidence and what happens when we make claims based on personal feelings instead of on facts. Yet, for all that, Lessing understood that there was a great divide in his life.

Lessing was a lonely man who struggled with depression, anxiety, and intense general fear about his health and life (something called *hypochondria*).[40] For all his academic swagger and intellectual ability, he was a man who desperately wanted certainty, security, and the knowledge that his life had meaning. His desperate adherence to his personal spirituality, which he claimed was summed up in the sentence "Little children, love one another," seems also to be the plea of a young child yearning to be loved by his father.[41] For all his tough-minded writings, Lessing was in many ways a tender-minded soul who longed for purpose, meaning, and certainty in a world that seemed so dark and devoid of love.

Many people today feel the same way. History, they say, has nothing to offer us but cold, dead, unfeeling facts, most of which are probably a pack of lies (or, at the very least, grossly biased) anyway. It may be interesting, but it's not of much spiritual use to us. Popular spirituality is personal, passionate, and vibrant—everything that history isn't.

Yes, Lessing was right. Modern-day agnostics, those who think that truth is unknowable, get part of the story right too. There *is* a gap between the finite and the infinite, between *truth* and our experience. Christianity has a different sort of name for this great divide: sin.

Sin is the ditch that divides sinner from Creator, finite from infinite. Lessing exhausted himself trying to leap across the divide only to fail again and again. We, too, fall into the pit of despair if we attempt to leap across the divide to touch the face of God. It can't be done. The gap between us is, in essence, a divide between two separate worlds.

Perhaps this is what C. S. Lewis had in mind when he wrote the following exchange in *The Voyage of the Dawn Treader*. Lucy, the youngest of the Pevensie children to have visited Narnia, has suddenly realized that she will never be able to return to this beloved country. There is a separation between her world and the world of the Great Lion Aslan.

> "Oh, Aslan," said Lucy. "Will you tell us how to get into your country from our own world?"

> "I shall be telling you all the time," said Aslan. "But I will not tell you how long or how short the way will be; only that it lies across a river. But do not fear that, for I am the great Bridge Builder."[42]

Is there a way from history to eternity, from the finite to the infinite? Yes, there is a Way.

Years before you were born, a musical duo named Simon and Garfunkel released a hit song called "Bridge over Troubled Water." Maybe you've heard it—it has been covered by musicians ranging in style from Elvis to Celtic Woman. The chorus finds the singer comforting his "silver girl" that he will stay by her when all else fails. "Like a bridge over troubled water, I will lay me down," he sings, meaning that he will be the solution to the darkness and uncertainty of the world around her. He will help her get through the troubled times in life to the shining dreams she so ardently desires.

From Lessing to Elvis to today's tender-minded seeker, the desire stays the same. The Ditch is there, but the dream is that there is a way across it, a way to know for certain that there actually *is* a shining Grey Haven, as Tolkien named his Elven paradise, and that there is a way we can actually reach it. No human love, no matter how sincere, could bridge that divide.

And so God sent us His Son not only to reach us poor sinners huddled on the far side of the Ditch but to Himself be the bridge by which we can be welcomed into the Father's presence. Immanuel shocked the sensible intellectuals of the ancient world by choosing to become man, born of a virgin. The infinite chose to clothe Himself in finite form, not to urge us to more sincerely tolerate one another, but in order to reconcile a broken world that He so desperately loves. The point of history is not focused on us and our imperfect loving of one another but on the ultimate act of love our Savior performed on Calvary's cross.

Christianity is founded entirely on one historical, testable truth claim: the resurrection of Jesus Christ.[43] Investigate the evidence. We're not asking if it's possible for the finite to contain the infinite. We're asking if it *happened* in the incarnation of God in Jesus. Test the claims of the New Testament authors, cross-examine the witnesses, and examine the facts for yourself.[44] Absolute certainty is possible—but not by analytical means. Dr. Montgomery offers the following explanation, a fitting closing for this section on history:

> Absolute proof of the truth of Christ's claims is available only in personal relationship with Him; but contemporary man has every right to expect us to offer solid reasons for making such a total commitment . . . We must present clear testimony to the Thomases and to the Stoics of our day that God did indeed come in the flesh and "showed himself alive after his passion by many infallible proofs" (Acts 1:3).[45]

Lessing's Ditch is real. Glory be to Jesus that He chose to enter our reality and reveal infinity to us, becoming our bridge to the Father and the final answer to all troubled waters.

Assignments and Discussion Questions

1. Read through one or all of the following and examine the historical tests that can be applied to Christianity. How does this fit with Lessing's Ditch? How does this fit with the history curriculum you are currently using?
   a. *History, Law, and Christianity*: at least chapters 1–5
   b. *The Defense Never Rests*: at least chapters 6–8
   c. *Religion on Trial*: at least chapters 4 and 5
2. Choose one aspect of historical apologetics that interests you and write a paper or create a presentation on it. Maybe it's Lessing's Ditch, or maybe it's researching how historians investigate truth claims. Choose something that you want to know more about. Use the resources at the end of this section as a starting point, but don't stop there!
3. Investigate the impact of Lessing's Ditch on our postmodern society. That's not as scary an assignment as it sounds! Do some research and reading, then role-play with a friend or teacher. One of you will be "Lessing" (or a postmodernist) and one of you will

be the "apologist." If you're playing Lessing, your job is to bring up objections; if you're playing the apologist, you need to respond appropriately. Once you've got the hang of it, switch roles. Was it harder to play one role than another? Why or why not?

   a. Pertinent reading:
      i. *Understanding the Times* (chapter 17)
      ii. *Postmodern Times* (pick out sections with your teacher)
      iii. *Finding Truth* (all of it is relevant; with your teacher, perhaps start with chapters 1 and 2)

4. Read the essay "A Vote of Thanks to Cyrus" by Dorothy Sayers. How does "compartmentalizing" history harm our apologetic task? In what ways can we treat history holistically in apologetics *and* in our everyday life?
5. Think of the platypus example that I discussed earlier. What other examples of someone believing that something *cannot* be true (only to be proved wrong later) can you think of? With your teacher's help, find a mystery story to read (*Nancy Drew*, *Encyclopedia Brown*, or any of the *Cam Jansen* mysteries would be a good choice). In what ways is apologetics like a detective story?
6. How has Lessing's Ditch been used by well-meaning Christians who think we *shouldn't* do apologetics? How has it influenced their argument that you can't argue someone into believing or that you can't provide evidence for miracles?

Unit Resources: History

As with all sections, parents and teachers are encouraged to read along with their child and to review materials for age-appropriate content. Some content, especially material concerning postmodernism, will contain themes that might be too mature for some students.

Beechick, Ruth. *Adam and His Kin.* Pollock Pines: Arrow Press, 1990.

Rationale: A unique read that weaves together history in a lyrical style, blurring the lines between literary prowess and historical knowledge. Especially helpful for encouraging the mind-set that history is not dull, boring, and lifeless and that "Bible characters" did not live in a box cut off from the rest of history.

Clifford, Ross. *Leading Lawyers' Case for the Resurrection.* Edmonton: Canadian Institute for Law, Theology, and Public Policy, 1996.

Rationale: A good survey of legal apologetics from prominent authors in the field. Note that a newer version (updated in 2015) is now available.

Montgomery, John Warwick. *History, Law, and Christianity.* Edmonton: Canadian Institute for Law, Theology, and Public Policy, 2002.

Rationale: An excellent resource detailing the historical evidences for Christianity. Note that this book was updated and reissued in 2015.

———. *The Shaping of America.* Minneapolis: Bethany House, 1981.

Rationale: A survey of American heritage that is, to quote the back cover of the 1981 edition, a "readable yet scholarly assessment of what makes an entire nation tick, and how the ticking began." Some of the reading may be beyond the ken of younger students, but it is an in-depth exposition that, with the help of a discerning parent, may be a good resource for those who wonder *why* our country is in the state it is in—and what can be done about it. The chapter on Enlightenment thinking may be especially helpful for a refresher on what it was and why it matters.

Parton, Craig. *The Defense Never Rests: A Lawyer among the Theologians.* St Louis: Concordia, 2015.

Rationale: Chapters 6, 7, and 8 deal directly with legal and historical apologetics. If your child reads nothing else from this resource list, at least have him read these sections—and read them with him. The second edition of this book (published in 2015) is now available.

———. *Religion on Trial.* Eugene: Wipf & Stock, 2008.

Rationale: See especially chapter 4, "Christianity on Trial," for an excellent summary of the bibliographical, internal evidence, and external evidence tests.

Pearcey, Nancy. *Finding Truth*. Colorado Springs: David C. Cook, 2015.

Rationale: See its description under Unit One Resources for more information.

Sayers, Dorothy. *The Whimsical Christian*. First Collier Books Edition. New York: Macmillan, 1987.

Rationale: This wonderful volume contains eighteen essays by one of the truly great female apologists. All are worth reading, but if nothing else, at least read *A Vote of Thanks to Cyrus*.

A Note on History Curricula

For those looking for a unique, integrated way to learn about history, I recommend *The Mystery of History* series by Linda Lacour Hobar.[46] Sensitive Lutherans may find Reformed thinking and interpretations throughout, but it is an excellent resource for a holistic view on world history.

For additional suggestions, consult pages 37–42 of the following:

Swope, Cheryl, and Heine, Melinda. *Curriculum Resource Guide for Classical Lutheran Education*. 2nd ed. CreateSpace Independent Publishing Platform, 2015.

Notes

1 Beechick, *You Can Teach Your Child Successfully*, 298.

2 Ibid., 296.

3 Ibid., 297.

4 Dorothy Sayers, *The Whimsical Christian* (New York: Macmillan, 1987), 53.

5 Ibid., 54.

6 Ibid.

7 Ibid., 55.

8 Dr. Ruth Beechick suggests that children write down questions that they want to investigate before and during history readings and instruction. This engages the child's mind more than simply providing answers to test questions. I encourage students of all ages to use this approach. See *You Can Teach Your Child Successfully*, chapter 16.

9 "History," *Merriam-Webster*.

10 Parton, *Religion on Trial*, 32.

11 William Bristow, "Enlightenment," *The Stanford Encyclopedia of Philosophy*, Summer 2011 edition, ed. Edward N. Zalta, accessed February 19, 2016, http://plato.stanford.edu/archives/sum2011/entries/enlightenment/.

12 Quoted in John Warwick Montgomery, *The Shaping of America* (Minneapolis: Bethany House, 1981), 48.

13 Ibid., 48.

14 Ibid.

15 Rolan Stromberg quoted in ibid., 48–49.

16 Ibid., 48–49.

17 Wilhelm Windelband, *A History of Philosophy: Volume II: Renaissance, Enlightenment, and Modern* (New York: Harper and Brothers, 1958), 420 (see also 439–40).

18 Ibid., 398.

19 Gotthold Lessing, *Lessing's Theological Writings: Selections in Translation with an Introductory Essay*, trans. Henry Chadwick (Stanford: Stanford University Press, 1957), 53, 55.

20 Ibid., 31.

21 Ibid., 30. *A priori* means "relating to or derived by reasoning from self-evident propositions," or something that is known beforehand simply because of the nature of the argument or statement in question ("A priori," *Merriam-Webster*).

22 Ibid., 31.

23 Ibid., 42–43.

24 Ibid., 52, 55.

25 Lessing's personal spirituality was based upon the supposed last words of John the Evangelist: "Little children, love one another" (see ibid., 58). He based many of his writings on the ideal of complete tolerance and brotherly love.

26 Parton, *Religion on Trial*, 29.

27 Ibid., 32.

28 Ibid.
29 Lessing, *Lessing's Theological Writings*, 31.
30 Parton, *The Defense Never Rests*, 90.
31 Ibid., 91.
32 Montgomery, *Tractatus Logico-Theologicus*, 109.
33 "Platypus," *English Oxford Living Dictionaries*, accessed February 19, 2016, http://www.oxforddictionaries.com/us/definition/american_english/platypus. Only the males have venomous spurs.
34 Clifford Ross, *Leading Lawyers' Case for the Resurrection* (Edmonton: Canadian Institute for Law, Theology, & Public Policy, 1996), 105.
35 George Agnew, "History of the Platypus," *Platypus Organization*, accessed February 19, 2016, http://www.platypus.org.uk/facts-history.htm#discovery.
36 Ibid.
37 Ross, *Leading Lawyers' Case for the Resurrection*, 105.
38 Quoted from *The Sign of Four* in Parton, *Religion on Trial*, 21.
39 Ross, *Leading Lawyers' Case for the Resurrection*, 105.
40 Hugh Bar Nisbet, *Gotthold Ephraim Lessing: His Life and His Works* (Oxford: Oxford University Press, 2013), 435.
41 Lessing, *Lessing's Theological Writings*, 58.
42 C. S. Lewis, *The Voyage of the Dawn Treader*, Harper Trophy ed. (New York: HarperCollins, 2000), 247.
43 1 Corinthians 15:14.
44 See the Resources and Assignment section for help.
45 John Warwick Montgomery, *Faith Founded on Fact* (Newburgh: Trinity Press, 1978), 40–41.
46 You can find more information at their website: http://www.themysteryofhistory.com/.

CHAPTER 2

Creative Writing

Subjects and Subcreators

> A novelist works not to cure a patient but to persuade a reader that for a moment he is not alone. Whereas psychiatry is to conduct the shipwrecked to dry land . . . fiction is to let him know that someone is swimming by his side.
>
> —Bernard DeVoto, *The World of Fiction*[1]

A Note to Instructors

I vividly remember one of the first "grown-up" books I read entirely on my own. I was surrounded by literature from a very young age and was blessed to grow up in a home where reading aloud was the norm, so it wasn't my first foray into the world of books—but it was one of the first times I had taken that journey entirely alone. I must have been six or seven—in any case, well under ten—when I read *Imprisoned in the Golden City* by Dave and Neta Jackson. The title page had a picture of a roaring tiger, and some of the illustrations frightened me, but I was determined to read it.

When I came to the last page, I remember sobbing uncontrollably. While the story of Ann and Adoniram Judson, missionaries to Burma, was not entirely happy, the ending was completely hopeful. I wasn't crying because the story was sad. I was crying because the story was *over*, because I wouldn't experience the novelty of the story I loved so much again—and because there was something about this book that I couldn't quite explain, a kind of melancholy that was brand-new to me. It was something like grief, but I didn't know what I was grieving. A loss of some kind, I knew, but a loss of what?

Maybe this sounds subjectively sloshy to you. Maybe you'd like to explain this away and say that I was tired when I finished reading the book, or I was hungry, or anything else. Children simply don't *feel* things like that. But I did. And I'm not the only one.

You see, someone far wiser than I named this haunting emotion that almost broke my childlike heart. The description is definitely not a sloshy one. Some things truly are so beautiful they would break your heart. It was, as C. S. Lewis explains, "an unsatisfied desire which is itself more desirable than any other satisfaction."[2] I was experiencing what Lewis calls *joy*—the same longing that made me want to cover my ears when an especially beautiful hymn was played at church.

> The books or the music in which we thought the beauty was located will betray us if we trust to them; it was not in them, it only came through them, and what came through them was longing. These things—the beauty, the memory of our own past—are good images of what we really desire; but if they are mistaken for the thing itself they turn into dumb idols, breaking the hearts of their worshippers. For they are not the thing itself; they are only the scent of a flower we have not found, the echo of a tune we have not heard, news from a country we have not visited.[3]

Over the years, I have experienced many things that have stirred this longing inside of me, this "fleeting glimpse of Joy, Joy beyond the walls of the world, poignant as grief"[4]—books, places, events, and sounds—but one of the greatest things I discovered was that not only did I *feel* these things, but it was *all right* that I did.

Perhaps I should explain that. In an apologetics handbook, the last thing good Lutherans expect to find is some kind of charismatic, touchy-feely essay on emotion. We don't dance in the aisles on Sunday morning, and we *definitely* don't base our religion on anything as flighty as human emotion. I'm not advocating either (although, truth be told, I'm not necessarily advocating *against* liturgical dancing, but that, as they say, is another can of worms). Lutherans are historically tough-minded souls who become uncomfortable if someone mentions "feeling" the peace of God or "sensing" His presence. Or, as one of my college professors remarked about a colleague, "She's German. She doesn't cry."

Yet there are those who can sense wild mountain heather on the breeze gusting down a bustling Chicago street. They're the ones sitting in a concert hall with tears streaming down their faces as the orchestra plays J. S. Bach—or the ones sitting alone in a basement, clutching a book and weeping. They know there's *something* out there, something that's missing, but they don't know what it is.

They are the tender-minded, the dreamers, writers, thinkers, and dancers. Of course they often have "typical" day jobs, even in traditionally "tough-minded" sectors (one thinks of law, the physical sciences, and medicine). Some even masquerade as tough-minded individuals in day-to-day life, and of course, most of us are not entirely tough-minded or entirely tender-minded. But that doesn't change the fact that they will be more moved by something beautiful than by something factual.

We need an apologetic that speaks to the heart as well as to the mind. We need some way to reach others with objective truth in a personal, warm, and beautiful way. Blaise Pascal, inventor and prolific writer, understood that all humans are born with this desire, this longing for something just out of reach, etched into their souls:

> What else does this craving, and this helplessness, proclaim but that there was once in man a true happiness, of which all that now remains is the empty print and trace? This he tries in vain to fill with everything around him, seeking in things that are not there the help he cannot find in those that are, though none can help, since this infinite abyss can be filled only with an infinite and immutable object; in other words, by God himself.[5]

This quote, incidentally, is often abridged as some variation of "There is a God-shaped hole in men's hearts that God alone can fill." St. Augustine, with eternal eloquence, simply states, "You have made us for Yourself, and our heart is restless until it rests in You."[6]

What can be done in the realm of tender-minded apologetics? How can we uncover this longing and provide a solution to it? One way is through creative writing, as I will discuss in the following note to students. This isn't the only way, of course, but it is a starting point. Storytelling has always been a part of human history, as novelist Edgar Lawrence Doctorow explains: "Stories were as important to survival as a spear or a hoe. They were the memory of the knowledge of the dead. They gave counsel. They connected the visible to the invisible."[7]

Humans have always desired to know that they are not floundering alone in the sea of life. If fiction's role is to let a reader know that someone is swimming by his side, the role of literary apologetics is to introduce a sinner to that *someone* who not only entered the ocean to save him but is continuing to carry him through the storm. This unit will provide a starting point for tender-minded apologetics.

As always, the resources at the end of this section will provide a springboard for further study, and I encourage you to look at them and select which ones you wish to investigate with your child. Use this section in tandem with whatever curriculum or plan you are currently using to introduce your child to literature and writing. I'm of the opinion that in order to learn how to write, children should read not books on how to write (at least, not exclusively) but books of varying genres, descriptions, and lengths subject to their maturity levels.

A word of warning: don't turn reading into a chore, and don't have your child analyze every book she reads! It is important for the development of discernment that your child learns to think critically, but there's no quicker way to kill the curiosity of a young mind than to load it down with book reports on a subject that's duller than dirt. Strive to creatively incorporate this section into your current literature or English curriculum. Writing alternative endings to stories and discussing books aloud work wonderfully for some children. Others would prefer to draw storyboards or act out their stories. You know what works for your child. Mold this section to your child, as Dr. Beechick would say—not the other way around!

A Note to Students

There's something about a good story that sticks with you. Even if you're not a huge fan of reading, we can all remember a story—in a book, movie, television show, or old-fashioned radio drama—that affected us in some way. Did you know that stories can be a powerful apologetic to the tender-minded? Did you know that they can mirror an even deeper story that is beautiful beyond our wildest dreams?

Our postmodern society has sky-rocketed subjectivity to new heights. The idea that something is "true for you but not for me" is everywhere in our culture. There are even people who shrink back from cold, hard science, blaming it (and anything that claims to be "objectively" true) for "pollution, depersonalization," and all sorts of other social ills.[8] The tender-minded soul is not interested in the facts of Christianity or whether it is objectively sound but in seeking personal meaning for life, suffering, and the entire human experience. People will search for meaning just about anywhere (in illegal activity, through meditation, and by test-driving various religions). Is there a way that we can help them discover the *truth?*

That's what we will investigate in this section. Out of necessity, we will focus on one aspect of "the arts" for our purposes: creative writing. At this point, you are probably having one of two reactions. You are either jumping up and down in joy or running away in terror—or, if you're not quite that emotional, you're either pleased or disappointed, depending on whether or not you like writing. If you love to write, this section will (hopefully) foster that love. If you're not at all sure about this whole writing business, perhaps it can help you discover different ways of storytelling. Not all storytellers use word processors or pen and ink, you know! Some speak their stories, act them out, sing them, compose them, or paint them. This is only the tip of the iceberg for tender-minded apologetics. Don't be afraid to investigate other ways of going about this! I'll provide resources at the end of this section, as always. For now, let's see what goes into making a story—and how we can use that to our apologetic advantage.

The Storyteller's Spell

Apologetic approaches for the tender-minded, in one way or another, appeal to a person's imagination. The dictionary defines imagination as "the ability to imagine things that are not real: the ability to form a picture in your mind of something that you have not seen or experienced" and "the ability to think of new things."[9] Storytellers should not only have good imaginations themselves, but they should be able to enhance and support their reader's (or listener's, viewer's, or hearer's) imagination. In order to do this, they need a framework upon which they can construct their ideas—what renowned author Eloise Jarvis McGraw terms the "techniques" or "tools" of fiction writing.[10]

I attended a writing workshop with authors Dave and Neta Jackson when I was thirteen or fourteen.[11] They gave a simple four-word explanation of what constitutes a story that has stuck with me, partially because it's so fun to say. All writers, they told me, need a HSGA.

You read that correctly—a HSGA.

What on earth is a HSGA? Pronounced "his-guh," it's an acronym for the four key components of fiction. (Astute readers will point out that I could term this GASH, HAGS, or SHAG instead, and if that's easier for you to remember, by all means, change up the acronym. Personally, I think that HSGA is the most memorable.)

HSGA stands for "hero, setting, goal, and anti." These are the four components that all fiction *must* contain. A story without a HSGA is like a house without a frame—but what, you may wonder, does HSGA actually look like out in the real world?

Every story needs to have a *hero*. As we'll see later in this section, this doesn't necessarily mean the typical "good guy." When we use the term "hero" in the broadest sense, we mean the main character (or characters) that a story follows. We can also mean a character who sweeps in to save the day. For example, in *The Lion, the Witch, and the Wardrobe* by C. S. Lewis, we can see that Lucy is one of the main characters, along with the other Pevensie children. There isn't always simply one hero in a story, and sometimes the main hero is not the most obvious character. Think of the Great Lion Aslan, who is (to say the least!) an extremely important figure. In many ways, he is the true *hero*—the true focus of the story and the one who makes all things right.

The "setting" of a story is the environment (or environments) in which it takes place. In *The Lion, the Witch, and the Wardrobe*, there are two main settings—our world and Narnia—and countless sub-settings such as the Beavers' house and the Stone Table. In addition to the environment, time is also an important part of the setting. For the Pevensies in our world, the year is in the 1940s. This is important because it's wartime in England, and the children need to be evacuated from the bombings in the city to a home in the country. If the setting were different, the story itself would change. If Lucy's life were already perfect, would she be as willing to enter into Narnia? Would her motivation change? If the wardrobe weren't in a secluded country mansion but in a bustling city museum, how would the heart of the story change? Far from being a mere green-screen background, the setting of a story plays a truly vital role in creating the mental and emotional pull of a book.

All stories have at least one "goal," or something that the *hero* needs to accomplish. Many times a story will have subgoals built into it too. In *The Lion, the Witch, and the Wardrobe*, Edmund feels that he must convince his siblings to come to Narnia to meet the White Witch. Lucy thinks that she must save Mr. Tumnus and, eventually, Edmund. And Aslan, well, he has his own goal—a far deeper magic than the children could ever dream. The *goal* of the character is usually tied up with his or her purpose in life and, more often than not, this leads the reader to experience a taste of what it feels like to achieve that goal. Perhaps, as Lewis suggests in *The Last Battle*, the reason we love certain stories so much is that they give us a hint of the fulfillment we are—consciously or unconsciously—seeking in our own lives.

This brings us to the "anti," which is anything that prevents the *hero* from reaching the *goal*. This can be environmental challenges (deep snow or, when the spring finally touches Narnia, the lack of snow for the White Witch's sledge!), mental or emotional conflicts, or a villain figure. What antis can you identify in *The Lion, the Witch, and the Wardrobe?* Can you begin to see how an *anti* is a necessary part of fiction? Without it, there's no gripping story. We'd just be reading a bunch of sentences strung together. Earthly fiction needs conflict—and perhaps there's a correlation to be drawn between fiction and our own lives, as well. The higher the stakes in the storyworld, the more opportunities the author has for drawing in and captivating the reader.

There you have it—a brief overview of HSGA! Some people would say that this is a simplistic view of writing. To some extent, they would be right. For example, the *anti* category could be expanded to encompass the three *c*'s—namely, "conflict, complications, and crisis."[12] The reason HSGA works, however, is because it's simple. It's easy to remember. We've come across another acronym in this handbook: do you remember MESH-AGE? It stands for "man, evil, salvation, history, authority, God, and ethics"—the seven points that any worldview has to address in some way. How does this tie into HSGA?

All stories must have at least one character. In HSGA, I term this character a *hero*. In MESH-AGE, *God* and *authority* could fit into this category. God is not a nebulous concept but a triune deity who is the only source of good. The Second Person of the Trinity, Jesus Christ, is the Word made flesh, who not only put His stamp of approval on the Bible but is Himself the fulfillment of all its prophecies.

Are all heroes in stories good? Not necessarily. *Antiheroes* blur the lines between what is heroic and what is villainous; "the usual good qualities that are expected in a hero" are noticeably absent in an antihero.[13] We typically think of heroes as knights in shining armor: brave, noble, kind, strong, and beautiful (inwardly if not outwardly). Antiheroes, by contrast, can be selfish, tormented, unsure, and may have questionable motives. Popular antiheroes include Katniss Everdeen, Anakin Skywalker, and, some would argue, Gollum.[14] As the name implies, an antihero is often at least part of the broader *anti* category.

This is reminiscent of *evil* from our MESH-AGE acronym and for good reason. They both recognize that something is wrong, that something goes against the way things *should* be. For the storyteller, this can be an antihero—or a villain, a snowstorm, a herd of cattle crossing the street—*anything* that keeps the *hero* from reaching the *goal*. Evil is whatever causes conflict, complications, and crises in everyday life—the role of the *anti* in literature. For a Christian apologetic, evil is anything that is contrary to the will of God. Remember the unholy three that I discussed earlier in this handbook: the devil, the world, and our sinful natures. All are sources of continuing evil. Man fits into this category. We are our own *anti*.

As much as we each want to paint ourselves as the valiant hero, a returning Aragorn or fearless Éowyn, we're much closer to the Dark Lord than most of us care to admit. We muddle around in our own lives and end up making things worse. A type of tender-minded apologetics (called the *via negativa*) highlights this fact, which I will discuss shortly.

How does the *setting* fit into the MESH-AGE paradigm? All stories take place *somewhere*—in dystopian America, ancient Greece, or on a faraway planet. Even if the story takes place entirely in one place (think of one-act plays), there is something about the place that makes the story work. History is the setting of the story of Christianity. God chose to inspire human minds to write the Bible in a language we could understand; Jesus became man and lived, breathed, and walked on the earth at a specific place and time in human history; and history is vitally important to understanding the human condition, as I've explored in a previous section.

That just leaves us with the *goal* and our two final MESH-AGE components: *salvation* and *ethics*. These three have much more in common than a passing glance would suggest. You see, *salvation* implies that there is something from which *we must be saved*. This may seem painfully obvious, but if there is no *evil*, there is no need for—or anticipation of—*salvation*. If there is no *anti*, there is not going to be a climax leading to the end of the story.[15]

Throughout history, ethical theories have offered competing views on what is proper behavior. For example, how many wives should you be able to marry—and may only a man marry a woman, or may a woman marry a woman? How should a husband treat his wife?[16] Why do we behave in a certain way and not in another? Why do we even want to?

You see, not following an ethical code has consequences. In some societies, those consequences can mean going to jail, being shunned, or losing some kind of privilege (perhaps a driver's license). Dr. Montgomery explains that "if the consequences of the moral acts are removed, their moral character disappears."[17] We're very quick to point out when others are behaving "unethically," because we want them to be punished. We're much less eager to point out our own ethical shortcomings. What happens when we fail ethically? We've broken something seemingly sacred, and someone has to pay the price: pay the fine, serve the sentence in jail, or otherwise make restitution. I've described that we are in many ways our own *antis*. If we've added to the *evil* (*anti*) by acting unheroically, we've pushed ourselves further from our *goal*.

What is the *goal*, though? Most people will tell you that it's "being happy" or "staying true to yourself." There are all sorts of ways people try to achieve the *goal*: through relationships, hobbies, jobs, and countless other things. The tender-minded world is desperate for something that provides it with meaning and hope. Now that we've examined how MESH-AGE interacts with HSGA, let's investigate more deeply just what we're supposed to make of all this—and how we can reach out to the tender-minded through it.

Review

How is HSGA linked to MESH-AGE?

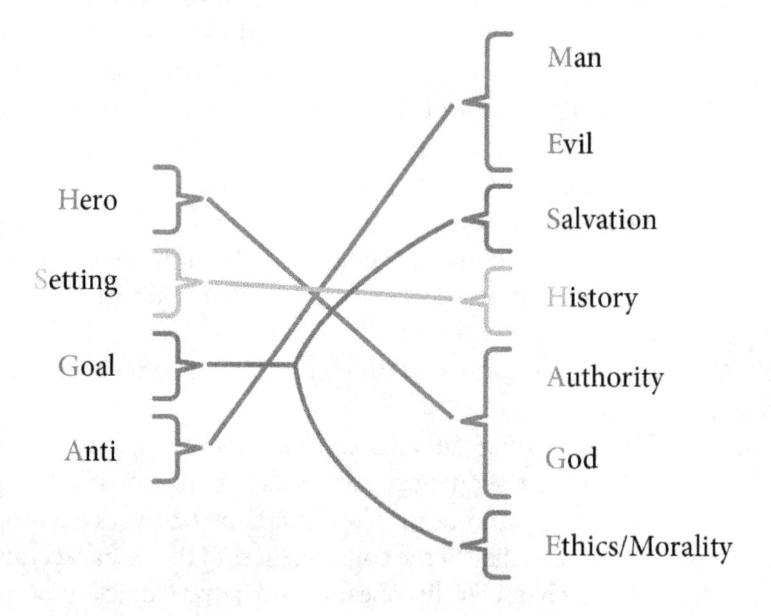

The Problem with Heroes (Hero)

> Without a weakness or two any hero will remain a [mannequin]; so will a villain without some trace of good. *And it is around one significant weakness of the main character that we can build a plot.*
>
> —Eloise Jarvis McGraw, *Techniques of Fiction Writing*[18]

I have discussed that, for Christianity, the *hero* is God—more specifically, the God-man Jesus Christ. The gospel is the beautiful story of how the *hero* came from the "blessed country" to fight *evil* and save those whom He had created—and those who rebelled against Him.

This poses a difficulty for Christian storytellers who want to reflect the *truth* in their stories. As Dr. Montgomery notes, "No literary character can in fact **be** the historic Christ, so the character's inadequacies and sins will automatically create tension with the biblical picture of the Savior, and to that extent reduce the effectiveness of the literary portrayal as an apologetic."[19]

If we create characters in *our* image, as it were, we are much more likely to produce monsters and demons than we are to give birth to saints and deities. Assuming, for the sake of argument, that we *could* create such a perfect character, we have an issue. The issue is named Marty Stu.

Also known as Gary Stu (or Mary Sue, if it's a woman), Marty Stu is an irritatingly angelic character who has few or no discernible flaws.[20] Marty Stu also "expresses the ideas, questions, personality, and morality of the author"—in other words, he becomes the poster boy for preachiness.[21] The character is so perfect, so well equipped for every trial, that he becomes unapproachable and unrelatable to your readers. Readers are especially irritated by "goody-goody" characters who are too picture-perfect. Don't believe me? Read critiques of *A Little Princess*, *Rebecca of Sunnybrook Farm*, and even the *Twilight* series. While some readers will tolerate Mary Sues or Marty Stus, many will become frustrated with a story and very vocal regarding their displeasure with it. (Ironically, this shows how twisted our concept of perfection really is. It takes a warped mind to be irritated by the straightness of perfection, because the mind sees it as something that it itself *should* be but isn't. It is, perhaps, a sort of literary jealousy on our part.)

Another issue with well-meaning Christian fiction writers is the overemphasis of the Christ image or Christ figure. Some people attempt to read allegorical (symbolic) meaning into figures when there is simply no symbolism to extract. Not *every* heroic figure is meant to mirror Christ. You can get into many strange situations—such as reading Christian symbolism into Winnie-the-Pooh, as entertainingly demonstrated by Frederick Crews[22]—if you insist on making mounts of transfiguration out of literary molehills.

How, then, are we to reflect, however dimly, the glory of a perfect God in imperfect literature? Is it even possible? Is it apologetically wise? Perhaps there is a way.

Archetypes and the Christ Image

There are things so deeply imbedded in human consciousness that they almost appear to be mystical. Regardless of what you think of psychology, there are recurring patterns and themes that can be found in everything from historical myths to a twenty-first-century student's dreams. It is astonishing how many writers report vivid dreamlives that transmit inspiration during a typical night's sleep.[23] There are "set[s] of images," or concepts, "that [seem] to capture the basic themes of human experience and universal human need" that occur over and over again throughout human history.[24] Twentieth-century psychoanalyst Carl Gustav Jung recognized these "fundamental and universal symbolic patterns" and termed them "archetypes."[25]

What are these archetypes that human beings seem wired to identify with so readily? One of the most important is the concept of the *hero* who is striving to do *something*, or reach some goal. Other common archetypes are the "Wise Old Man, Earth Mother, the Persona [the version of ourselves that we show to others], and the Witch or Trickster."[26]

Think about the truly great works of literature. J. R. R. Tolkien's *The Lord of the Rings* trilogy and C. S. Lewis' *Chronicles of Narnia*, for example, contain startling instances of the archetypes. Gandalf is almost a stereotypical wise old man. Jadis even has "Witch" in her title as the White Witch. Consider one of your favorite works of fiction, and one of the archetypes is bound to appear, regardless of the book's time period or cultural background. The idea of a *hero* claiming (or reclaiming) something, a victorious conqueror capturing the prize, exists throughout fiction.

How could we ever hope to present a *hero* worthy of tenderminded apologetics? Isn't it a hopeless cause, since readers *don't* want perfect characters, nor do we want to encourage Christ figures where none exist?

First, we must realize that, as was stated previously, literary characters *cannot* be Christ. They can reflect certain divine aspects, but we must be cautious lest we create a god in our own image. All analogies will fail at some point. Remember, we don't need to create a perfect character. We want to start the conversation with the tender-minded so that we can introduce them to Christ, the only perfect man. We're not trying to paraphrase the Bible or create a more easily understood religion. We want to get them thinking, not set up our own watered-down version of Christianity. We can prod imaginations into examining aspects of divinity, but for the real deal, we have to read the "real history"—that is, the Bible.

Consider C. S. Lewis' character Aslan from the *Chronicles of Narnia*. He is, perhaps, one of the most easily recognized "Christ figures" in literature, yet no Christian would say that Aslan *is* Jesus. He isn't. He does, however, reflect several key aspects of Christ's character that can help us understand more deeply who our Savior is.

Aslan is wild. Not in the out-of-control five-year-old sense but in the untamable, haunting beauty of someone who is truly free. He is wild like an Irish moor, a pounding sea, or a painted mustang galloping under a desert sky. He is, in the words of Mr. Beaver, "not like a *tame* lion."[27] He comes and goes as he pleases, this great Son of the Emperor Across the Sea. When Lucy timidly asks Mr. Beaver if the great lion is safe, Mr. Beaver replies, "Safe? . . . Who said anything about safe? 'Course he isn't safe. But he's good. He's the King, I tell you."[28]

This kind of power reflects a characteristic of the hero archetype. The idea that something (or someone) can be stronger than any other force is both comforting and terrifying. The eighteenth-century poet William Blake wrote "The Tyger" in an effort to understand just such a concept. How could something as violent and passionate as a tiger "burning bright in the forests of the night" have come to exist?[29] Something even wilder, more dreadful, and stronger than the fiercest tiger must have made the dread creature itself. But what could be more fearsome than a prowling tiger? Well, said Blake, the One who created it, since the tiger would answer only to Him.

Many people seem to want to cage the tiger and approach its Creator on their own terms. They want a safe, cherub-faced Savior who smiles benevolently upon all from his plush manger filled with glittering hay. A god who is completely understood or, in effect, "caged," is extremely appealing to humans. We like things we can understand, and we like things we can control even better. Sometimes we need to be confronted with the tiger's teeth so that we can understand just how small we are, how desperate our situation is. Author Gene Edward Veith Jr. explains:

> It is natural for us to want to save ourselves, to cultivate a spiritual independence and self-sufficiency, so that we can be in control of our spiritual lives. No wonder we have such a fondness for religions of Law, theologies of glory, which allow us to center on our own achievements, merits, and accomplishments. That we keep failing to achieve, merit, and accomplish what we think we should—however we evade our failures by rationalization or dishonesty—by no means alters the goal of spiritual self-sufficiency. In a truly evangelical spirituality, however, this attitude must be broken, so that we awake to our need and put our trust in Christ rather than in ourselves. In the Gospel, our sense of independence is replaced by a sense of dependence.[30]

You can't have Jesus on your own terms. You can't choose to cling to His eternal love while ignoring His holiness and justice. The tiger cannot be caged.

Our literary Christ figures will never measure up to the glory, beauty, power, and majesty of Jesus Christ. It's not possible. Tread carefully when creating Christ figures, and use human fallibility to your advantage. Even the most beautifully invented character will have flaws, but you can use those flaws to point to the One who was without sin. Don't try to cage the tiger; let the ferocity of God be, and strive to capture a blurry imitation of it in your writing.

Remember that you have other characters as well, who should be easier to create—flawed sinners that you can bring to life, different archetypes to interact, fight, and struggle through the story together. Does your hero have to be the character you spend the most time on? No, of course not. Can you get away without a Christ-image figure? Yes. Redemption, however, in art as in life, is hollow without a redeemer—just remember that a redeemer made of ink will never match a Redeemer who took on human flesh and dwelt among us.

Einstein's Gulf: Perfect Myth and Perfect Fact (Setting)

> Everyone has read fiction which possesses—and projects—a remarkable sense of reality, drawing the reader into its setting until it seems to him he is not merely reading about this place, he is *there*. He knows the very smell of the apples rotting under that old tree, the creak of boards on the sagging porch, the indefinable atmosphere of the main character's house—he is living totally in the character's world, and for the space of his reading it seems as vivid and tangible as his own.
>
> —Eloise Jarvis McGraw, *Techniques of Fiction Writing*[31]

The importance of the setting in storytelling cannot be overemphasized. A believable setting makes a good story a great one. A poor setting can kill the magic of reading with astonishing speed. Setting deals with physical location, time, and anything that can be experienced through the senses. How do we create a convincing setting that has any sort of apologetic weight?

Know Thy Setting

The setting must be real to you, the creator, before it can ever be real to your readers. Whether you are writing something set in modern-day America or a vaguely medieval fantasy world, you must know the details of the setting as well as or better than you know your bedroom, house, and city.

No matter what time period or planet you set your story, there are some things that are simply natural to humans: a sense of home, the fear of darkness, and the "orneriness of *things*" such as door-jambs on which to stub toes, hot water to spill on hands, and clothing over which to trip.[32]

How do we show our readers what the setting is like? For one, we can cash in on the five senses: sight, hearing, touch, taste, and smell.[33] What does that old castle smell like? What does it feel like to wear a spacesuit? Does water from the Fountain of Youth really taste like Cherry Coke? Let your reader experience the setting rather than just writing a bunch of descriptions that he will inevitably skip.

Now, you may be thinking that all this is just fine and dandy, but what does the setting of a story have to do with apologetics?

Eloise Jarvis McGraw brings up a fascinating device that she uses to make the setting of a story come alive to a reader. "It consists [of]," she says, "linking the universal-and-familiar with the specific-and-strange by placing them side by side."[34] She uses the example of inserting a dog into a story in ancient Babylon. The reader, who may feel overwhelmed by the extreme foreignness of it all (how they store their drinking water, their clothing, their speech, etc.), is put at ease by the presence of an old hound dog lounging in the courtyard.

Imagine you have just walked into a large birthday party for one of your friends, but you don't know *anybody* there. Even the most outgoing among us would feel a bit uncomfortable! Then you spy your friend weaving toward you through the crowd, and you're filled with relief. Finally, a familiar face in the midst of the chaos!

That's also what you want in apologetics. It's uncomfortable for sinful humans to think about things like perfection and punishment, and death and the afterlife are equally unnerving. We don't want to make the gospel *so* familiar that we change it into a fluffy, happy-go-lucky religion that floats in the sky like a cheerful haze; nor do we want to make it so inaccessible to people that, upon entering the party, they turn right around and head for home. We need something familiar for people to cling to. They need a bridge, some way of experiencing the unknown while still feeling safe.

Think about it. Aslan was a lion because the inhabitants of Narnia were beasts. That was their link, though he was the link for the children, as well, at the end. He reached out to them, came into their setting, their world, and shared their experiences.

When writing a setting, attempt to meet your readers where they are. Do the same thing in apologetics. The tender-minded soul's world is beautiful, sensory, and deeply personal. If you are to reach out to them with something that is universal and familiar, you must *know* what is familiar to *them*.

Remember that only one story can fill a universal and familiar need with a specific and strange answer. This is the beauty of the incarnation. Jesus Christ not only *linked* the familiar with the strange, He chose to *be* both. He chose to be man and God, to enter into a setting that all humans knew, and to become what we could never find apart from Him. If you hadn't noticed, humans can't shake Einstein's Gulf. It follows us everywhere like a shadow that's always just out of sight. There's only One answer to this divide, and literature is a perfect place to introduce the tender-minded to this.

This is what Tolkien meant when he said that "art has been verified."[35] The *setting* of our wildest dreams—and the bridge across it—is true:

> The Gospels contain . . . a story of a larger kind which embraces all the essence of fairy-stories. They contain many marvels—peculiarly artistic, beautiful, and moving; "mythical" in their perfect, self-contained significance; and at the same time powerfully symbolic and allegorical . . . There is no tale ever told that men would rather find was true, and none which so many sceptical men have accepted as true on its own merits . . . Legend and History have met and fused.[36]

The *hero* entered our *setting*, destroyed our *anti*, and won for us the *goal*. The more we can encourage a *setting* that mirrors our human condition, the more we can truly speak to deep-seated needs. The *setting* is analogous to *history*, after all. A fictional story deals with a history that never was, in an effort to reach a reader where he currently is. And our *hero*—Christ—appeared in real history, as C. S. Lewis so poignantly states:

> Here and here only in all time the myth must become fact; the Word, flesh; God, Man. This is not "a religion" nor "a philosophy." It is the summing up and actuality of them all . . . For this is the marriage of heaven and earth: Perfect Myth and Perfect Fact: claiming not only our love and our obedience, but also our wonder and delight, addressed to the savage, the child, and the poet in each one of us no less than to the moralist, the scholar, and the philosopher.[37]

Yearning for Paradise (Goal)

The idea of a happy ending is an archetype with deep roots in the human consciousness. Religious studies expert Mircea Eliade explains:

> At the "beginning" as well as at the "end" of the religious history of Man, we find the same "yearning for Paradise." If we take into account the fact that the "yearning for Paradise" is equally discernible in the general religious attitude of early man we have the right to assume that the mystical memory of a blessedness without history haunts man from the moment he becomes aware of his situation in the cosmos.[38]

In other words, it appears that there was some moment in man's history where the "yearning for Paradise" was fulfilled, because whatever man desired, man had within his grasp. Something must have happened, some unspeakable tragedy must have occurred, to propel ancient humans to desperately try to keep the memory of that beautiful utopia alive.

Why do these ideas appear across practically all cultures and throughout history? Why are the stories surrounding archetypes often so poignantly moving? C. S. Lewis offers an answer that is both simple and profound:

> The Christian says, "Creatures are not born with desires unless satisfaction for those desires exists. A baby feels hunger: well, there is such a thing as food. A duckling wants to swim: well, there is such a thing as water . . . If I find in myself a desire which no experience in this world can satisfy, the most probable explanation is that I was made for another world."[39]

This desire for paradise, so closely interwoven with the archetypes of literature, binds all humans together. Regardless of skin color, ethnicity, or gender, we find ourselves struck with the same nameless longing.

Eloise Jarvis McGraw says that stories end when a simple question is answered: "Does [the main character] get what he wants, finally, or does he not?"[40] If the character gets what he wants (or something even better), we say the story has a happy ending. If he doesn't, the story ends tragically. The theme of the story hinges upon the deepest desire of the character and how his longing is resolved.

The Christian apologist should be especially sensitive to this yearning. Themes of going home, reaching a safe haven, and finding fulfillment speak powerfully to a soul who knows that the world is not all as it should be. The pull of a "happy ending" is almost universal. Yet why do we long for it? Why should it matter?

Eucatastrophe: And They All Lived Happily Ever After

> The Birth of Christ is the eucatastrophe of Man's history. The Resurrection is the eucatastrophe of the story of the Incarnation. The story begins and ends in joy. It has pre-eminently the "inner consistency of reality . . ." It is not difficult to imagine the peculiar excitement and joy that one would feel, if any specially beautiful fairy-story were found to be "primarily" true, its narrative to be history, without thereby necessarily losing the mythical or allegorical significance it had possessed . . . The joy would have exactly the same quality, if not the same degree, as the joy which the "turn" in a fairy-story gives: such has the very taste of primary truth. (Otherwise its name would not be joy.) It looks forward (or backward: the direction in this regard is unimportant) to the Great Eucatastrophe. The Christian joy, the Gloria, is of the same kind; but it is pre-eminently (infinitely, if our capacity were not finite) high and joyous. Because this story is supreme; and it is true. Art has been verified. God is the Lord, of angels, and of men—and of elves. Legend and History have met and fused.
>
> —J. R. R. Tolkien, *On Fairy-Stories*[41]

A eucatastrophe is, in essence, the happily ever after so often desired in fiction and fantasy. In Tolkien's words, it is "the sudden happy turn in a story which pierces you with a joy that brings tears."[42] Just when all seems lost—when the conflict is too great, the crisis too severe, or the complications too deep—something changes. What once seemed impossible is brought near, and the *goal* suddenly comes within reach.

Imagine this: a *hero* unjustly slain, his beloved subjects scattered, his kingdom in the quiet grasp of despair. He was not strong enough, it seems, to conquer the *anti*. He has been conquered and now lies in a stone-cold tomb.

Eucatastrophes, it seems, tend to coincide with death of some kind. Perhaps this is because death is, as they say, the final conflict, the last crisis. Death is something that everyone must face.[43] It's the deepest fear of some and the greatest puzzle for others, and no matter how hard we try to explain it away to ourselves or to others, it's unnatural. Death is the killer of all goals, hopes, and dreams—you can't take anything with you when you go, after all. Death is the end.

Now imagine this: a *hero* who doesn't just sidestep death, but who experiences it, and who emerges from the grave fully alive. Death hasn't been cheated; it's been swallowed up forever. Its grip on the *hero* has been broken, shattered forever, and he stands victorious. Not only has he achieved the *goal*, but he has removed any and all doubt that he fully and completely accomplished his purpose. Nothing has been left undone.

It's the happily ever after that all the storybooks try to mirror. The prince saves the princess; the king returns; the lion makes all things right. We long for it because our lives are hurtling closer to our catastrophe every day. Every moment we edge closer to our deaths, when all earthly goals are cut off and cast into the grave—finished or unfinished. And if there's a goal beyond this life? We'll have passed the deadline for figuring out what it is and how to achieve it.

Even tragic endings point us to eucatastrophe. We are saddened by them because we realize that something's not quite right. That's not how it was supposed to end, we murmur to ourselves. And yet why not? Why should we expect any sort of happy ending? Perhaps because we're designed to.

The hopes, joys, and storybook endings stir in us a deeper desire than can be accounted for by mere psychological conditioning. Perhaps we see reflections in Galadriel's pool because there is something real above it. Maybe we cling to elven (or Dunadan) warriors because we long to be loved with an everlasting love, to dwell in the shelter of *someone* higher than ourselves.

A happy ending doesn't occur for some nameless, faceless character for whom no one cares—it happens to a character we know and have grown to love. In our quest to defend the great eucatastrophe of the incarnation (the resurrection), we must never forget that Christ lived, died, and rose again—yes, for the whole world, but also for you. For *you*. You are not a nameless face but a precious soul with whom the *hero* desires to spend eternity. Fiction can draw that deeply personal connection out, highlight it, and point to the risen *hero* who speaks our name as He emerges from the tomb—the same *hero* who will one day open every grave and call His saints to Himself in the great eucatastrophe to come.

Via Negativa (Anti)

> [There are] two vital ingredients of any story, *plot* and *character*... Now to make a plot you must have a *theme*; you must have at least one *character* in a situation of *conflict*. You must have *complications* which prevent him from getting what he wants, you must build the complications to a *crisis*, resolve this in a *climax*, and draw the whole thing to an *end*.
>
> —Eloise Jarvis McGraw, *Techniques of Fiction Writing*[44]

The *anti*, as I've already stated, is anything that comes between the *hero* and the *goal*. It contains *conflict* (between the character and "his situation, his era, his fellows[,] or himself"[45]), *complications*, and a *crisis*.

Conflict is one of the most relatable human experiences. It in many ways defines us, and there are numerous ways of reflecting human conflict in stories. One way of particular apologetic note is the *via negativa*, or "negative path."

> Here an effort is made to show that secular literary classics (1) depict the sinful, fallen human condition in exact accord with biblical anthropology, and (2) demonstrate that all contemporary secular ways of salvation are deceptive and unable to solve man's dilemma. By process of elimination, then, the reader is brought to a consideration of the Christian answer as the only, or at very least the most meaningful, solution to his fallen condition.[46]

Consider dystopian novels of recent history: *The Hunger Games* trilogy, the *Maze Runner* series, and the *City of Ember* books. Each of them shows, in their own way, the corruption of human beings and the very real presence of evil in the world. Since spoilers are somewhere between paper cuts and ingrown toenails in my hierarchy of evils, I won't go into too many details. If you're curious, read the books.[47] Suffice it to say, modern fiction, ironically, on some level recognizes that our human condition is in a sorry state of affairs.

The *via negativa* can also appear in apologetic works of fiction. Man's depravity apart from God is a hotbed of conflicting ideas—left to our own devices, humans are sadly overequipped to come up with all manner of dark and evil deeds, both real and fictitious. After reading *The Hunger Games* series, I remember being struck by how utterly hopeless it was. It presented a world where humans were entirely on their own and where even the bravest efforts to do the right thing fell shockingly short of the goal. Evil could take many forms—and not only in the way that was expected. "Good" was tinged with more than a shade of "bad." There was no one who did good—not even one. How utterly fitting for a series so blatantly devoid of any kind of transcendent deity—or any god at all other than the god of self-preservation.

Sin isn't pretty. The *via negativa* can serve to highlight our hopeless human condition, and writers should remember that sinful humans (or characters), when left to their own devices, generate enough conflict to fill up the world's store of history books (which, of course, we have). The problem is that once we recognize our depravity, we're very quick to "fit other answers into the empty space in [our] heart[s]" and "[imagine] the possibility of solutions for the human dilemma so realistically described in modern secular literature."[48] We've gotten ourselves into this mess, so we should be able to get ourselves out—or so we think.

And so we exchange one *anti* for another. We've swept the house clean of ugly demons just in time to let in the new tenants. Instead of *murder* we let in *hatred*. Instead of *violence* we let in *gossip*. For some, it's much easier to deal with demons when they look like angels—and it can be difficult to discern between the two.

Think of how many times in literature the hero or heroine is betrayed by a friend or discovers a hindrance that once looked like a help. Or consider how easy it is to identify evil "out there" as opposed to evil lurking and festering inside of you. The prophet Nathan, for example, when confronting King David with his sin, told him a story of a rich man and a beautiful little lamb. David, a former shepherd, was outraged that someone would harm—let alone kill!—another man's animal friend. Can you imagine his reaction when Nathan turned to him and said, "*You* are the man"? You, King David, are this hideous murderer.

So are we all. We are all murderers, liars, thieves, and dealers in dark arts, the very worst *anti* you could imagine. We're not alone, either—we have our cohorts of original sin, the devil, and the sinful world to provide backup.

Fiction is a powerful mirror. It can show the deepest, darkest parts of our souls that we'd really rather gloss over and forget. It can highlight how corrupt the world is, how crafty the great Adversary, and how lost we are. It can also reflect the immense need for a *hero* who is able to attain the *goal*. Whether it's by highlighting mankind's depravity or personal failings, the *anti*—like the law in doctrine, if you think about it—can be a truthful mirror into the hidden desires of the human soul.

Further Up, Further In

> It was the Unicorn [Jewel] who summed up what everyone was feeling. He stamped his right forehoof on the ground and neighed, and then cried:
>
> "I have come home at last! This is my real country! I belong here. This is the land I have been looking for all my life, though I never knew it till now. The reason why we loved the old Narnia is that it sometimes looked a little like this. Bree-hee-hee! Come further up, come further in!"
>
> —C. S. Lewis, *The Last Battle*[49]

Where do we go from here? The time has come for you to take the helm. The world desperately needs apologetics for the tender-minded, and this is a need that you can help to fill. Whether you long to write, sing, paint, draw, act, or dance, HSGA, MESH-AGE, and the allure of storytelling can start you on an exciting and timely journey in apologetics. Let me leave you with two pieces of advice.

First, read. Read a lot. Read any and every chance you can get, and read *good* books. Read Tolkien, Lewis, Chesterton, Sayers, and MacDonald. Read fantasy, detective stories, historical fiction, and biographies. Fill your mind with the "true myth" in the form of Bible study and catechesis. Practically anyone can teach you the technical side of writing (nouns, verbs, sentence structure, and the like); the heart and soul of a story is something that, for the most part, is unlearned and unteachable. This thrills the tender-minded soul—don't let it discourage you!

Second, write. Or dance, sing, or paint. Not because you think you should or because you want to preach at somebody, but because it gives you enjoyment and fulfills some nagging part of your heart. Have something unique to say, and don't be afraid to say it. Discover a character and plunk him down in the middle of a conflict. Sit back and see what happens.

This section is meant as a springboard to bigger and better things. It's meant to inspire you to delve into an area of apologetics that is so often overlooked and underappreciated. What moves you? Have you ever experienced anything so beautiful that it almost broke your heart, so wonderful that you almost couldn't stand it? *That's* your experience of joy, the echo of a eucatastrophe that was just beyond your full comprehension. Take that experience and run with it.

Fiction can be an escape from life and an escape to it. Fantasy, especially, is "in constant dialogue with reality both as it is and as it could or should be."[50] Stories have the power to influence the way we view the world—how and what we think, feel, act, and, yes, even believe. Fantasy can draw us further up and further in, where we can discover that perhaps we aren't quite as alone in the world as we thought. In stories, we find that as we dig deeper into myths, we discover not only that we have that joy, that longing for something outside of our grasp, but that we are in good company. We, like Jewel, suddenly find ourselves among our dearest friends—some unknown to us up until that point—running "further up and further in," deeper into the "true myth" that alone is the source of endless joy. And like the prodigal son, we find that our *hero* is racing toward us, nail-pierced hands spread wide, ready to greet us in the greatest eucatastrophe our hearts could ever imagine.

Assignments and Discussion Questions

1. Using HSGA, create a story (written, spoken, sung, or painted). Think about the archetypes I discussed and focus on capturing an essence of joy. Having trouble? Think of illustrations for each section of the Nicene, Apostles', or Athanasian Creeds, and either illustrate them or write something based on them. How is this a "tender-minded" apologetic?

2. Investigate the "literary" apologetics of J. R. R. Tolkien, C. S. Lewis, and G. K. Chesterton. A good resource is *Myth, Allegory, and Gospel*, edited by Dr. John Warwick Montgomery. How does each apologist use beauty to point to *truth?*
3. How does the liturgy in Lutheran churches provide an exposition on doctrine *and* a possible apologetic to the tender-minded unbeliever?
4. Now that you've investigated all four subject areas, evaluate a worldview in terms of MESH-AGE by incorporating the four areas of study. For example, how does a worldview's perspective of man influence its perspective of the arts? How does its view of evil influence its view of history? Keep at it and attempt to draw parallels between all of the seven areas! Note: You must evaluate a worldview other than the one that you personally hold.
   a. You can approach this in several ways, with your instructor's approval: you can evaluate the worldview of a fictional character from a book, movie, or TV show; or you can choose to go a more "traditional" route and do research on a documented worldview (e.g., Islam). Note that the previous statement is an *exclusive or* statement: choose only one of the options to complete! Once you have selected your method of research, decide upon a medium for presenting your findings. You could create an art project with a seven-pointed shield, labelling each section one of the MESH-AGE letters and drawing an explanation of how it ties into the seven areas of study. You could write an essay detailing the idiosyncrasies of the worldview. You could give an oral presentation, a dramatic performance, or anything else you can think of—with your instructor's permission, of course. Be creative.
5. Read the poem *Seven Stanzas at Easter* by John Updike. What is the theme of the poem? How can one fall into the trap of "mocking God with metaphor" as it relates

to the resurrection? How does this poem express a tough-minded truth in a tender-minded way?

6. Select one of the following poems to read and discuss with your teacher. Why are poems and stories good starting points for apologetics? How do the following poems provide their own unique apologetic starting points?
   a. *The Tyger* by William Blake. How does Blake describe the tiger? How does he use this description to elaborate on an aspect of God's nature?
   b. *Journey of the Magi* by T. S. Elliot. (Best for more mature students.) What is the death that the wise men ponder? What about this poem is most useful for apologetics?
   c. *The Temper (I)* by George Herbert. Are feelings constant or changing in one's faith life, according to the poet? Do feelings have a place in faith and apologetics and, if so, to what extent and in what way?

Unit Resources: Creative Writing

Investigate the following resources with your teacher. I also encourage you to pick your favorite fiction author and research him or her. What is his worldview? Can you find echoes of MESH-AGE in her books? What other resources can you think of to help you investigate tender-minded apologetics?

Lewis, C. S. *The Chronicles of Narnia*; *Mere Christianity*; *Surprised by Joy*; *God in the Dock*.

Rationale: Lewis is a masterful thinker, and his writings provide insight into many aspects of apologetics. Even if he doesn't use the terms "tender-minded" and "tough-minded," he addresses both types of apologetics and presents them in an honest and clear fashion.

McGraw, Eloise Jarvis. *Techniques of Fiction Writing*. Boston: The Writer, 1959.

Rationale: Scour websites and used bookstores for this out-of-print gem! McGraw has an excellent writing style and a gift for encouraging up-and-coming writers to learn, mature, and most of all, *write!*

Montgomery, John Warwick, ed. *Myth, Allegory, and Gospel.* Edmonton: Canadian Institute for Law, Theology, and Public Policy, 2000.

Rationale: A collection of essays that examine the literary apologetics of several noted authors, including C. S. Lewis, J. R.R. Tolkien, and G. K. Chesterton.

Pearcey, Nancy. *Finding Truth.* Colorado Springs: David C. Cook, 2015.

Rationale: See its description under Unit One Resources for more information.

———. *Total Truth.* Wheaton: Crossway, 2004.

Rationale: An impressive volume that examines worldviews, how we got where we are in our culture today, and the holistic nature of truth.

Pittenger, Tony. *Messiah: The Greatest Sermon Ever Sung.* Minneapolis: KnockOut, 2012.

Rationale: A beautiful work that highlights how truth can capture a tender-minded soul as well as a tough mind.

Tolkien, J. R. R. *The Lord of the Rings; The Hobbit.*

Rationale: No explanation is likely needed for these classic stories with beautiful themes!

———. *A Tolkien Miscellany.* New York: Houghton Mifflin, 2002.

Rationale: A must for any Tolkien fan, this book contains several lesser-known works by the master who brought us *The Lord of the Rings* and *The Hobbit.*

Notes

1 Quoted in Eloise Jarvis McGraw, *Techniques of Fiction Writing* (Boston: The Writer, 1959), 204.

2 C. S. Lewis, *The Weight of Glory* (New York: Macmillan, 1966), 18.

3 Ibid., 4–5.

4 J. R. R. Tolkien, "On Fairy Stories," reprinted in *A Tolkien Miscellany* (New York: Houghton Mifflin, 2002), 136.

5 Pascal, *Pensées*, 45.

6 John Ryan, trans., *The Confessions of Saint Augustine* (New York: Doubleday, 1960), 1.

7 Edgar Lawrence Doctorow, "Ultimate Discourse," *The Conscious Reader*, 10th ed., ed. Caroline Shrodes, et al. (New York: Pearson Longman, 2006), 394–96.

8 John Warwick Montgomery, ed., *Myth, Allegory, and Gospel* (Edmonton: Canadian Institute for Law, Theology, and Public Policy, 2000), 20.

9 "Imagination," *Merriam-Webster*.

10 McGraw, *Techniques of Fiction Writing*, 3.

11 Attempts to find published proceedings from this workshop were unsuccessful. Ideas in the following section were greatly influenced by Mr. and Mrs. Jackson, and readers are encouraged to investigate their works.

12 McGraw, *Techniques of Fiction Writing*, 22.

13 "Antihero," *Merriam-Webster*.

14 "Anti-Hero," *Literary Devices*, n.d., accessed February 19, 2016, http://literarydevices.net/anti-hero.

15 McGraw, *Techniques of Fiction Writing*, 22.

16 Parton, *Religion on Trial*, 7.

17 Montgomery, *Tractatus Logico-Theologicus*, 157.

18 McGraw, *Techniques of Fiction Writing*, 50.

19 Montgomery, *Myth, Allegory, and Gospel*, 25.

20 The term was first coined in 1973 in a *Star Trek* parody by Paula Smith. Several writing books and articles reference this, including Heidi Hood, "Avoiding a Mary Sue Character," *Book in a Week: Big Girl Blue*, last modified July 27, 2014, http://www.book-in-a-week.com/2014/07/avoiding-a-mary-sue-character.

21 Ibid.

22 *The Pooh Perplex*, quoted in Montgomery, *Myth, Allegory, and Gospel*, 24.

23 Examples of this abound. Though not particularly accessible to younger readers and filled with content that may be considered of questionable worth, *Writers Dreaming* by Naomi Epel claims to interview twenty-six writers on dreams that have inspired them.

24 Sean McDowell, *Apologetics for a New Generation* (Eugene: Harvest House, 2009), 100.

25 Montgomery, *Myth, Allegory, and Gospel*, 26.

26 McDowell, *Apologetics for a New Generation*, 100. There are, of course, many more archetypes that Jung and other psychologists have identified.

27 Lewis, *The Lion, the Witch, and the Wardrobe*, 182.

28 Ibid., 80.

29 William Blake, "The Tyger," *Poetry Foundation*, accessed February 19, 2016, http://www.poetryfoundation.org/poem/172943.

30 Veith, *The Spirituality of the Cross*, 62.

31 McGraw, *Techniques of Fiction Writing*, 134.

32 Ibid., 142.

33 Ibid., 134.

34 Ibid., 140.

35 Montgomery, *Myth, Allegory, and Gospel*, 118.

36 Ibid., 117–18.

37 Quoted in ibid., 30–31.

38 Quoted in ibid., 27.

39 C. S. Lewis, *Mere Christianity* (New York: HarperOne, 2000), 137.

40 McGraw, *Techniques of Fiction Writing*, 25.

41 Quoted in Montgomery, *Myth, Allegory, and Gospel*, 117–18.

42 J. R. R. Tolkien, *The Letters of J. R. R. Tolkien*, ed. Humphrey Carpenter and Christopher Tolkien (New York: Houghton Mifflin, 2000), 100.

43 Two notable historical exceptions being Enoch and Elijah.

44 McGraw, *Techniques of Fiction Writing*, 22.

45 McGraw, *Techniques of Fiction Writing*, 24.

46 Montgomery, *Myth, Allegory, and Gospel*, 21.

47 These books deal with dark themes and a fair amount of violence, so it's possible they may not be right for you to read at this moment in time. Check with your teacher first.

48 Montgomery, *Myth, Allegory, and Gospel*, 23.

49 C. S. Lewis, *The Last Battle*, First Harper Trophy Edition (New York: HarperCollins, 2000), 196.

50 Holly Ordway, "The Gospel as a Good Catastrophe," *The City* 8, no. 2 (2015): 66.

CHAPTER 3

Get Your Armor On

> [We] let our young men and women go out unarmed in a day when armor was never so necessary. We who were scandalized in 1940 when men were sent to fight armored tanks with rifles, are not scandalized when young men and women are sent into the world to fight massed propaganda with a smattering of "subjects"; and when whole classes and whole nations become hypnotized by the arts of the spell binder, we have the impudence to be astonished.
>
> —Dorothy Sayers, "The Lost Tools of Learning"[1]

Many individuals seem to think that apologetics is too advanced a subject to deal with in any meaningful way before a student reaches high school. Not only is this an affront to *you*, the middle school student, but it is something which, if left unchecked, can create serious issues in your faith life.

I'm sure you've heard before that life is a war zone. Whether we live in middle-class America or a war-ravaged developing nation, we all face spiritual attacks every single day of our lives. Satan is not some cartoon character hopping around in laughable indignation. He is a powerful force of evil, prowling about looking for someone to devour (1 Pet. 5:8). He is also well capable of taking the form of an angel of light (2 Cor. 11:14)—or as the thing that you desire most in this world.

This handbook has attempted to introduce you to both tough-minded and tender-minded apologetics. There is so much more that could be said, and it is my prayer that you will investigate the resources I've provided and continue to grow in the grace, knowledge, and truth of Christ Jesus. I want to turn your attention now to two challenges that you will face in your apologetics journey.

You see, I've discussed *how* you can do apologetics. I've discussed *why* you should do apologetics and *what*, exactly, we are defending. However, I haven't touched on *what happens* when you do apologetics—and how this can affect you.

I will tell you this: apologetics will change your life. No one is ever the same after embracing a serious commitment to defending the Christian faith. It isn't safe, easy, or convenient. Like warfare, it isn't glamorous or heroic. When you're under direct attack, you can't pause to wonder if you're ready to defend yourself and if you thoroughly understand every aspect of your opponent's attack before responding. By that point, it's too late. If, however, you strive to prepare yourself for any prospective confrontation *before* you're challenged, you may find it easier to provide a defense. You've already considered possible moves and countermoves, attacks and defenses, and you're ready to put them into action.

This does not mean that everything will go perfectly. Giving 100 percent of your effort into something does not mean that it will "succeed," especially if your vision of success is a Hallmark-movie ending. Allow me to speak more subjectively in this section and discuss with you some of the personal aspects of doing apologetics, what you can expect, and how to live through the aftermath of the defense.

Addressing Evil and Suffering

> The closer you get to the light, the greater your shadow becomes.
>
> —*Kingdom Hearts*[2]

The so-called problem of evil is a hot topic in apologetics. Dr. Montgomery summarizes it in the question: "How can there be a God who is both perfectly good (and therefore opposed to evil) and all-powerful (and therefore capable of eradicating evil), when the world displays the presence of evil on so many levels?"[3]

The problem of evil has been dealt with in numerous books and articles. It is most definitely a question that you will run across in the course of defending your faith, and it is worth understanding. It has, however, been addressed, and addressed well, in other apologetics materials (see the resources for a complete listing). Instead of rehashing old material, let's take a look at a different facet of the "problem of evil": namely, how it can hit far too close to home for the apologist.

Unbelievers aren't the only ones who ask "Why?" when something bad happens. The problem of evil isn't something that only the pagan world struggles against. We don't have to look any further than the book of Job to see that, yes, bad things happen to believers too.

Even Christians can fall into the trap of believing that the goodness and mercy that are to follow us all the days of our lives (Ps. 23) are intended to manifest as worldly success. Oh, many of us don't want the *typical* worldly goods. Many times we sincerely believe that what we desire is a *spiritual* good—and herein lies the rub. There are many spirits at work in our world who are eager to bring pain and suffering to all who bear the name of Christ. More on that later.

The Christian knows that God is all-powerful and also perfectly good. The apologist is able to address the problem of evil with unbelievers. Yet sometimes we are unable to address it with ourselves. It's often much easier to address someone else's suffering than it is to confront your own.

In our market-driven world, we expect actions to produce results. We make this assumption every day. Do you want a good grade? Study. Do you want to be an athlete? Train. Do you want to be a musician? Practice. Over and over we are told, explicitly or implicitly, that if we try harder or dream bigger, we will be able to meet our goals. The student will get a better report card, the athlete will make the team, and the violinist will finally master that selection from Vivaldi's *The Four Seasons*. And the apologist who ardently applies herself to study, prayer, and doctrine—what will she get?

Apologetics can seem deceptively simple. In fact, that's one of the criticisms I hear most often from other Christians who shy away from any sort of defense of the faith: "It's too simple. Life doesn't have quick fixes like that. You can't just present a five-step plan for defending the faith." This highlights a common misunderstanding about apologetics that can occur among apologists themselves: that apologetics is somehow the answer to more converts, more souls saved, and more battles won under the banner of Christ.

Before you rush out into the world, wide-eyed, optimistic, and overflowing with apologetic zeal, you need to understand the problem of evil and how it applies to you.

Our sinful natures have a way of twisting everything around to meet our supposed needs. In Greek mythology, sirens were mystical beings who drew sailors to their deaths with beautiful songs. Enchanted by the music, sailors steered too close to dangerous rocks and ran aground trying to reach the source of the songs. The "tempter" is the greatest and craftiest siren of all. He knows exactly what you desire most in the world, oftentimes better than you know yourself.

Think back to the section on creative writing. I discussed *joy*, the nameless longing that we all experience in unique ways. This same joy can be twisted into your own personal torment, the reef upon which you crash and break. Unbelievers and even fictional characters seem aware of this horrible irony. Consider the villain's chilling remark at the end of *The Hunger Games: Mockingjay Part I* film: "Miss Everdeen," he intones to our heroine, Katniss, "It's the things we love most that destroy us."

C. S. Lewis experienced deep darkness after the death of his wife, Joy. After his struggles with the silence of God in the face of despair, he made an incredibly insightful comment:

> Not that I am (I think) in much danger of ceasing to believe in God. The real danger is of coming to believe such dreadful things about Him. The conclusion I dread is not "So there's no God after all," but "So this is what God's really like. Deceive yourself no longer."[4]

Each one of us can identify with this statement on some level. For Christians who are experiencing the reality of pain and suffering, the fear can become not "There is no God" but "There is a God, but he isn't good." Oftentimes the more you grow in your faith, the deeper the darkness around us seems. History is full of strong Christians who struggled with despair—think of Martin Luther, C. S. Lewis, and Dorothy Sayers, just for starters. Unbelievers aren't the only ones who cry out to God, "Why?" And this, ironic as it sounds, can be a powerful tool in real-world apologetics.

Unbelievers aren't interested in hearing from cheerleader Christians who live in ivory towers and beam benevolently on the world. You're doing no one any favors if you bounce around acting like life is perfect the way it is and you have everything under complete control. It isn't and you don't. People, according to Craig Parton, are not impressed by displays of so-called personal piety.[5] If you're worried that your spiritual life is not up to snuff, congratulations. You're right. That's why your testimony, if used at all, should *not* be about how Jesus infused you with the power to become a straight-A student or to obtain other earthly successes. Your testimony should talk about your sin and the depravity and evil that rages inside you. If you puff yourself up with spiritual ego, people will write you off as just another prideful windbag. Honesty really is the best policy.

Evil and suffering will touch you. Sins that you do (sins of commission), sins of not doing things you *should've* done (sins of omission), and the fallen world around us will wound us. You will experience sorrow. You will question God—the psalmists did! There will be days when the knowledge that God is perfectly good and all-powerful doesn't seem like enough, and it is in those moments that Christ draws us out of our self-centered views to gaze upon the One we have pierced. Only in Christ can we experience the goodness and power of God; only in what seems like the most heinous crime ever committed to a man who appeared completely powerless do we see the glory of God.

When you address the problem of evil, whether in your own life or with an unbeliever, never forget that Jesus wept. So will you, many times throughout the course of your life. And when you do, take comfort in Jesus' simple statement: "In the world you will have tribulation. But take heart; I have overcome the world."[6] This victory over death is the only answer to all evil—Christ the only One who swallowed up death forever. Only here can the tender, bruised heart find solace and the keen mind something worth clinging to. Only here had God become a man of sorrows, when the fullness of time had come, and only here can the wandering heart and the searching mind find perfect rest and the healing of all harms.

Mourning for Jerusalem

> Then Jesus said to the crowds and to His disciples . . . "O Jerusalem, Jerusalem, the city that kills the prophets and stones those who are sent to it! How often would I have gathered your children together as a hen gathers her brood under her wings, and you were not willing! See, your house is left to you desolate. For I tell you, you will not see Me again, until you say, 'Blessed is He who comes in the Name of the Lord.'"
>
> —Matthew 23:1, 37–39

One of the hardest things in life is parting from someone we love. Whether it's saying good-bye to a visiting grandfather who has to return home to California, bidding farewell to a family friend who will be attending college in another state, or leaving a friend's house where you've been having the time of your life, good-byes are difficult. Movies and books capitalize on this and display gut-wrenching good-bye scenes: Westley and Buttercup in *The Princess Bride*, Frodo bidding farewell to Sam in *The Return of the King*, and the one-sentence, hollow farewell at the end of *The Hunger Games: Mockingjay—Part II*. Even thinking about those good-byes can cause our eyes to become a bit misty.

Apologetics can bring about some of the most painful good-byes you may ever experience. The reason many people avoid discussing "divisive" topics (typically religion and politics) is that it can lead to serious conflict. You see, religious beliefs are held by people. They're not disembodied concepts that we can deal with and expect to come out unscathed. The whole reason we need an apologetic (a defense) is because we're in the middle of a war, and no one—no one, friends—comes out of war unbroken.

One of the quotes that has profoundly impacted my life is a simple reminder of what we are supposed to be doing in apologetics: "We aren't called to be successful. We're called to be faithful."[7] If I can be permitted a pop-culture reference that will be obsolete by the time you read this, Aunt May reminds a discouraged Peter Parker of the same thing in *Spider-Man 2*: "Sometimes we have to be steady and give up the thing we want the most—even our dreams."

We are called upon to cling firmly to our faith above all else, and sometimes this means that we may lose friends. There are those who, upon finding out the depth and ramifications of your convictions, will no longer want to be around you. It's one thing to read about this, and it's quite another to experience it—but perhaps hearing that it may happen in advance can encourage you and, at the very least, let you know that you're not alone.

Koukl, whom we heard from in the section on computer science, offers this piece of advice: "If they want to go, let them leave . . . When the conversation becomes a monologue (yours), it's time to let it go."[8] In context, he is referring to someone with whom, it's assumed, you don't have a particularly close relationship. The same holds true, however, when you're speaking with someone who is very near and dear to you.

Does this mean that you should cut off all contact and only have upright, orthodox Lutheran friends? No, of course not—but if someone is so put off by your beliefs that he chooses to walk away from you, let him leave. How do you know when to walk away—and when to let someone go?

If someone keeps coming back to the same arguments or refuses to argue consistently using principles on how one lives everyday life, Dr. Montgomery says that it's time to walk away.[9] In the same manner, if someone says to you flat-out that she wants no more discussion, you've done all you can. There's nothing more that can be said that your friend is willing to hear. This is something that is very easy to read about and excruciatingly difficult to do. There's an immense difference between seeing words on a page and hearing someone you care about deeply say, "That may be true, but I can't accept it," "No more religious discussions," or "I don't care enough to look into the 'truth.'" When a relationship is on the line, it takes dreadful strength to cling to a faith that will drive a wedge between you and your friend. It will leave scars.

It's tempting to count these situations as abject failures. They feel like it. Remember, however, whose battle you're fighting. Victory belongs to the Lord, and "He will bring the next ambassador along to pick up where you left off."[10] As Koukl reassures:

> Do not be discouraged by outward appearances. Don't get caught in the trap of trying to assess the effectiveness of your conversations by their immediate, visible results. Even though

> a person rejects what you say, you may have put a stone in his shoe nonetheless. These things often take time. The harvest is often a season away.[11]

Now, this is all fine and dandy if you're dealing with someone you don't know very well. While the same encouragement applies when you're dealing with close friends, it feels radically different. Rejection from a stranger, while uncomfortable, is one-and-done. Rejection from someone with whom you used to be close is messy, and it's something that remains painful for quite a long time.

It can be a real temptation to water down your faith for the sake of maintaining friendships. "The desire to be accepted" by others, according to professor and theologian Gene Edward Veith Jr., "may be the most subtle and damaging temptation of them all."[12]

Being alone is one of humanity's deepest fears and sometimes it's one of the things from which grown-ups will try to shield you. Loss, however, is a part of life while we live here on earth. The reason I'm mentioning it to you now is because this is an often overlooked side-effect of apologetics. Truth brings division. Jesus Himself said that He came "not to bring peace, but a sword."[13]

Walking away (or letting someone leave) requires both a tough-minded adherence to the "uncompromisable" (what C. S. Lewis terms "mere Christianity") and the tender-minded assurance that it's worth it. It requires the realm of objectivity (what is true) to have incredible bearing on the realm of subjectivity (what truth means for me). This can only be found in the answer to Einstein's Gulf—Christ Himself. I can't equip you to not feel pain, but perhaps I can provide you with resources for healing after your battles.

There is a reason that the Holy Spirit inspired the writer to the Hebrews to record, "Let us consider how to stir up one another to love and good works, not neglecting to meet together, as is the habit of some, but encouraging one another, and all the more as you see the Day drawing near."[14] The church, Dr. Veith rightly notes, is an extraordinarily precious and terribly underused resource for the Christian.[15] When we attend our local church, we are expressing our unity of belief with others there and with the saints who have gone on before us. It is the hospital where battle-torn soldiers are visited by the Healer of Souls and the Captain of the Army.

There is no failure so deep, no pain so real, and no regret so strong that His forgiveness is not deeper, realer, and stronger. The Lord who knit us together in the secret places well knows our deepest longings, fears, and sorrows. Like a groom comforting an anxious bride, He visits us in word and sacrament. Will you find true friendship in your church? Perhaps. I pray that you do. But even if you don't, remember that we don't go to the hospital expecting other patients to heal us. No one can truly understand your pain except the One who looked forward two thousand years to you and your hopes, failures, and sins and who still chose to say, "I am willing."[16] He was willing to die the most gruesome death you can imagine so that, by His blood, you can be cleansed of all unrighteousness and sin—both sin that you have committed and the guilt and loneliness that accompany all failures.

Losing your soul doesn't always look like something evil to be avoided. Sometimes it looks like everything you've ever wanted: acceptance, comfort, love. When the narrow way grows narrower still, even the flames of eternal torment seem to offer us a guiding light through the darkness. Sometimes the thriving of the wicked and those who really don't seem all that bad entices us to focus not on the cross and the Desire of Every Nation but on our own hearts and our own dreams. C. S. Lewis said it best: "If you look for truth, you may find comfort in the end: if you look for comfort you will not get either comfort or truth—only soft soap and wishful thinking to begin, and in the end, despair."[17]

The *truth* that you are seeking is really seeking you. Like Aslan gently told Jill, we would not be calling to Him unless He was already calling to us.[18] Our Savior is a man well acquainted with every sorrow, every failure, and every battle-scar we try so desperately to hide. Use the resources He has given you—His word, the sacraments, the church, fellow Christians—and cling to the comfort that "this light momentary affliction is preparing for us an eternal weight of glory beyond all comparison."[19]

If Only in My Dreams

You have most likely heard it said that just because someone else—or everyone else—is doing something, that doesn't mean that you should. The example some adults are fond of quipping is "If everyone jumped off a cliff, would you follow?" What they mean is that if everyone was doing the wrong thing, something that would be dangerous for you, would you willingly go along with it? The implied answer is a resounding "No!"

I don't know about you, but that example often falls flat for me. I mean, come on—if my friends go cliff jumping, it would be into some glassy sea in the Caribbean and not into the rocky Grand Canyon. It's perfectly safe; people do it all the time. It looks fun, exciting, and validating. You would be somebody special if you did it. If you don't, well, you're just not brave, smart, or strong enough.

That's what it can feel like when discussing religion—and worse. If you don't go along with the crowd, or if you get in anyone's way, you're an outsider. And besides, the dreams most kids are chasing—the cliffs they're jumping off of into a serene ocean—aren't really all that ugly, are they? The books they're reading are pretty cool. The church my best friend goes to is way more fun than mine. Her boyfriend goes to a synagogue and they get along just fine, so what's the big deal with defending the faith, anyway?

You see, we have this expectation that if we do "the right things," good results will follow. Some people take this so far as to say that if you have sincere intentions, things will work out all right in the end. Follow your dreams! Be true to your heart! Surround yourself with those who love you! We've heard it before . . . but the difficulty is that dreams are very often not what we expect them to be, even if we all agree.

Consider the passage from C. S. Lewis' *The Voyage of the Dawn Treader*. In the midst of their quest for the missing lords of Narnia, King Caspian, two of the Pevensie children, and Eustace Clarence Scrubb (among others) come across a mysterious black expanse of sea. While traversing it, they pick up a bedraggled, wild-eyed stranger who urges them to leave at once. When asked what could possibly be so horrid, he responds, "This is the Island where Dreams come true."[20]

Immediately, everyone wants to stay. One sailor remarks that he would be married to his beloved on such an island, and another realizes that he would find his close friend alive again. Notice that each of these dreams involves someone the person loved very much. Their dreams of a loving relationship and that most elusive human longing for desirability and acceptance would be fulfilled—perfected, even—on such a glorious island. Momentarily, their quest to find the seven missing lords is forgotten. What other land could ever fulfill the deepest desires of their heart as the "Island where Dreams come true"?

Perhaps you, too, have experienced an island where dreams come true. Have you been in a situation in life where something you've wanted seemed to be in your grasp? Was it friendship, acceptance, some great athletic or musical feat, or perhaps the first awakenings of love? Here, at last, you think, is where you belong. However, this island can appear dark—it can be difficult to discern what exactly lies over the hills rising out of the sea. As the sailors in the book paused to ponder, the mysterious stranger, with staring eyes and a voice trembling with passion, breaks into their musings.

> "Fools!" said the man, stamping his foot with rage. "That is the sort of talk that brought me here, and I'd better have been drowned or never born. Do you hear what I say? This is where dreams—dreams, do you understand—come to life, come real. Not daydreams: dreams."
>
> There was about half a minute's silence and then, with a great clatter of armor, the whole crew were tumbling down the main hatch as quick as they could and flinging themselves on the oars to row as they had never rowed before . . . For it had taken everyone just that half-minute to remember certain dreams they had had—dreams that make you afraid of going to sleep again—and to realize what it would mean to land on a country where dreams come true.[21]

When people speak of dreams coming true, they imagine an island paradise full of light, love, and acceptance. They never expect a world full of their worst nightmares and deepest fears. Their dreams would come true, all right—but it wouldn't be in the way they expected.

Simply because everyone believes a thing to be true does not make it so. Tragedy results when we depend on the desires of our own fallen hearts or the best intentions of our fellow humans. Some of the greatest atrocities in our history have been committed by people *who were convinced that they were doing the right(eous) thing*. Think of the story of Paul, who actively persecuted the young Christian church based on an incredibly deep, passionate, and sincere belief. Supported by his fellow Jews, he sought to destroy others for the sake of his dream.

But we don't even have to go as far back as Paul. Have you looked in the mirror today? Have you examined the deepest desires of your own heart? Dear one, the world will tell you to set aside everything else and pursue your dream at the expense of your relationship with your Savior. What it won't tell you is that every dream that has not been redeemed, every melodious vibration of your heart that is not tuned to His will, shall lead to your eternal death.

This is why apologetics matters. If Christianity is true, Christ is *the* only way. All other ways are dark islands in a sea of changing cultures, no matter how beautiful they appear. Every dream to which we entrust our hearts will fail to save the true dream, the story of salvation that is both fully true and completely beautiful.

It is never an easy thing to see friends and loved ones eagerly rowing toward the dark island. The call of the world is strong, and our temptation is to join with them, to journey toward the dream together. Conversely, sometimes we believe that if only we can open our friends' eyes to the danger, it will suddenly and magnificently change them, and we will have won our friends back to us. Are we reaching out to our friends with the gospel—the truth—motivated by our deepest desire to be accepted, loved, and welcomed? Will we water down our defense if the waves become too choppy or if the island appears too beautiful? Or do we realize that we must stay the course even when others willfully ignore the warning?

Let me articulate what I have been talking around and about this entire course: it is not your job to be successful. It is heart-breaking when we fail—when we have proclaimed and defended our faith, and still we are mocked, scorned, and cast aside. The out-come is not in your hands. Your calling, by grace, is to always be ready to give a defense. That isn't an optional suggestion based on the likelihood of your success. It's a mandate that the Holy Spirit equips you to enact.

Circling back to the Chronicles of Narnia again, think of *The Lion, the Witch, and the Wardrobe*. Lucy's siblings didn't believe her when she first told them about Narnia. Her own brother, Edmund, even *after* he had experienced the land inside the wardrobe, refused to back up her claims. Again in *Prince Caspian*, Lucy spots the Great Lion Aslan in the woods and eagerly tells her siblings. They dismiss her, saying she must be imagining things. When Lucy next sees Aslan—at night, alone—he tells her that she must immediately go and tell the others that he has come. If they refuse to follow, she is to strike out after him—on her own, without her family.

That is the calling of the Christian. We are sent to a world that is dying of a disease it refuses to acknowledge: sin. After the proclamation of this and of the gospel, we are called to defend. We give positive evidences, clarify what we mean, and refute challenges to our faith.[22] And then, if we are rejected and prohibited from continuing our discussions, we are to follow the Lion of Judah regardless of who is or is not beside us.

I would encourage you to read (or reread) the Chronicles of Narnia again. C. S. Lewis was adept at tender-minded apologetics—and tender-minded support *for* apologists. Read the psalms where the writers question and grapple with suffering, evil, and confusion. Sit with Elijah under the broom tree and cry out with Ezekiel that God would make the dry bones within our hearts alive with Pentecostal fire. The battle is the Lord's and the victory is sure. Stand firm and see the coming salvation of the Lord.

Assignments and Discussion Questions

1. Investigate the "problem of evil" and how it has been addressed by apologists such as John Warwick Montgomery, Craig Parton, C. S. Lewis, and others. Find solid resources and build an assignment (whether writing, drawing, or acting) around it with your teacher's permission. How would you respond to someone who asks how a loving God can allow evil and suffering in the world?
2. Investigate apologetics resources—books, devotionals, and so on—that you can use within your family devotions, studies at church, or devotions with friends. How can apologetics fit into the continuing education of a Christian? What comfort is there to be found for the lonely in apologetics?

3. Would a tough-minded or a tender-minded apologetic be more welcome during a time of sorrow? Why do you think this is?
4. Read *The Last Battle* by C. S. Lewis (assuming you have read the other Chronicles of Narnia books—if you haven't, read the entire series!). Have you ever felt like Lucy did when she tried to reach the dwarfs in the stable (chapter 13)? How did Aslan transform perceived failures into good? Is our success in doing apologetics dependent upon the outcome of our interactions with others? What is the purpose of doing apologetics at all?
5. How can the trials that you face in your life actually help you in doing apologetics? Why is Christianity uniquely equipped to address mankind's pain and suffering (think specifically about Jesus as a man of sorrows)?
6. The great composer J. S. Bach ended his compositions with the letters *S. D. G.*, meaning *Soli Deo Gloria*—"Glory to God alone." Does God bring glory to Himself through broken things (or broken people) as well as through beautiful ones? Does this hold true in apologetics as well, and if so, how?

Notes

1 Sayers, "The Lost Tools of Learning."

2 *Kingdom Hearts*, video game, directed by Tetsuya Nomura (2002: Square, 2006), PlayStation 2.

3 Montgomery, *Tractatus Logico-Theologicus*, 153.

4 C. S. Lewis, *A Grief Observed* (San Francisco: Harper San Francisco, 1996), 5–7.

5 Craig Parton, "The Apologetics Task Today" (presentation, International Academy of Apologetics, Evangelism, and Human Rights, Strasbourg, France, July 8–9, 2014).

6 John 16:33.

7 Menuge, "The Apologetics of C. S. Lewis."

8 Koukl, *Tactics*, 191.

9 John Warwick Montgomery, "Philosophical Apologetics" (presentation, International Academy of Apologetics, Evangelism, and Human Rights, Strasbourg, France, July 8–9, 2014).

10 Koukl, *Tactics*, 191.

11 Ibid., 199.

12 Gene Edward Veith Jr., *Loving God with All Your Mind*, rev. ed. (Wheaton: Crossway, 2003), 98.

13 Matthew 10:34.

14 Hebrews 10:24–25.

15 Veith, *Loving God with All Your Mind*, 97.

16 Matthew 8:3.

17 Lewis, *Mere Christianity*, 32.

18 C. S. Lewis, *The Silver Chair*, First Harper Trophy Edition (New York: HarperCollins, 2000), 24–25.

19 2 Corinthians 4:17.

20 Lewis, *The Voyage of the Dawn Treader*, 183.

21 Ibid., 183.

22 John Warwick Montgomery, "Christian Apologetics in the Light of the Lutheran Confessions," in *Christ as Centre and Circumference* (Hamburg: VKW, 2012), 149.

Unit Three Review

Review Questions

1. What is Lessing's Ditch? Why did Lessing separate facts into two "truth categories"? In what ways do you see Lessing's Ditch still present in our society today?
2. What does it mean to say that "the finite cannot contain the infinite"? Why is this an unprovable (and irrational) claim to make?
3. What does HSGA stand for? How can it help us with the apologetic task we are facing?
4. What is a "eucatastrophe"? How can fictional and historical eucatastrophes provide us with ammunition for making a tender-minded apologetic?
5. What does it mean to be "successful" when doing apologetics? What is our goal in doing apologetics?
6. This unit was loosely based on a medieval concept of the transcendental "Beautiful."[1] How does beauty correlate to the concept of reasoning for (or about) something? What does it mean to "reason"? In what ways does beauty influence the way we reason? Why is this important for apologetics?
7. What was one surprising thing that you learned in this unit? Why was it surprising?

Vocabulary List

archetypes: As defined by Carl Jung, a set of concepts that are fundamental and universal symbolic patterns.[2]

eucatastrophe: As defined by J. R. R. Tolkien, "the sudden happy turn in a story which pierces you with a joy that brings tears."[3]

HSGA: The four main components of fiction: Hero, Setting, Goal, and Anti.

joy: As defined by C. S. Lewis, "an unsatisfied desire which is itself more desirable than any other satisfaction."[4]

Lessing's Ditch: The view of Gotthold Lessing, which states that since we can never achieve 100 percent certainty concerning the truth of historical claims, we cannot gain any degree of religious certainty from historical testimony of the life of Jesus Christ.

via negativa: The "negative path" in literature, which shows that sinful humans are utterly fallen, wicked, and unable to save themselves.[5]

Resources

The following are resource suggestions for finding support when you are experiencing the painful side of apologetics. As always, use this as a starting point—and don't neglect the help of Christian parents, pastors, and mentors.

Nonfiction

The Bible.

Howard, Grace. "Truth Detector." *WORLD Magazine*. Last modified January 28, 2012. Accessed February 13, 2016. http://www.worldmag.com/2012/01/truth_detector.

Rationale: I'm including this resource because it was an encouragement to me, and also because it contains a quote I have clung to through many a lonely day and night: "Leadership is lonely." Sometimes it's helpful to see that we are not alone in our loneliness.

Veith, Gene Edward, Jr. *Loving God with All Your Mind.*

Rationale: Although this book is written for a slightly older audience, it contains immense encouragement to the Christian who desires to think well. The third part, especially, reminds readers that they are connected to the eternal communion of saints—a wonderful reminder for battle-weary apologists.

Zacharias, Ravi. *Can Man Live without God?*

Rationale: Again, although sections of this book will be difficult for younger readers, it is a profound affirmation of the impact of Christianity on one's life.

Fiction

Adler, David, et al. *Cam Jansen Series.*

Rationale: Delightful detective series that will sharpen your critical-thinking skills.

Englemann, Kim. *The Joona Trilogy.*

Rationale: An imaginative fantasy with thought-provoking themes.

Keene, Carolyn. *Nancy Drew Series.*

Rationale: One of the most beloved literary sleuths uncovers facts and employs discernment in order to solve the most challenging cases.

Levine, Gail Carson. *Ella Enchanted.*

Rationale: An easy read that deals with themes of absolutes, magic, and consequences.

Lewis, C. S. *The Chronicles of Narnia.*

Rationale: Unquestionably one of the most beautiful examples of tender-minded literary apologetics ever, Lewis is a master at conveying archetypes that touch both the mind and the heart.

McGraw, Eloise. *Mara, Daughter of the Nile.*

Rationale: A brilliant, beautifully crafted novel set in ancient Egypt. The Egyptian religion heavily influences the flavor of the book and the actions of the characters, providing insight into a world shaped by its worldview.

Murdock, Catherine Gilbert. *Princess Ben.*

Rationale: Dealing with themes of identity, security, and vengeance, this book highlights the importance of truly understanding others. (And it's just plain fun.)

Riordan, Rick. *Percy Jackson and the Olympians.*

Rationale: Worth reading for his razor-sharp humor alone, Riordan paints a world influenced by gods and goddesses and competing worldviews.

Sobol, Donald. *Encyclopedia Brown Series.*

Rationale: Another charming detective series to sharpen critical-thinking and fact-seeking skills.

Notes

1 Again, see Goris and Aertsen, "Medieval Theories of Transcendentals."

2 See Montgomery, *Myth, Allegory, and Gospel*, 26.

3 Tolkien, *The Letters of J. R. R. Tolkien*, 100.

4 Lewis, *Surprised by Joy*, Kindle edition (Houghton Mifflin Harcourt, 1966), 18.

5 See Montgomery, *Myth, Allegory, and Gospel*, 21.

A Parting Word

This is it. You've made it. You have completed this course, and it is my prayer that you have grown in the grace and knowledge of our Lord Jesus Christ. The time has come for you to venture off on your own into the world of apologetics—but, of course, you're never alone. Not really. We are surrounded by a countless host of witnesses and blessed with the word of God, the greatest weapon of all.

This course undoubtedly did not answer all of the questions you have about apologetics. It wasn't designed to do so. It was designed to provide you with an introduction, a brief glimpse into an aspect of our faith that is so desperately needed in our world today. Investigate the resources for continuing education (including the following bibliography of works that influenced me to write this course), and if you have questions, ask. Ask your teacher, parent, or pastor. Search the Scriptures and know them. When you become discouraged, call to mind the words of the inspired prophet Isaiah:

> For as the rain and the snow come down from heaven
> and do not return there but water the earth,
> making it bring forth and sprout,
> giving seed to the sower and bread to the eater,
> so shall my word be that goes out from my mouth;
> it shall not return to me empty,
> but it shall accomplish that which I purpose,
> and shall succeed in the thing for which I sent it.[1]

The will of God shall be done, on earth as it is in heaven. The life, death, and resurrection of our Savior testify that God is faithful and that He will act. Lift up your heads, you who are called by the King of Grace to be His knights. Though you live in a battle zone, the war has been won for you. May you heed our Savior's call to "hear and understand" (Matt. 15:10), and may you rest securely in the knowledge that those who hold fast to the true confession (Heb. 4:14) are being held securely by the One who was, who is, and who is to come.

Note

1 Isaiah 55:10–11.

Acknowledgments

This handbook began as one of two ideas for a thesis for the International Academy of Apologetics, Evangelism, and Human Rights headed by Dr. John Warwick Montgomery. In spite of my best efforts to ignore this topic, I finally selected it and, with very little hope, submitted it as a thesis topic. Although this topic was closest to my heart, I fully expected a rejection. I'm not an educator, nor do I have children of my own, and I felt vastly underqualified to write this. Instead, I received an almost immediate acceptance. And that was about the time I realized a tiny bit of what sort of hole in which I had chosen to plunge myself. If you've never experienced the moods a writer goes through when creating a written work—one thinks of the scene from the Disney movie *Tangled* in which the heroine, Rapunzel, oscillates between utter glee and absolute despair—you may not be able to empathize with my family members and close friends as much as they deserve. Compound that with my admitted lack of background in teaching, and I knew I was in for a wild, glorious, and indescribable ride.

This handbook is, necessarily, focused on a specific age range. (In youthful naïveté, at the outset of this project I had suggested that it could be used "for elementary, middle, and possibly high school," at which point Mr. Parton gently brought me back down to earth and suggested that I select one age range. I am forever indebted to him for his tact and sound advice.) This book should be seen as a starting point. Perhaps, God willing, there will be more books for elementary, high school, college, and beyond. Perhaps that is a task that will be laid upon someone else (maybe even you, the reader?). There is still much that can be said and written, and our task as apologists and educators is far from finished. It is my hope that this little handbook may, in some way, be a part of helping to instruct the next (and current) generations of defenders of the faith.

There isn't room to mention all of the individuals who have influenced, encouraged, and supported me during the writing of this course. I would like to highlight a few and especially thank those who edited and fact-checked my work. Any errors, omissions, or snafus (theological, logical, or otherwise) in this work are entirely my own. I offer my thanks to the following individuals:

Dr. John Warwick Montgomery and Mr. Craig Parton. Apart from being adept apologists, these gentlemen offered valuable insight, support, and critiques to this work. The section on history began as an essay in Dr. Montgomery's class "Religion and the Law" at Concordia University Wisconsin in Fall 2014, and the brunt of the work would not have been accomplished without his review and encouragement. I am indebted to both of these men for their critiques concerning the handbook as a whole. To say it has been an honor to learn and grow under their instruction would be a vast understatement, and I have no qualms about saying that God used (and is using) them in a powerful way to influence countless lives.

Dr. Brian Morley, instructor in residence at the 2016 International Academy of Apologetics, Evangelism, and Human Rights in Strasbourg, France. My thanks to him for his thoughtful and encouraging discussion and his gentle and well-tuned critiques for this work. I'm honored to have been one of his students, if only for two short weeks.

Dr. Don DeYoung, chair of the science and mathematics department at Grace College, in Winona Lake, Indiana. I am deeply indebted to Dr. DeYoung for his review of the section on mathematics in unit two and for his kindness to me and to my family. What a wonderful thing to have a brilliant thinker and strong Christian for a true friend!

Dr. Steven Nelson, professor of English at Concordia University Wisconsin. Dr. Nelson not only accepted me contacting him out of the blue to review my section on creative writing, but he did so willingly and thoroughly in a short span of time. My thanks to him, also, for making my dream of being a writer seem like something attainable.

Dr. Gary Locklair, chair of the computer science department at Concordia University Wisconsin. Aside from the gratitude I owe him for obvious reasons (existence is a wonderful thing—thanks, Dad), he was instrumental in the compilation, fact-checking, and conceptual framework for the computer science section in unit two. The idea of computer science as a liberal art and the modern-day analogy to classical astronomy is very much at the heart and soul of his work, and I am grateful that he allowed me to use that and expand upon it.

Mrs. Karen Locklair, former instructor of five children and current greatest inspiration for each. For all the patience (especially during the stages of "volatile writer's syndrome" that occurred in moments of high stress), cheerleading, and grammar editing—thank you. Above all, thanks to you and Dad for your undaunted focus on Christ as the answer to both objective questions and the deepest longings of our hearts. You both have sacrificed your time, talents, and dreams to support my own, and though "thank you" will never be enough, please know that I am but one of the countless redeemed who ardently pray Philippians 1:3–11 with you in mind. Mom, your vocation and your Christian discernment make you more than deserving of the highest degree possible (really, ask Dr. Martin Luther).

Finally (but certainly not last in gratitude), Dr. Angus Menuge, professor of philosophy at Concordia University Wisconsin. To paraphrase E. B. White, it is rare to find someone who is both a sound thinker and a true mentor, and Dr. Menuge is both. The masterful way in which he issues challenges and encourages responses is uniquely orthodox without being stuffy. His phrase "We aren't called to be successful, we're called to be faithful" was the inspiration for the title of this course and, in many ways, the inspiration for my continued learning in the field of apologetics.

May any good in this book reflect the One who alone is good, and may any error within it in no way diminish the light of His radiance. If you wish to see the source of light, look not to the pockmarked moon with her inconsistent reflections—look to the Son and live.

Soli Deo Gloria, Allelu-YAH, Amen.

Selected General Bibliography

Abeka. "2015 Homeschool Scope and Sequence." *Abeka.com*. Accessed September 25, 2015. http://www.abeka.com/HomeSchool/ScopeAndSequence.aspx.

———. "Getting Started with Homeschooling." *Abeka.com*. Accessed September 25, 2015. http://www.abeka.com/HomeSchool/StartingHomeSchool.aspx.

Archer, Gleason. *Encyclopedia of Bible Difficulties*. Grand Rapids: Zondervan, 1982.

Bauer, Susan Wise, and Wise, Jessie. *The Well-Trained Mind*, 3rd ed. New York: W. W. Norton, 2009.

Beechick, Ruth. *Adam and His Kin*. Pollock Pines: Arrow Press, 1990.

———. *You* Can *Teach Your Child Successfully: Grades 4–8*. Fenton: Mott Media, 1999.

Bentley, Vicki. "Lesson Plans." *Hslda.org*. Accessed September 25, 2015. https://www.hslda.org/earlyyears/LessonPlan.asp.

Berquist, Laura. *Designing Your Own Classical Curriculum*, 3rd ed. San Francisco: Ignatius, 1998.

Cain, Susan. *Quiet: The Power of Introverts in a World That Can't Stop Talking*. New York: Crown, 2012.

Campbell, Sarah, and Campbell, Richard. *Growing Patterns: Fibonacci Numbers in Nature*. Honesdale: Boyds Mills, 2010.

Christian Worship: A Lutheran Hymnal, 9th printing. Milwaukee: Northwestern, 2008.

Concordia: The Lutheran Confessions. St. Louis: Concordia, 2005.

Copan, Paul. *How Do You Know You're Not Wrong?* Grand Rapids: Baker Books, 2005.

———. *Is God a Moral Monster?* Grand Rapids: Baker Books, 2011.

Cornerstone Curriculum. Accessed September 27, 2015. https://cornerstonecurriculum.com.

Crews, Frederick. *The Pooh Perplex*. New York: Dutton, 1963.

Edwards, Bruce L. *The Taste of the Pineapple: Essays on C. S. Lewis as Reader, Critic, and Imaginative Writer*. Bowling Green: Bowling Green State University Popular Press, 1988.

Garland, Trudi. *Fascinating Fibonaccis*. Palo Alto: D. Seymour Publications, 1987.

Home School Legal Defense Association. *Hslda.org*. Accessed September 25, 2015. http://hslda.org.

———. "Homeschooling Toddlers to Tweens." *Hslda.org*. Accessed September 25, 2015. https://www.hslda.org/earlyyears/What_Teach_20103190.asp.

Homeschool Tracker. "Record Keeping." Accessed September 25, 2015. http://www.homeschooltracker.com/features/#record-keeping.

James, William. *Pragmatism and Four Essays*. New York: Meridian, 1955.

JSTOR. Accessed September 26, 2015. http://www.jstor.org/.

Koukl, Gregory. *Tactics*. Grand Rapids: Zondervan, 2009.

Kreeft, Peter. *Socratic Logic*. South Bend: St. Augustine's Press, 2010.

Lewis, C. S. *Christian Reflections*. Grand Rapids: Eerdmans, 1995.

———. *The Chronicles of Narnia*, full color collector's ed. boxed set. New York: Harper Trophy, 2000.

———. *The Great Divorce*. New York: HarperOne, 2001.

———. *A Grief Observed*. New York: Bantam, 1976.

———. *God in the Dock*. Grand Rapids: Eerdmans, 1970.

———. *Mere Christianity*. New York: HarperOne, 2000.

———. *Miracles*. New York: HarperCollins, 2001.

———. *Out of the Silent Planet*. New York: Macmillan, 1965.

———. *Perelandra*. New York: Macmillan, 1978.

———. *The Problem of Pain*. New York: Macmillan, 1944.

———. *The Screwtape Letters*. New York: HarperCollins, 2001.

———. *That Hideous Strength*. New York: Macmillan, 1965.

———. *The Weight of Glory*. New York: Macmillan, 1949.

———. *Till we Have Faces*. Orlando: Harcourt, 1984.

Lutheran Service Book. St. Louis: Concordia, 2006.

The Lutheran Study Bible. St. Louis: Concordia, 2009.

Luther's Small Catechism with Explanation. St. Louis: Concordia, 1986.

Macaulay, Susan Schaeffer. *For the Children's Sake*. Westchester: Cross Way Books, 1984.

MacIntyre, Alasdair. *After Virtue*. Notre Dame: University of Notre Dame Press, 1984.

McDowell, Josh. *The New Evidence that Demands a Verdict*. Nashville: Thomas Nelson Publishers, 1999.

McGraw, Eloise Jarvis. *Techniques of Fiction Writing*. Boston: The Writer, 1959.

Menuge, Angus. *Aslan's World*. St. Louis: Concordia, 2006.

Menuge, Angus, ed. *C. S. Lewis: Lightbearer in the Shadowlands*. Wheaton: Crossway, 1997.

Montgomery, John Warwick. *Christ as Centre and Circumference*. Hamburg: VKW, 2012.

———. *Christianity for the Tough Minded*. Edmonton: Canadian Institute for Law, Theology, and Public Policy, 2001.

———. *Christ Our Advocate*. Edmonton: Canadian Institute for Law, Theology, and Public Policy, 2002.

———. *Crisis in Lutheran Theology*. Minneapolis: Bethany Fellowship, 1973.

———. *Faith Founded on Fact*. Edmonton: Canadian Institute for Law, Theology, and Public Policy, 2001.

———. *God's Inerrant Word*. Minneapolis: Bethany Fellowship, 1974.

———. *History, Law, and Christianity*. Edmonton: Canadian Institute for Law, Theology, and Public Policy, 2002.

———. *In Defense of Martin Luther*. Milwaukee: Northwestern, 1970.

———. *The Law above the Law*. Minneapolis: Bethany Fellowship, 1975.

———. *Law and Gospel*. Edmonton: Canadian Institute for Law, Theology, and Public Policy, 1994.

———. *Law and Morality: Friends or Foes?* Luton: University of Luton, 1994.

———. *Myth, Allegory, and Gospel*. Edmonton: Canadian Institute for Law, Theology, and Public Policy, 2000.

———. *The Shaping of America*. Minneapolis: Bethany House, 1981.

———. *Slaughter of the Innocents*. Westchester: Cornerstone Books, 1981.

———. *The Suicide of Christian Theology*. Minneapolis: Bethany Fellowship, 1970.

———. *Tractatus-Logico Theologicus*, 5th ed. Eugene: Wipf & Stock, 2013.

Myers, Jeff, and Noebel, David. *Understanding the Times*. Manitou Springs: Summit Ministries, 2015.

Parton, Craig. *The Defense Never Rests: A Lawyer among the Theologians*. St Louis: Concordia, 2015.

———. *Religion on Trial*. Eugene: Wipf & Stock, 2008.

Pascal, Blaise. *Pensées*, rev. ed. London: Penguin, 1995.

Paustian, Mark. *Prepared to Answer: Telling the Greatest Story Ever Told*. Milwaukee: Northwestern, 2004.

Pearcey, Nancy. *Finding Truth*. Colorado Springs: David C. Cook, 2015.

———. *Total Truth*. Wheaton: Crossway, 2004.

Pittenger, Tony. *Messiah: The Greatest Sermon Ever Sung*. Minneapolis: KnockOut, 2012.

Robot Ethics. Edited by Patrick Lin, Keith Abney, and George Bekey. Cambridge: MIT Press, 2012.

Ross, Clifford. *Leading Lawyers' Case for the Resurrection*. Edmonton: Canadian Institute for Law, Theology, and Public Policy, 1996.

Sayers Classical Academy. Accessed September 26, 2015. http://www.sayersclassical.org.

Sayers, Dorothy. *The Mind of the Maker*. Edited by Susan Howatch. London: Continuum, 2004.

———. *The Whimsical Christian*, First Collier Books ed. New York: Macmillan, 1987.

Schaeffer, Edith. *The Hidden Art of Homemaking*. Wheaton: Tyndale House, 1982.

Schmidt, Alvin. *How Christianity Changed the World*. Grand Rapids: Zondervan, 2004.

Schuldheisz, Sam. Contributor at *1517 Legacy Project* blog. Accessed September 27, 2015. http://www.1517legacy.com/contributors/sam-schuldheisz.

Sire, James. *The Universe Next Door*. Downers Grove: InterVarsity, 1997.

Stanford Encyclopedia of Philosophy. Accessed September 26, 2015. http://plato.stanford.edu/.

Summit Ministries. Accessed September 27, 2015. http://www.summit.org.

Swope, Cheryl, and Hein, Steven, et al. *A Handbook for Classical Lutheran Education.* CreateSpace Independent Publishing Platform, 2013.

Swope, Cheryl, and Heine, Melinda. *Curriculum Resource Guide for Classical Lutheran Education*, 2nd ed. CreateSpace Independent Publishing Platform, 2015.

Tolkien, J. R. R. *The Lord of the Rings*, Three-book boxed set. Boston: Houghton Mifflin, 2002.

Tolkien, J. R. R, and Tolkien, Christopher. *The Monsters and the Critics, and Other Essays.* Boston: Houghton Mifflin, 1984.

Updike, John. *Collected Poems.* New York: Knopf, 1995.

Veith, Gene Edward, Jr. *Loving God with All Your Mind.* Wheaton: Crossway, 2003.

———. *Modern Fascism.* St. Louis: Concordia, 1993.

———. *Postmodern Times.* Wheaton: Crossway, 1994.

———. *The Soul of the Lion, the Witch, and the Wardrobe.* Colorado Springs: Cook Communications Ministries, 2005.

———. *The Spirituality of the Cross*, rev. ed. St. Louis: Concordia, 2010.

———. *State of the Arts.* Wheaton: Crossway, 1991.

Veith, Gene Edward, Jr., and Kern, Andrew, *Classical Education*, 3rd ed. Washington, DC: Capital Research Center, 2015.

Wallach, Wendell, and Allen, Colin. *Moral Machines.* New York: Oxford University Press, 2009.

Wilder-Smith, A. E. *He Who Thinks Has to Believe.* San Diego: Master Books, 1981.

Wilson, Douglas. *Recovering the Lost Tools of Learning.* Wheaton: Crossway, 1991.

Zacharias, Ravi. *Can Man Live without God?* Dallas: Word Publishing, 1994.

About the Author

Valerie Locklair is a sinner saved by grace alone through faith in Christ alone (1 Tim. 1:15; Gal. 6:14). Along with her four siblings, she was homeschooled from kindergarten through high school. She graduated from Concordia University Wisconsin with a degree in information technology and cofounded GRACE, the first officially sanctioned women-in-computing organization at a private college in Wisconsin. Motivated by a growing interest in apologetics and gnawing doctrinal questions of her own, Valerie attended the International Academy of Apologetics, Evangelism, and Human Rights in Strasbourg, France. After studying under Dr. John Warwick Montgomery, Mr. Craig Parton, Dr. Angus Menuge, and other distinguished professors, and prompted by a growing need for a personal apologetic approach in her own life, Valerie completed both the fellowship and the diploma of the academy. Her areas of interest include apologetics for the next generation, connecting branches of knowledge to the defense of the faith, and investigating Einstein's Gulf and its impact on societal thinking.

Valerie is a student and assistant instructor of Taekwon-Do at a local dojang. In her spare time, she enjoys traveling to far-off places and playing with her horses using natural horsemanship methods. She lives in Wisconsin with two rescued horses, one rescued dog, and an unknown number of rogue rabbits. She has weaknesses for philosophical discussions, *Murder, She Wrote* reruns, and Diet Coke (and has been known to indulge in all three simultaneously).

Printed in the USA
CPSIA information can be obtained
at www.ICGtesting.com
JSHW012242180923
48467JS00011B/133

9 781945 978654